Corporate Cure

How To Build A High-Engagement,
High-Performance Company
That Will Last

By John Owens

GREEN CASTLE
publishing

GreenCastle Publishing

GreenCastle Publishing
137 Cross Center Road, Suite 239, Denver, NC 28037
www.greencastlepublishing.com
704.483.7283

Credits:
Cover Design, Sandra Ketchie
Creative Director, Sherré DeMao
Interior Layout, Rosemarie Printz
Editor, J. Kevin Toomb Ph.D.
Indexer, Wendy Allex

Library of Congress Control Number: 2014948140

ISBN 978-0-9841051-2-0

Printed in the United States of America.

For rights or permissions inquiries, please
contact GreenCastle Publishing at 704.483.7283
or info@greencastlepublishing.com.

For information about special quantity sales, premium
or corporate programs, contact GreenCastle Publishing
at 704.483.7283 or sales@greencastlepublishing.com.

This book is dedicated to my children,
Alexa Paige, Nicklaus Ryan, and Jack Riley Owens in
being my everyday inspiration for the choices I make.

Table of Contents

Preface

When you looked at the cover of this book, you may have been thinking one of a few things. One thought might have been wishful thinking about your company accomplishing some of the accolades listed. Another thought may have been that you noticed some recognitions your company has achieved, but other achievements that have escaped you, yet you would love to add them to your list.

This book isn't about how to win awards or be recognized. The Corporate Cure needed in American companies isn't to win awards or be named to some prestigious ranking. The Corporate Cure is about how to build a high-engagement, high-performance company that will last – just as the subtitle suggests. The beauty of building such a company is all of the companies featured within this book that are doing it right understand what it takes to build a company of endurance, and coincidentally also have a list as long or longer than my arm of awards, accolades, and high rankings.

I was inspired to focus on the accolades companies can realize for the cover because if you build your company right, it will be award worthy. However, most important and more relevant, your company will be a place that is embraced by employees, customers, your marketplace, and industry as one to emulate and celebrate for all the things _you_ are doing right.

Introduction

Running multiple businesses for more than two decades has been a roller coaster ride, but not the thrill-seeking kind that you would expect it to be as an entrepreneur. No...for me it has been heart and gut-wrenching because three of these multiple businesses were the same business that was restructured again and again. The first business, a retail mortgage company that I established in 1995, grew to servicing $5 million home mortgages a month with over 60 employees, and then we were forced to restructure in 1999, laying off 30 employees as a result of the retail side taking a hit literally overnight. We resurfaced with a focus on the wholesale mortgage business. By 2005 we were processing $100 million in loans per month. Being named among the Inc. 500 in 2005 and 2006, it seemed we were unstoppable. A year later, we were forced to dissolve when our sole credit facility folded like a house of cards, leaving companies likes ours to clean up the mess. Now, with my current company, a private mortgage, wealth management and insurance services firm, I believe that three is a charm, but not without being constantly reminded of the exhilarating ups and devastating downs my team, my family and I have had to endure.

What I know now is that market conditions and the actions of an industry can put a well-run, good company into a coma in the blink of an eye. When you've been through the super highs and the debilitating lows that I have been through, you learn a lot. A hell of a lot! Being in the financial services industry, I didn't just learn from my mistakes and assumptions. I learned even more from the mistakes that others made, many of whom are no longer in the business or industry because they just couldn't take it anymore.

I also am a baseball fanatic and lover of the sport as a result of my days as a collegiate player for the University of North Carolina - Charlotte (49ers). When you are at the home plate, you don't want to strike out. You want that home run. You want to anticipate any curve thrown at you and knock it out of the park, making it tomorrow's news. For me, I was at the business plate and felt like I had struck out twice, in spite of doing what I thought was exactly right for my business, my family and the people in my company. My big 'aha' came as I was determining how to pick up the pieces and rebuild my business again, for the third time in a volatile industry. A big fan of the book, Good to Great, I asked myself what would be the defining factor that would make this third company great?

As I looked around at others in my industry faltering all around me, it hit me. I hadn't struck out at all, but was able to do in each case what others could not do. In the first case, I made a hit to stay in the game because I was determined that the balls being thrown at me weren't going to put me down and out. I just needed to play the game a little differently. The second time, I walked the bases to regroup and not let the ineptness of my industry get the best of me. I was able to reach deep into my company and uncover that ray of hope and belief within my core team that convinced them we could get through it, rebuild and succeed in spite of the conditions and the road blocks. I didn't realize the extent of this until this third go-around, because my full playbook hadn't been written until now.

The key to going from good to great comes down to building a company that can endure in spite of what comes its way. If you truly want a company that can endure over time, regardless of what could get in its way internally or externally, it is about revival, not survival. And if you really do it right, it becomes sustainable and seamless in its ability to adapt and flow. As I reflected back, it hit me, like a fast ball hits a bat on impact. Nothing can resuscitate a company faster and more resiliently than a strong corporate culture. And better yet, a strong corporate culture can actually help you anticipate those curves and keep the bases loaded in your favor time and time again. The first two times, I took it for granted. I was doing some of what it took to build a corporate culture, but not all of what it encompassed. This third time, I knew with certainty that corporate culture was both the heart and central nervous system of a company.

As a result, it became my passion, obsession and focus as the visionary to nurture, cultivate, appreciate, and necessitate our ideal corporate culture at all levels. And as its powerful effects took hold within my company, others wanted to know my secret. I was asked to speak about how I was able to do it when so many others in my industry couldn't. Other company CEOs wanted to grab a cup of coffee and understand how they could bring a corporate passion into their organization. Before I knew it, another entrepreneurial enterprise in the form of a consulting group was taking shape to provide solutions. Shortly thereafter, I opened a baseball academy with the exciting ability to shape its corporate culture from the very beginning.

As I continued my due diligence with a dedicated team studying and documenting corporate culture successes and failures across the country, my belief of how important corporate culture is for every organization in any industry became steadfast. It doesn't matter whether the business is for profit, not-for-profit, or the government; its effectiveness is reliant on having a strong and aligned culture, which is a culture best suited for them in what they do and why they are doing it. Our findings resulted in the development of a proprietary corporate culture assessment tool that I tested with companies with profound, eye-opening results for these organizations. This only fueled my desire to show others what I have learned and is now culminated in this book.

Your organization is as strong or as weak as the corporate culture holding it together or tearing it apart. My hope is that this book will be as eye-opening for you as the journey I have been on, but without the roller coaster ride.

SECTION I

About Culture

CHAPTER 1
What is Culture?

In my college days as a pitcher for college-level baseball teams, the level of passion, love of the game, and commitment to "the team" in being the best, doing our best, and winning games was exhilarating. The level in which we were committed to the university, our coaches, and to one another as teammates was almost cult-like. We had each others' backs on and off the field, and were united in what we set out to accomplish each time we practiced or played a game. As I moved into the business world, I longed for that level of team camaraderie – that belief in our abilities and capabilities, which went beyond what we did, but what it represented in the long-run. It wasn't until I was in the business world that I truly understood what I had realized as a part of that baseball team. We had an aligned culture in how we approached being as individuals in a team and for the team. As a part of an educational institution, we had our own form of corporate culture that has kept us connected even decades after moving on to our other lives.

The idea of corporate culture in Corporate America is nothing new. However the ideal of corporate culture has become more debated than ever before since we have witnessed corporate giants crumble before our eyes. Their once goliath presence and power to impact an entire industry or globally vanished into economic debris. The irony is that these companies and their cultures were at the very heart of not only their ultimate self-destruction, but the economic meltdown as a whole. Their misguided focus on power, elite status, short-term material gain, profits at others' expense, unethical practices, and ego-driven agendas resulted in a fragmented, broken secret society that could no longer maintain its elusive smoke and mirrors existence.

So, what is the ideal culture? How can it be defined? How can it be cultivated and become the powerful foundation of a business that it needs to be? Putting cultivation and culture together is a good starting point. It is also a critical evolving and problem solving point.

The word "Cultivate" means "*to produce; promote; improve growth by labor and attention; and improve growth by education and training.*" Isn't growth what you hope to achieve for your company? And who is the source of the labor necessary for that growth? Your people! Whose attention do you require to attract for this growth to occur? The people you employ and resource, as well as and the people who are your customers.

The meaning of the word "Culture" includes: "the quality in a society that rises from a concern for what is regarded as excellent in manners, pursuits, etc.; the characteristics and beliefs of a particular group." A person with culture, based in the first meaning, is one who possesses a level of sophistication and discernment. A company culture, based on the second meaning, is one in which everyone shares beliefs and characteristics.

What are the beliefs within your organization? What are your beliefs as a leader of your organization? Are they in alignment? What are the beliefs of your other managers and employees? Are they in agreement or in conflict? What do you believe are the ideal characteristics your company should possess to be successful? What are the ideal characteristics that people in their jobs should have to make the company successful? What is your idea of success?

All of these questions have relevance to your corporate culture. All of these questions and more need to be answered to get at the heart of what your culture is or is not right now, and then what it should be and can be for your business. To understand this better, let's gain a deeper understanding of culture in its root form.

Good Cult, Bad Cult

The root word "cult" has gotten a bad rap with most people thinking hideous thoughts of brainwashing, clueless followers, a charismatic and narcissistic leader, and an outcome of ultimate doom and destruction. Think about Charles Manson and Jim Jones, and you will begin to see what I mean.

Manson and Jones were revered and they used their power to mislead. They demanded respect, but respected nothing in return. Their followers were in awe of them and what they professed to be doing. Their followers were intensely loyal. However, their loyalty was not reciprocated by the leader, who would not hesitate to manipulate in order to achieve allegiance. The followers were dedicated to a person and his ideals, blindly accepting them without fully understanding them, believing in the person more than in the beliefs themselves. They were sheep following the wolf, so to speak, into the den.

Street gangs are another type of cult that appears in the daily news as they protect their territories and their people at all costs. Their territory is their object of devotion. Taking other people's possessions and property without hesitation is driven by their belief in their right to own and possess whatever they want. Their beliefs around the right to own and protect both their "streets" and their way of life are without question for those accepted into the gang. There is a sense of unified pride and ownership by everyone involved. Their strong unified beliefs are centered on maintaining possession and control of places, people and things.

In the case of the Manson/Jones cult following, the leader was self-chosen and pivotal to the cult's existence. The self-professed leader was responsible for everyone adhering to and staying in line with his teachings and preachings. Beliefs were dictated, not shared. In the case of street gangs, their shared beliefs are the adhesive that holds the group together. While gangs have leaders, the shared beliefs give the gang its power and the leaders their power. A gang leader is chosen by peers and respected for their ability to keep the group true to their beliefs.

Look up the meaning of the word "Cult" in the dictionary and you get: "a group or sect bound together by veneration (feeling of awe, respect) of a particular person, purpose, or thing"; or, "a group having a sacred ideology and a set of rites centering on their sacred beliefs." Two key words that stand out in the definitions are "respect" in the first definition and the word "sacred" in the second definition, which is especially poignant because its meaning is stated as "reverently dedicated to a person, idea, purpose or object."

The reality is that there is a good side and a bad side to everyone, everything, every situation, and every option. My opinion is that cult goes bad when it is ego driven (focused on a particular person), or materially driven (focused on a particular "thing" or possession). However, having a "cult following" in your company is not a bad thing IF it is built from a focus on purpose. This separates the good cult from the cult gone bad and powerfully clarifies why culture is so vitally important to the foundational effectiveness or ineffectiveness of an organization.

As a leader in your company, wouldn't your ideal be to have employees intensely dedicated to delivering your products and services because they see that they have a higher value and purpose? Wouldn't your ideal be to serve your customers with such an obsession because your purpose is to amaze them about how you do it better than anyone else? Wouldn't it be your ideal to have your entire organization bound together by a feeling of awe and mutual respect for the difference your company is making out in the marketplace? Wouldn't it be your ideal to have your marketplace recognize and revere your organization for its impact? Wouldn't it be your ideal to have customers so connected with your company that they are dedicated and loyal to your brand because it symbolizes something more to them than merely a service or product?

Once you have achieved brand loyalty for your company, you will essentially have a customer cult following. Put in these terms, cult doesn't sound so sinister, does it?

Right Culture, Wrong Culture

I know the right and the wrong side of corporate culture all too well. After all, I am in the financial services industry. For those of you reading this, you are probably thinking that because the Great Recession was directly impacted by financial empire practices in the United States, that any culture in the financial investment or banking industry was the wrong culture. I've seen already troubled cultures get worse and promising cultures go in the wrong direction. The financial industry is a study in culture in and of itself, no doubt. But it is not the only means of gauging what is right versus what may be wrong with your corporate culture.

It has been said that the best way to know what you want is to experience what you don't want. This gets at the very heart and soul of your beliefs. Knowing your values and beliefs are the first and most important aspects of defining what you want and don't want, and what you consider to be right or wrong.

Growing up as a policeman's son, I quickly learned what law and order and "my way or the highway" meant. You didn't question authority and you didn't have a say in the way things were being done. You were just supposed to do what you were told to do. Many of us grew up this way in an authoritarian environment, which also gave us the right structure and clearly defined lines not to cross. We learned what was right from what was wrong, but it was told to us versus discovered by us.

Fast forward to my first job out of college, and I was camping outside of people's doorsteps to collect their mortgage payments. This was in the 1990's, when the American Dream of owning your own home was alive and thriving, and foreclosures weren't an everyday item in the national news. The entire focus of my job was collecting money, not caring about the people, their circumstances, their situations, or their reasons for lack of payment or slow payment. My salary was dictated by what I collected. You couldn't repossess their house in the sense of latching it to a tow truck and lugging it off. But you could repossess their dignity. I didn't like this job very much. I worked quickly toward moving up to move out of that role and into one that would, hopefully, be more gratifying on both sides of the transaction.

My goal to move up and out of that role paid off in securing a role to help people restructure their loans so they wouldn't get to the point of foreclosure in the first place. It was my first exposure to the importance of making a good loan in the first place, not only for the company, but for the homeowners too. Even though I was in a more satisfying role in being of service instead of severance in relationships with customers, the industry as a whole was not embracing this idea of what was in the best interests for all concerned. It was, even then, about the all mighty dollar and what could be made.

Reflecting on this from a corporate culture standpoint, what I propose is that it isn't about one culture being good and another being bad. It is about a culture being right or wrong for you, the business you are in, and the type of company and contributor you want to be in your marketplace. A culture works when everyone in it believes and supports it at every level for all the same reasons and motives. I do believe there is an ideal culture for all businesses to strive to be for true sustainability and endurance.

❖

What this book strives to do in the following chapters is help you understand and define the culture that you believe will be the most effective for your company and its people ... the culture that the people best suited to work for your company will embrace and support ... and the culture that your customers will buy into and continue to buy, buy, buy.

CHAPTER 2
Why CULTure Matters

In 1994, I needed one more unit of closed business in order to receive the maximum bonus at the financial services company in which I was employed as a Regional Manager. I had moved my way up from the trenches to being a star performer, and the bonus that was being offered was a hefty sum, much larger than in years past. As I got closer to the goal, I sensed an underlying contention that almost seemed as though the management did not want me to reach this goal. Every move I made seemed to be getting blocked in unexpected ways. Management was not interested in assisting me, since I would get the bonus, not them. It was almost as if the profits lost by the bonus were deemed as not worth the unit sales gained. It was then that I learned that the bonus amount was set high for the specific reason that management did not think it could be obtained. It was a way of achieving the desired sales without having to reward the final result.

In spite of being in it all alone, I achieved that final unit bonus and as everyone was superficially applauding my accomplishment at the corporate event in February of 1995, it was at that moment I knew I was going to be leaving and starting my own company. And I vowed my company would define a better way to treat, reward and support employees.

The bottom line is that a company's culture is the root cause and effect of business success or failure. It also can be the cause and effect of individual success or failure. When people allow a culture to consume them to a point of losing their own identity, it is not a culture for them. Instead, it is placing them in a role that is not only uncomfortable, but also unfulfilling. An individual cannot know if a company's culture is or is not right without the company knowing its culture first. Otherwise, it is a guessing game on everyone's part.

Understanding the negative and positive sides of culture's root word "cult" can bring about great insight into defining what may be wrong with your current culture and give you the ability to identify and embrace the right corporate culture for either your company or for you as an individual.

Cults & Street Gangs

As I considered what makes one culture right and work well, and another culture wrong and ineffective in a company, I began to explore the root of the word cult and the fact that we have grown to associate the word cult with something bad and destructive. I asked myself, what would be constructive versus destructive? This resulted in me exploring this idea with an associate consultant and we made some unique and powerful discoveries and associations.

When you look at the destructive cults referenced in the previous chapter, both cults were assembled by the group recruiting individuals using coercive tactics based on the leader's beliefs and the intent to make his or her beliefs the cult followers' beliefs. Additionally, unquestioned allegiance to the leader's teachings is expected, as well as having it belonging to the group. Challenging or questioning these teachings would result in punishment or even death. Once you are a part of the group, getting out is not an option. There is no turning back or changing your mind. The leader is coveted and revered as an almighty figure, a supreme being who is viewed as better than those who are following him. The leader has acquired his place of power because he has been specially selected by a self-professed ultimate power.

When you look at street gangs, many underlying aspects are similar. Gang members are expected to have unquestioned allegiance to the gang and its leader. Challenging either the gang's activities or leader's authority would result in punishment or death. A coveted and revered gang leader is typically not self-appointed, but is selected to be the leader who other gang members view as having greater ability and worthiness. One of the key differences between cults and a street gang is in their approach to beliefs. Whereas destructive cults grow through recruitment based on coerced beliefs or individuals being brainwashed into adopting the beliefs of the cult, street gangs grow through individuals wanting to belong as a result of their communal beliefs or shared beliefs. It is considered an honor to be a part of the gang. This is why gangs tend to be driven by ethnicity because of the underlying beliefs of their ethnic culture. The cultural beliefs of the ethnic group become the basis for the gang's beliefs. These communal beliefs around their ethnic culture expand to include shared beliefs around property, possessions and power - ultimately shaping the core values of the gang, some of which are not the shared core values of their ethnic culture.

Interestingly, organized crime shares many of the same aspects as a street gang, but in a much more sophisticated way.

Destructive Cults		**Street Gangs**	
C	Coerced Beliefs	C	Communal Beliefs
U	Unquestioned Allegiance	U	Unquestioned Allegiance
L	Leadership Coveted & Revered	L	Leadership Coveted & Revered
T	Teammates Tested	T	Teammates Tested

Both Destructive Cults and Street Gangs are fear-based in their operations. The unquestioned allegiance combined with the tested teammates is why the fear exists. The leader in a Destructive Cult, such as a religious or satanic cult, is coveted and revered as a chosen one who has the direct line with the deity or satanic figure being professed as the almighty by the leader. The leader presents himself as the means to the end, keeping himself between the higher power and the people. A gang leader is coveted and revered as the one in power who has earned his place of status. Because the leaders are coveted and revered, they are not questioned for fear of disappointment, humiliation, retaliation, or punishment. Fear-based cultures exist in Corporate America. Many of you who are reading this book know this all too well as you are either working in one or have escaped from one. A fear-based culture means it has some of the destructive "cult-gone-bad" characteristics, with an emphasis on unquestioned allegiance and being continually tested.

The Right CULTURE

After exploring the destructive side of a cult, I wondered what would be the underlying factors that transform the cult aspect into a group of people having a positive and effective impact inside and outside of their organization. After all, the actual meaning of a cult is not sinister; it is what cults have grown to be associated with that has created the negative interpretation.

Taking a look at this from a positive perspective, I worked with an associate consultant and together we determined these powerful differences:

Destructive Cults		Constructive Cult	
C	Coerced Beliefs	C	Communal Beliefs
U	Unquestioned Allegiance	U	Unquestioned Allegiance
L	Leadership Coveted & Revered	L	Leadership Inspires & Motivates
T	Teammates Tested	T	Teammates Trusted

Communal Beliefs: Street gangs were on the right track by having communal beliefs. I have been using street gangs as an example for a while with my consulting clients, citing this positive aspect of their culture. They are always shocked when they realize the truth in this. Having communal beliefs means that everyone is sharing the same beliefs and feeling connected to one another as a result. It creates a sense of community with everyone because they are sharing the same beliefs. Shared beliefs are what bring a group of people together as opposed to coerced beliefs, which force people together. Communal beliefs are not the same as common beliefs. Communal takes it a step further. You can have beliefs that are in common, but they are not being shared at a deeper level of engagement to form a group dedicated to one another and adhering to and honoring their beliefs. The engagement factor is the key difference between common beliefs and communal beliefs.

This is important to realize when we take a look later at the different corporate culture models in the second section of this book. Beliefs being shared mean that those who share them feel connected and they believe they are connected on all levels. We will discuss this more in the second section, as well. Where street gangs go astray is in how they approach allegiance, leadership and teammates.

Unconditional Allegiance: Unconditional allegiance means that you trust and place no conditions on your commitment to belonging to the group. While there may be expectations, the right to be or not be a part of the group is the choice of the individual and not the group or the leader of the group. Unquestioned allegiance, as described earlier, is fear-based. There is a desire by leadership to undermine and intentionally focus on the weaknesses and confidence of their followers by instilling a feeling in them being viewed of lesser value than the leadership. Team members are expected to follow and not question the decisions and motives of the leaders. Once a part of the group, it is difficult to leave the group without serious repercussions or even life threatening consequences.

<u>Leadership Inspires & Motivates</u>: A leader who inspires and motivates team members is viewed as a critical part of the team by the team, and the leader views him or herself as a part of the team. The leader's title is less important than the end result of their leadership. This leader is focused on effecting mutually desirable results and outcome through others and for others. A leader who is coveted and revered is viewed by the team as a separate, higher ranking individual. The leader views the individuals within the group as followers or subordinates. Status and title are important to this leader and his or her focus is on effecting personally desired results and outcomes through the use of others.

<u>Teammates Trusted:</u> When you have a team of people who trust one another, they also have confidence in one another, faith in one another, and faith in the actions that will be taken on behalf of the team and the organization as a whole. In the right environment, leaders are considered to be a part of the team, and they are trusted, as well. In addition, they trust those they are leading to do the job they have been brought in to do. Individuals within a gang or destructive cult are continuously tested for their allegiance and worthiness. There is an underlying mistrust, not only between the members, but also between the leader and his or her followers. Hazings are a cult-based concept of testing allegiance and worthiness. While done in jest in fraternities, sororities, and sports or competition teams, many news reports have exposed harmful hazings that have crossed the line because of their cult-like tendencies.

❖

Acknowledging the good qualities of a cult is the true beginning to fully understand and embrace the power a strong corporate culture can have within an organization. In the next chapter, we will explore the underlying foundation that transforms a cult into a culture.

CHAPTER 3
Becoming a Culture

In 2005, I was standing in the reception area of the Ernst & Young Entrepreneur Awards banquet in which I was a finalist. I remember taking pride in witnessing my leadership team dispersed throughout the crowd, animated in their obvious pride for being a part of our company. They naturally and effortlessly spoke about the company, promoting its uniqueness and its accomplishments. I could hear our corporate culture being mentioned as the foundation of our success. They were all speaking the same language, but in their own passionate words.

Seeing your team embracing the company on an emotional level is gratifying to witness as a CEO, but also is a turning point for any company hoping to achieve a dynamic and effective corporate culture. That emotional connection means that each individual feels connected with the company. When there is a personal connection with the company, there is a personal commitment, as well.

As I shared in the previous chapter, the word cult has gotten a bad rap because it has been associated with a negative connotation. To have a truly powerful and effective corporate culture, it should be cult-like in that everyone who is a part of it believes in it, lives it, breathes it, works it, nurtures it, protects it, and feels connected to the company and to each other. What makes a cult become a corporate culture involves a shift into the positive aspects of cult reinforced with foundational best practices that are the keys to making it a successful and effective culture.

The Plus Power of Cult

As I worked with the management consulting company and also considered what I have seen and experienced through my career and building multiple businesses, I came to some powerful conclusions on what could be the ideal corporate culture. I determined that I would test these conclusions in building my corporate culture. The idea of a constructive cult fascinated me. So I asked myself: What makes it constructive beyond the surface level? What evolves it into a culture? What will make it sustainable within my company or any company?

As I investigated this further and brought in a team to conduct due diligence around this premise, it became clear that a corporate culture is a continuous building process. It isn't about building it and they will come. It is about building a foundation that can be continuously fortified and made stronger with everyone both inside and outside of the company playing important roles.

C	Communal Beliefs	=	Conscientious Consideration
U	Unconditional Allegiance	=	Unwavering Commitment
L	Leadership Inspires & Motivates	=	Leadership Drives Cohesiveness
T	Team Trusted	=	Team Working Together

<u>Communal Beliefs = Conscientious Consideration:</u> Having commonly shared values and beliefs about the way work should be done, the business should be approached, the company should operate, and a person should behave personally and professionally, the result will be a working environment where everyone at work "gets each other." By sharing beliefs and values, people feel more connected to each other and more willing to assist and help one another. Communication is not forced, but is a natural way of doing business and getting things done. Effort is made to achieve the desired outcome while considering what is in the best interests of the team, the company, customers, and others.

<u>Unconditional Allegiance = Unwavering Commitment:</u> A company with a strong corporate culture earns an unwavering commitment from its stakeholders versus just expecting it. Management understands that actions speak louder than words in professing to be and then actually being seen as professed. The stakeholders are not just the leadership and the internal team of employees, they also include customers, vendors, suppliers, shareholders and anyone else associated with the company. There is a passion and love of the company, what it stands for, and what its products or offerings are doing as a result.

<u>Leadership Inspires & Motivates = Leadership Drives Cohesiveness:</u> For the corporate culture to stay on track, the company's leadership must be its steward and shepherd. The leadership understands that the corporate culture is the glue that binds together the things that give the company competitive advantage on many fronts. Leaders who truly embrace the culture can keep it strong and effective no matter how large the company

About Culture

grows. Whether the company has 10 employees or 10,000 employees, a corporate culture can survive and thrive when leadership is at its helm making sure it does not go off course. From hiring the right people to continue to build upon and enhance the culture to reinforcing beliefs and values through his or her own actions and management style, the leader protects and cultivates the culture as a valuable intangible asset.

Team Trusted = Team Working Together: When teammates are trusted, they are more willing to work together and also support each other when demands or challenges occur. Everyone views anyone else in the company as a team member and also as someone to count on to work with and support the company's overall goals and objectives. There is a 'we are in this together" mentality. Trust among team members is essential for a team to work effectively, and trust reinforced throughout the organization enables departments to interact and support the others with confidence. Just like allegiance, trust is earned and cannot be expected.

From Cult to CULTURE

While one could argue that the CULT aspect of culture is enough to make it work when approached constructively and purposefully, it is not enough. It needs some foundational principles of operation to truly underscore and bring the organization's leadership and employees together to become a corporate culture.

C	Communal Beliefs
U	Unconditional Allegiance
L	Leadership Inspires & Motivates
T	Team Trusted
U	Unified Understanding
R	Respect & Responsibility
E	Expectations around Excellence

Unified Understanding: It is one thing to have common values and beliefs and another thing to have an understanding of what they mean in the big scheme of things within the company, to internal and external stakeholders, and out into the marketplace. This is accomplished by taking the values and beliefs to a higher level of consciousness with both a vision and mission for the company. This is where strategy also plays an important role. When the strategy encompasses the culture at its core, through a clear and unified understanding of the company's vision and mission, then it can be embraced by everyone involved in effectively implementing and measuring its effectiveness with confidence.

Respect & Responsibility: For a corporate culture to be effective, it also must have covenants around respect and responsibility about how everyone works together, approaches doing their individual jobs, and are accountable for what needs to be done. Dependent on the values and culture model, this can vary, but both respect and responsibility are addressed, expected and monitored. This is where ethics plays an important role, with leadership emulating for the entire company what this means by their actions in support of their words. Self accountability and upholding ethical standards according to what is deemed right and appropriate creates a trickle-down respect throughout the organization as each employee gains respect for the leadership and then one another. Team members who respect one another are self accountable to themselves in order to not let another team member down, and also are comfortable with holding teammates accountable due to the unified understanding.

Expectations around Excellence: A sustainable culture is one that realizes the impact of performing according to high expectations. Everyone is focused on doing their best to achieve the desired results based on the goals, objectives and the company vision, mission and purpose. With everyone sharing expectations around excellence, effort is energized into an enthusiasm that is contagious and focused. Goals that were once viewed as stretch goals are seen as achievable. Ideas that were considered unthinkable to achieve are now embraced with the possibility of becoming an igniting force bringing them into reality.

❖

With a foundational approach to building your corporate culture, it is sustainable and replicable. As a CEO, more than 50 percent of your time should be dedicated to being the steward and shepherd of the corporate culture. You have a basis from which you can continue to build and to take department to department, division to division, and company to company. Whether your company has 50 people or 50,000 people, your culture can hold strong and your company can last long.

CHAPTER 4

Values &
Corporate Culture

It is one thing to be challenged, and entirely another to be beaten down due to being continuously challenged. I saw the effects of this in a co-worker, shortly before leaving the corporation I was working for at the time to start my own firm. I witnessed a man who was beaten down, and literally reduced to a stature of submission and acceptance out of fear of losing his high-paying job that was keeping his family in a comfortable lifestyle. He was miserable, but afraid to leave. He had been with the company 25 years and his time to go elsewhere had long passed in his eyes. He had resigned himself to a reality where he knew his personal values were compromised and he had accepted this reality as his only means of survival.

Ever since I was a child, I liked challenges. I was always forming teams and leading peers, and as a college baseball player, I wanted to be the one with the baseball at the bottom of the ninth inning. I knew that I thrived on being under pressure and being challenged, but when the challenge compromises who you are as a leader, team player, or person, then it is cutting into your ability to be the absolute best that you can be for you and everyone around you.

After graduating from college, I dove into the world of financial services and banking. Within a few years, I had earned the status of top performer in the mortgage and financial services firm in which I was employed. I was successful because I didn't let any challenge get the best of me and before long I was training my co-workers despite my young age and relative inexperience. I was working constantly. My wife and one-year old child barely saw me, and I had another child on the way.

The pressure to perform in the company was intense for everyone. It was all about keeping your eyes on the prize and nose to the grindstone. No one enjoyed coming to work, let alone being at work. Since your pay was good and you had a family to support, you kept going into work even though you braced yourself for what was in store when you walked through that door.

Values Compromised

While I was proud of my financial and career success at such a young age, I was just as equally not proud of my role as a husband and father. I knew that if I did not breakaway soon, the job and company would start to own me. I loved the idea of being a part of a company where employees enjoy coming to work every day. The problem was, in my industry, that kind of company didn't exist, at least not back then. So, I decided to start my own mortgage company.

On March 1, 1995, Ameritrust Mortgage was established. Our start-up company mission is the same as it is today: To enhance the lifestyles of our customers and our employees. This was not the way any other financial services firm was operating at the time, making it exciting and also challenging to think I could build a company that could go against the way every other firm operated. That was exactly the kind of challenge for me!

With my savings and my wife's support, we opened our doors. By 1998, we had grown to 50 employees and were processing five million dollars in loans per month. It was during my first set-back in my business, in late 1998, that I realized the importance of having core values that help get you through the tough times.

In 1998, Ameritrust Mortgage was heavily invested in the retail mortgage industry. We were working directly with the customer or borrower and processed the loan from start to finish. As the dot-com era swelled into its impending bust, Asian markets crashed, and Russia defaulted on bonds owed to the U.S., there was not enough collateralization in the securities markets. Valuations dropped faster than you could adjust your cost structure, and the mortgage industry took a hit, literally changing overnight.

People began paying off their loans early, causing the market to face a lack of financial security within the industry and making the value of loans decline. We adapted by getting out of the retail business and moving into the wholesale mortgage business. We were now working for other brokers to sell and secure loans instead of working directly with customers. It appeared to be a wise decision at the time, because the company began to grow. We grew from $3 million in loans per month in 1999 to $100 million in loans per month in 2005. It was at this time that we established a program called CHIPP, an acronym that resulted from defining our five core values: Customer Obsession, High Trust, Integrity, Passion and Personal Growth.

Just as we had taken our vision and mission to another level by incorporating our values, our industry took another hit —this time from sub-prime mortgages that were brokered. Market interest rates began to adjust in 2005, and borrowers with prime and sub-prime adjustable rate mortgages, who could barely afford their payments when they secured their loans, began to default. By 2007, the mortgage industry as a whole was in trouble. Interest rates adjusted high enough to discourage new mortgages and prevented some customers from refinancing existing ones. Home ownership began to decline, and I knew I had to adapt again. I went back to my company vision, mission, and core values and dissolved the wholesale division, and decided to return to our roots in the retail mortgage industry. Our values spoke more to dealing with the end consumer, whom we had separated ourselves from by shifting to the wholesale.

I cannot help but wonder to this day if our industry leaders had maintained a credit-worthy standard instead of a greed for market share, if a few thousand, if not millions, of misguided homeowners could have been spared their grief by servicing them with integrity, including not issuing a loan that should never have been issued in the first place.

As counter intuitive that it may have seemed to everyone around us by getting back into the retail side of the business, which was a declining area nationwide, we knew this was exactly where we needed to be. We saw what was happening in the industry, and wanted to practice our corporate values where they could have the greatest impact in restoring confidence with the consumer.

Values Explored & Defined

Profitability and results are obviously important and necessary for business, but you can't reach those goals until you identify and maintain your corporate culture. Defining your corporate core values is where it all should begin to take shape. And as a leader in your organization, it begins with you.

Personal Values: Whether you can spout them off without hesitation or not, your core values as a person are in operation 24/7, either creating uneasiness in a given situation where they are being compromised, or an ease and even enjoyment when they are being honored. As a leader, being aware of your own personal values can help shape and confirm your alignment with your company values.

<u>Business Values:</u> No one should be forced to sacrifice or compromise their personal values in order to do business or be in business. No one! The way in which you engage employees to become aligned with the company's values is to have employees who naturally share and embrace these same values on a personal level. As values are explored and defined, you will realize that business values are derived from the personal values of the leadership of a company and then reinforced by everyone in the company if they are aligned and agreeable to them.

<u>Mission & Purpose:</u> The best way to reaffirm your mission and purpose as a person and within your company is to define your values. We actually did it backwards when we started our company. We knew our mission, but hadn't fully explored what it meant from a values proposition until we got broadsided by a situation that went against what we respected and believed to be right. Once we defined our values, we realized that the current business model of focusing on the wholesale side was not allowing us to fully live and work using our values, especially as it related to serving the end user, the homeowner. Our mission to enhance the lifestyles of our employees and our customers had gone off track because being in the wholesale business separated us from those ultimately being served.

<u>Non-negotiables:</u> With a strong set of core values, there will also be a strong set of guidelines for honoring and upholding these values in the way the company operates and approaches its business. Core values are non-negotiable because they are considered sacred to the company's well being, as well as to each individual's well being associated with the company. An example in our case is demonstrated through our values of High Trust and Integrity. Beyond the compliance measures dictated by our industry, we had documented protocol to assure that everyone in our company was conducting their jobs in an appropriate, client-centric manner. This protocol was non-negotiable because we knew it assured accuracy, proper documentation, and a seamless experience for the customer. We have a zero tolerance policy for any activity that could be construed as being not above board in our dealings. All choices made on behalf of the company or in serving a client were judged based on whether the choice would be one that would make the person proud to be associated with the company by its outcome.

    When I look at any set-back in my company's existence since being established in 1995, it comes down to our corporate values not being honored, either from the inside or the outside. In 2007, when we were forced to shut down and re-emerge as a result of Washington Mutual shutting down credit lines to wholesalers without warning, it became loud and clear that we had been dealing with and totally at the mercy of a company whose values were totally out of alignment with our core values. So clearly, having values does not protect you from mayhem and having a potential downfall. It is also about working, living, and, most important, aligning your values in every way, every day, without exception.

Practicing Your Values

Working Your Values: You can profess your values on signage, on your website, in employee manuals, and in marketing communication. However, if you are not practicing your values on a day-to-day, moment-to-moment basis, then they are just words on paper that make you feel good and look good. Everyone in leadership within your company should be an overseer of your company's core values, and so should every employee in your company.

Living Your Values: Values are values, and are plain and simple. What you believe is right and best at work also should be what's right and best in how you live your life. There can be no double standard, and if there is, then what you profess and what you truly believe are two different things. As the saying goes, "Actions speak louder than words." Often it is what leaders and individuals do outside of their work environment that exposes their true values, to the dismay and disapproval of onlookers. From political to corporate scandals, you can easily know what I am talking about by just reading the daily news.

Aligning Your Values: What I realized in my second setback, was that aligning values was critical not just inside the company with employees, but even more critical outside the company with any individual or company that you would be relying on to deliver your offerings as promised. Even if you are presented with a situation where you are given no choice, you do have choices, even if it means you must shift and adjust your original plan in order to keep your values aligned and protected for the greater good of all concerned.

❖

This was a painful lesson for me to learn. Even though, as a company, we were working on our values and the employees within the company were living our values, a company we relied upon had completely different values and brought us to our knees in a matter of 24 hours. My Inc. 500

fast-growth company had to be reduced from 180 employees to 35 employees in the blink of an eye, due to actions totally out of our control. The remaining troops were rolling up their sleeves in this third go-round in order to clean-up the mess and stay true to our values every step of the way.

CHAPTER 5

Strategy & Corporate Culture

I used to dread strategy meetings in my company because they were exhausting and unproductive. Our monthly leadership meetings were 10-hour marathons. They were dismal attempts at bringing the leadership team together. Everyone was jockeying for a personal agenda and alliances were being formed like the contestants on the popular TV show "Survivor" in preparation for battle to defend their turf, argue their point, and come out the winner. What I finally realized is that the reason the leadership meetings were so ineffective was because they weren't strategic meetings at all. They were bitching sessions and "Hey, look at me" sessions. We would come out of these meetings no more prepared to tackle issues and lead our teams of employees, because we had no clear course or strategic direction uniting us.

It was during my third business setback in 2007 that I recognized the importance of having a true business strategy, not just a business plan. I had learned in my first setback in 1998 that a vision and mission aren't enough if they are not backed by solid values to guide the mission home. This is when we realized that we not only needed values and a mission, but also a good culture, and began our journey toward culture re-engineering. As our new culture began to take hold, our second setback occurred when tough decisions about who fit and who didn't fit in the culture had to be made. This was also when an entire department packed up and left in the middle of the night. During the second setback we quickly realized that it was not a setback at all because with everyone who stayed onboard, our company catapulted into being one of the largest privately held mortgage companies in 2005/2006 because of the culture we had all embraced. Our third setback occurred when the economy kicked everyone's butts and we needed to adjust to what was happening within our entire industry. We realized how strong our corporate culture was when, in spite of this industry-wide chaos, our team was ready to roll its sleeves up and get to work in adapting and living our mission. While I had a business plan, I realized that I had not had a business strategy. A good business plan may have action and implementation behind it, but a great strategy has agility and business intelligence behind it. It was during this third setback that strategy became a pivotal part of how we operated from that point forward. Best of all, because of our culture, the strategy was a team effort that was truly embraced by everyone on our team.

When we decided to get back into the retail side of the business, having been there before, you would think that it would have been an easy shift and just a simple business model change. However, the emotional toll it brought onto management and employees was far more difficult to manage than you can realize until you are in the midst of it.

This is where it became clear how important the corporate culture was for building and then embracing a strategy for the company. A company that is united is a company with people able to focus and provide valued insights and perspectives for where the company needs to go and what it can achieve. A company that is divided will spend most of its time continually selling a strategy from within to get people onboard, versus developing and then implementing the strategy with everyone doing their part to make it happen.

Visioning with Passion & Purpose

Any company that seems to implement its strategy almost effortlessly is able to accomplish their strategy because everyone is totally committed to it and are playing a role in its creation. A strong corporate culture is the mind, heart and soul of your organization that gives your strategy wings to take flight and stay in motion.

A company vision and mission are essential to a strategy, but actual visioning is what takes the strategy to a much higher, more actionable level. This means taking your vision and mission into the company by going deeper into what they mean in every aspect of the company. What it looks like. What it feels like. To employees. To customers. To the marketplace.

When I started the company in 1995, my vision was to be the largest private mortgage company in the Southeast. It was all about becoming big and being a leader. It was, quite frankly, about ego (my ego). I liked being a winner and that meant being viewed as on top of the mountain. When we switched to handling wholesale mortgages, the same premise held true in being the biggest and a leader. We accomplished this, servicing wholesale mortgages in 38 states, cranking out 100 million mortgages a month, and receiving national recognition as an Inc. 500 fast-growth company. From the beginning we had a clear mission. But it wasn't until the second time around that we established our values. The problem was, while we defined our values, we did not take them fully into the company in what they meant in operating the company at every level. Our values were concentrated on the customer, the end user, and we had removed ourselves from this when we went wholesale. Had we realized this sooner, we may have determined to shift to retail mortgages before the bottom fell out from under us on the wholesale side.

Today, we have taken our core values literally into every aspect of our company strategy to support our vision and our mission. Core values drive every decision, from hiring to firing an employee. Core values define how we work together and serve customers. Core values determine how we approach running and growing the business. Core values help us define additional offerings to take into the marketplace. Core values dictate the choice and decisions we make.

From SWOT to SOAR

The basics of developing a strategy dictate that you look at your company's strengths, weaknesses, opportunities and threats (SWOT). The problem with too many companies is that SWOT is where they get stuck and cannot seem to move beyond. They get into analysis paralysis, scrutinizing everything, and discussing everything. Everyone has their opinions and rationale. Getting caught in SWOT is exactly why companies have 10-hour strategy meetings that end up draining everyone and accomplishing nothing. Believe me, I know. I have been there, done that.

So, even though MBA classes are still teaching the SWOT analysis approach to building a business strategy, I determined a different methodology that transformed our 10-hour marathon leadership meetings into three-hour strategy pulse meetings. Instead of SWOT, we focus on SOAR.

Strengths: It always amazes me how companies will profess strengths without really going deep enough to understand the "why" and "how" to best leverage themselves against competition. If it cannot be leveraged as an advantage, then it is not a strength. Your strategy should not just look at the surface level for identifying company strengths, but also look at the individual strengths of the people within your company. What this also will identify is the necessity of documentation, cross training, or the need to establish a knowledge database of references built from specific individuals so that the company is not caught off guard if a person is not accessible. If your company's key strengths are reliant on a specific person's capability, this makes your corporate culture critical to assuring this person stays on board. But more critical is creating an environment where one person's strength can be shared and become several people's strengths.

Opportunities: One of the reasons that our leadership meetings were so laboring was that everyone believed the opportunities they were bringing to the table were the ones the company should be focusing on. These opportunities were driven by personal agendas because we did not have a well-defined corporate agenda. The reality is that even in what appears to be the most dire of economic circumstances, there are opportunities all around you. The trick is to focus on the opportunities that make the most sense for your business, your employees, your customers, and where you want the business to go for long-term value and advantage.

Advantages: By studying your strengths and potential opportunities, you are naturally going to recognize any threats and potential weaknesses or vulnerabilities. At least, you should be recognizing them. After all, how can you honestly state something as an advantage unless you have looked at what may be a threat to your business or a potential weakness? The difference is that by creating the desired outcome about defining your advantages, you are putting less emphasis on getting caught-up in the threats and weaknesses. They are no longer the focal point. They are the qualifiers and justifiers to your advantages. You are acknowledging them in order to hone in on where you have true advantage and what strategically sets you apart. As one of the few private firms, it would have been easy for us to get caught up in the threat of being in the back yard of some of the biggest banks and financial institutions in the world. However, focusing on the advantages and opportunities enabled us to see what was being missed, including the personal approach and being local in our approach to serving customers.

Reach: Reach is about who you are trying to reach beyond the surface level and down into the emotional level where your and their values, mission, and purpose breathe alongside yours. You want to reach them because they will embrace your advantages as their advantages. They are your customers, your team members, your vendor partners, etc. This is why your corporate culture matters and matters in a big way. It is your culture that will ultimately be the "secret sauce" that truly reaches and speaks to your customers, your employees, and all the stakeholders in your company. Once you truly know who you want to and need to reach, then you can focus on how to and where to reach them most effectively.

By focusing on SOAR, you are taking your strategy to the next level. You are not just doing a situation analysis based on where you are currently; you are looking at where you expect to go in order to soar your business to greater heights in market share, sales, profitability, loyalty, and yes, sustainability.

It was a painful process as the CEO to get the leadership team in a SOAR mindset over the SWOT mindset. Part of how I achieved the shift was to have a series of meetings versus one long marathon meeting. I would begin each meeting with a clear outcome for what that particular meeting was going to focus on in the strategy development process. Instead of trying to solve all the company's issues, we used the meetings to take the pulse on one aspect of the business and resolve to prioritize the best solutions based on the desired outcome, always being cognizant of our core values, vision and mission. Once the strategy was completed with everyone's contributions, subsequent meetings continued to take a pulse on how we were doing with a very clear agenda

Strategy Essentials

Innovating Around Values & Passion: If your values truly speak to you, and you are truly passionate about the differences your offerings can make, then innovating will be a natural result and a critical differentiating success factor in your business strategy. Innovation is not just for technology companies. A company with strong core values and with people passionate about the difference their offerings can make is inspired to innovate on an ongoing basis in order to serve their customers better than anyone else. For instance, our passion for customers and our value of trust and integrity enabled us to develop innovative processes designed to accurately and efficiently serve and communicate with our customers, which resulted in shorter closing timeframes and more satisfied customers.

Being Obsessed with the Customers: Any company with a strong cohesive corporate culture also sees an unwavering passion and obsession for serving its customers. Our due diligence confirmed this when looking at a multitude of companies with strong corporate cultures. Even though it is a value, it is a core value for any of the successful cultures I later describe in this book. It merits mentioning here because the strategy dictates how you will bring that obsession to life in what you offer, how you offer it, and why it will matter to your customers. Our customer obsession, in combination with our values supporting our mission, is exactly why Ameritrust is the brand-name for three different companies: Ameritrust Mortgage, Ameritrust Wealth Management, and Ameritrust Insurance. Our mission inspired us to diversify and get each diversified team totally committed to seeing the mission and our core values through serving their customers. By diversifying, we were solidifying our stability as a company while also more fully touching customers' lives and enhancing customers' lifestyles.

Measuring & Monitoring: A strategy without a means of monitoring and measuring its effectiveness is not a good strategy. Defining what is to be measured and how it is to be measured is essential to knowing what is working and what needs adjusting. We determined several measurement points in our strategy and then put systems and procedures in place to monitor and get feedback for decision-making. Areas we determined that were essential to measure included customer referrals, customer satisfaction, employee retention, employee satisfaction, and sales profitability. Sales in and of itself was not a benchmark, because over the years we had learned that you can have skyrocketing sales with plummeting profits or the wrong kind of sales generating no profits. Our strategy measurements shifted from being about volume to being more about value — long-term, sustainable value.

Decision Making Made Easier: A well-conceived strategy also makes decision-making at all levels of the company easier. The strategy can literally guide decisions when situations arise because the plan is so well thought through and documented that all stakeholders within the company have reference for guidance. A company strategy should not and cannot be empowered without it being effectively and clearly communicated to the entire team. By empowering decision making in your company at a strategic level, you are giving your strategy life on a 24/7 basis. For instance, by understanding the combined importance of customer obsession, high trust and integrity, when a loan was questionable and deemed too risky our underwriters and loan officers worked together to determine any options, and then educated the homeowner. If options are limited, then they direct the homeowners to resources to help them improve their circumstance for reconsideration later. When we were focused on high volume and being the biggest, the loan officers we had in place would quickly drop the loan like a defect on an assembly line versus seeking ways to add value to the end customer. Once the core values became our strategic drivers, we hired more customer-centric people who shared our core values.

Accepting & Embracing Adversity: You cannot ignore problems, challenges, mistakes, or setbacks in your business. But you also can't allow yourself to get into a quagmire over them either. Having a solid foundation with a vision, mission, and values helps you be more able to deal with adversity and make better overall decisions. You can look at the facts, accept responsibility where necessary, or identify the root of the problem. You acknowledge what is out of your control, and then you define solutions and preventions and put systems and processes into place as a result. Most important of all, you learn from the adversity, and then let it go and move one. Another interesting caveat to having strong core values in association with a vision and mission is that you are more likely to sense something is not right, and, therefore, can anticipate, investigate and shift before adversity hits. Your values give you a stronger base of gut instinct that should never be ignored. If it doesn't feel right, chances are something isn't right.

Agility & Continual Evolution: Strategies today must operate from the knowledge that markets are dynamic and shifts occur often, and sometimes unexpectedly. In order to minimize fluctuations, you must build a strategic plan that can anticipate and capitalize on market shifts instead of just reacting to them. What we also realized is the value of not having all our eggs in one basket. Diversification guided by our core values has made us more agile by not being dependent on one stream of business, but multiple streams of business.

❖

As a result of this deeper exploration of our mission and values, our vision shifted from being the biggest to being the best. Everything we did from that point forward was driven by being the best place to work, the best place to obtain a mortgage, the most trusted place to get financial advice, and the most reliable place to obtain the right insurance for a family or an individual's needs. As you explore strategy and corporate culture in your own business, you might find that your vision will shift too, in very gratifying and exciting ways.

CHAPTER 6
Leadership & Corporate Culture

I was eyes down at my desk reviewing some reports when the fill-in receptionist popped her head into my office and said that we had a serious problem. The employees were unhappy and action needed to be taken now. On the surface level, this could be viewed as impressive that a temporary employee could be so bold to come prancing into the CEO's office and make such a proclamation. I must have made this person feel welcome, appreciated and motivated. Not the case! This fill-in employee was my wife and, quite frankly, I wouldn't be telling the truth if I didn't admit that my initial reaction was irritation, annoyance, and that I didn't have time for this. But the reality was that I wasn't happy about my company or about doing my job either, and hadn't been for a while.

The toughest part about being a leader is when you must look in the mirror and see how you are leading, or rather, not leading. It is not something you can do effectively on your own. No matter what type of leader that you are, if you stop learning you stop growing. And this means seeking to learn and continuing to grow as a leader through others.

One of the things that made me successful in the beginning of my career was that I was hungry for knowledge and I had great teachers. I wanted to learn from everyone. In the first five years, my company was growing fast, which was propelled by my interest in and focus on learning … what I needed to know, what others needed to know, what worked, what didn't work, what could be improved, and what others were doing that we should be doing. The problem with growing very fast is that you can easily get caught up in the momentum of the growth and forget to keep growing yourself. The focus becomes more about managing and reacting to the growth.

About Culture

After a while, I was going into work, but I was just going through the motions. The company was managing me, instead of me leading the company. I was in a rut and had lost sight of the very things I had been doing in the beginning that made me and my company successful.

So on that fateful day in October of 2001, when my wife receptionist made me look in the mirror, I accepted that I didn't like the reflection I was seeing in me or my company. I had known this for a long time, but just didn't want to admit it, because that would make me feel too much like I was failing.

Clarity and Courage

The first move I needed to make was a mental one. I needed to decide to get out of my own way, put my ego aside and get help. I needed to make the time even though I felt like I had no time to spare. I needed to allow myself to transform if I was going to see my company transform.

I hired a consulting firm that specialized in developing leaders and organizational culture, and began working with a leadership coach who helped me see how my own leadership style was creating much of the problem. This required me to take a look inside myself and learn how I was wired.

As the son of a New York police officer, I was raised to face problems head on and fight back when cornered. I didn't run from controversy. I almost lived for it. As a result, when conflict arose in my company, I took charge and nipped it in the bud. I dictated what needed to happen to fix it and I expected people to jump through hoops to get the situation handled. While I felt in control, my hands-on confrontational approach was not working for me or for my employees, and was part of the reason things were getting out of control.

As a star baseball player in college, I enjoyed being in the spotlight. I also enjoyed the competition and always being the one on top, the winner, and being the one getting the accolades and recognition. I liked being the one making things happen. If it was the bottom of the ninth, I wanted the ball hit to me so I could be the hero. This attitude defined my leadership style with my employees. If something wasn't getting done, I'd tell them to hand it to me. I wanted to be the one making the final play. My executive coach made me realize that by wanting to be the star all the time, I was basically telling all of my employees that their contributions meant nothing. It was all about me and my company instead of about them and what they were doing to make the company successful. I needed to shift from being the only star to leading and coaching my employees to be stars too.

If you haven't utilized executive coaching, I recommend it. As a matter of fact, I think it is essential when it comes to any type of professional or corporate transition. No-one can operate in a vacuum or expect to know the answers and what to do at all times. Being able to look honestly at yourself means allowing yourself to be vulnerable and being willing to expose and share that self with others.

Mover & Shaker

Being a Mover and Shaker in the business world has come to be synonymous with someone who is making things happen. From a leadership standpoint, I have a slightly different view of Mover and Shaker. As a leader, you can be a Mover & Shaker, or be just a Mover or just a Shaker. The ideal, in my opinion, is to be a Mover. In doing my own self discovery and analysis of my leadership, I realized the difference and it has stuck with me.

Mover Leader

M   = Motivator & Manager
O   = Opportunities Embraced
V   = Values Driven & Value Drives
E   = Excellence through Engagement
R   = Return on Investment (Black Zone)

The Mover Leader is both a motivator and a manager. This leader's role is focused on managing the accountability of the team through a unified understanding based on an underlying purpose. Communicating and clarifying what everyone's contribution is being made to the end result creates self accountability in each of the team members. By motivating with a big-picture understanding, managing employees becomes easier because they are managing themselves. This leader's high expectations focus on embracing opportunities with optimism and confidence in the team's contributions and abilities, therefore everyone is more effective at moving things forward. The Mover is a leader who is both core values-driven and value-driven. There is a strong set of core values in how the leader approaches business, works with the team, manages the company, and makes decisions that are also at the very core of how the company builds value in its offerings and to its stakeholders and shareholders. The Mover also understands that the desired end game for the company is directly tied to how well the employees are engaged in the process. A Mover realizes that excellence is driven when employees are engaged. The

About Culture

result is that the company realizes a solid return on investment with sales growth and profitability, as well as with employee and customer retention.

Shaker Leader

S	=	Self-Focused
H	=	Hard Driving
A	=	Action Driven
K	=	Kick Starter
E	=	Excellence through Exhaustion
R	=	Return on Investment (Red Zone)

The Shaker Leader is self-focused and everything the team does is about what it ultimately will mean in advancing the leader's agenda. This leader's confidence is driven by his or her own abilities, and not necessarily by the team's ability. High expectations combined with self-focus results in micro-managing employees to achieve results in pursuing opportunities. In many cases, this leader will take the ball back to get things moving the way he or she wants them to go out of a belief that he or she is the one that always makes things happen. The Shaker doesn't care to be a motivator of employees, even though they may profess that they do. The truth is that this leader just wants to see action being taken and a continuous flow of activity in the business. Looking busy is how members of the team react whenever this leader enters their work area. This leader is always in the mode of kick-starting people, projects and efforts for short-term results that intend this to bring long-term effectiveness, but having short-lived momentum due to the volatility in which this leader operates. Since the focus is on this leader's own idea of what he or she envisions as the ultimate end game or success strategy, being able to anticipate or fully know what this leader is really wanting is exhausting, confusing, and worrisome. While this company may realize short-term growth and profitability, the environment does not support a long-term ability to sustain sales or retain employees.

The Mover & Shaker Leader is like a roller coast ride with ups and downs, sharp turns, and deep plunging emotional effects. This leader motivates by being hard-driving with no mercy or consideration for what may be occurring for team members. There is an element of fear-based motivation with this leader, with team members more concerned about not screwing up versus doing a good job. It is all about the end result and moving things forward at all costs for the Mover & Shaker. As long as things are moving in the direction desired, this leader can be enjoyable at times to be around, but when things start heading in an undesirable direction, all hell breaks loose because this leader will shake to the very core to get to the bottom of why things are not occurring as planned. When the company is profitable, the team members are not feeling or receiving the rewards, and if the company is not profitable, the team members are the ones being blamed by this leader. The result is that the company goes through roller-coaster highs and lows in growth, profitability and morale.

Once I realized that the Shaker characteristics were causing me to get in my own way, I understood better what I needed to be as a leader in order to have a true team behind me and working well for my company, and not just in my company. It created a shift in my style and approach that has served me more effectively ever since.

❖

In Section III, Chapter 15, I explore Leadership Engagement, and in Section IV, I dedicate the entire section to Leading the Culture according to what works the most effectively dependent on the corporate culture model being used. Consider how your leadership style may be shaking up your business in unsettling ways instead of shaping it in powerful ways.

CHAPTER **7**

Communication & Corporate Culture

An underlying hush came over everyone in my company whenever I would enter the office. The energy level was not what I was used to feeling and I sensed something was different, but wasn't sure what or why I was feeling this way – I just knew something had changed abruptly. Employees would glance at me and look away. I could see confusion and pensiveness in their eyes. It was like they wanted to say something, but didn't dare. This continued for several days with tension and the entire atmosphere continuing to shift. It was unsettling and clear that it was not my imagination. One member of my management team was able to get to the bottom of what was happening. There was a rumor going around that my marriage was in trouble. Someone had seen me leaving the fitness center where I worked out without having my wedding band on my finger. In that brief period of not putting my wedding band on until I got home, an entirely alternative reality was born.

My marriage was not in trouble, but my entire company somehow believed that this was the case. The manager who shared this suggested that I should call a team meeting to address it with the team. My first reaction was "It is none of their damn business what is going on in my personal life, and they should know better." After all both my wife and I worked at the company together and they saw how well we worked together. The entire situation, in my opinion, was ludicrous and not worth my time or energy in justifying or wasting company time in addressing.

Regardless of my initial reaction, I did need to address it. This wasn't just about employees being concerned about my marriage. This was also about them being concerned about the company and what it would mean to their roles. If my marriage were to break up, does that mean the company would fall apart too?

A team meeting was called and my wife, Stacy, and I addressed the group together. With reassurance and everyone laughing in the end, the rumor was put to rest and their energy returned. Faith and trust was restored.

While the rumor I just shared was of a very personal nature, rumors occur all the time of a professional nature internally and externally that have brought businesses to their knees. Rumors are more than just damaging. They can take you by surprise and reach right into your gut because of how personally they affect you, especially when you are passionate about what you do and why you are doing what you do. While ignoring it and just letting it pass over may have worked for you in middle or high school – in business and in the adult world it's not that simple. And as a leader, rumors that continue to grow and take a life of their own mean that communication has been disrupted or has ceased altogether.

The fact that the rumor about my marriage being in trouble was not squelched immediately by other employees indicated that there was a bigger issue at stake. There was not a unified understanding. A level of trust also had diminished because of the perception that I was not honoring my marriage by wearing my wedding band. The value of commitment to my wife and family I had professed also was tied to my commitment to the company. Doubt about what I really stood for had entered people's minds by the simple act of not wearing that wedding band for a few hours on one day.

A mentor once told me that "No Communication = Make Sh*t Up." Think about it for a minute. How many times have you not known what was going on, so your imagination began thinking of all kinds of scenarios? We humans are good at doing this - jumping to assumptions and then determining what is going on without any actual tangible facts or information, just our overactive imaginations.

To be an effective leader, it is your job to make sure everyone has a unified understanding of the company, its vision, mission, purpose, and their roles in making it happen. But communication doesn't and shouldn't stop there. It must be seamless, ever flowing, consistent, clear, effective, and reinforcing. It must be embraced as the critical success factor that it is. It must be a priority in every company from the inside out and the outside in.

Inside Out, Outside In

When you make communication a priority in your organization, it can quickly become a competitive advantage because communication is so rarely done on a consistent basis in business in general. To assure communication is fully embraced and understood throughout your company, various aspects of communication should be addressed and clearly understood including: reinforcing corporate values, vision and mission; flow of communication; documentation around communication; handling of external/internal communication, and measuring the effectiveness of communication.

Reinforcing Values, Vision and Mission: Communication should recognize your core values on a consistent and ongoing basis in what is being communicated and why. At Ameritrust, our corporate values are not just in the employee handbook, they are posted in the office where everyone can be reminded of what we stand for each and every day. They are described on our website so that customers know and can expect these values to shine through our actions and how our customers are treated. They are spoken in our words and carried out in our actions as we make decisions and serve each other and our customers. Reinforcing your values in communication on an ongoing basis reinforces everyone inside and outside of the company to know why what you do matters, and why everyone should care and take pride in what they are doing. This also will give everyone permission to share and communicate any instance that is not in alignment with the corporate values, so that corrections or a particular situation can be addressed.

Communication Through Action: What you communicate to your team by the actions you take is even more important and critical to demonstrating your commitment to the values, vision and mission. When it came to my attention that some of our sales team, led by a particular manager, were out partying and conducting themselves in an inappropriate and unprofessional manner, other team members shared their concern that it did not fit our family-friendly environment. It was up to me to set the expectations, including reprimanding anyone's behavior that was not in alignment with what we considered to be honest, high integrity, customer focused, and professional. In spite of this particular manager producing top sales figures for our company, his behavior was having a derogatory effect on the rest of the team. After I made the tough decision to terminate his employment, I realized just how much this person and others who would leave as a result of his being fired were holding back the rest of the team. We experienced double the volume in sales the following month as everyone, relieved by who was no longer there, rallied together to demonstrate what they were all capable of doing.

<u>Flow of Communication:</u> Defining who takes responsibility for specific communication so that a gap does not occur is a key to success. And quite frankly, this must start from the top down, and be a priority from the top down. Identifying what types of information should be the responsibility of specific departments or individuals leaves no room for confusion or finger pointing because something didn't get communicated. Not only should accountability be incorporated into your organization's communication process, but expectations should be, as well. It is easy to take some aspects of communication for granted and assume it is being done when it is not when everyone thinks someone else is handling the specific communication.

<u>Documentation for Clarification:</u> Misunderstandings in communication occur because of a lack of follow-up, clarification, or confirmation of understanding. Having a process for documenting communication within your company is important so that everyone is approaching communication in the same manner. Whether you are conducting memorandums, policies for email and letters, marketing messaging standards, or other forms of communication, the most important thing to remember when it comes to documentation is to first communicate why it is important. What is a blessing, and yet sometimes feels like a curse, is the level of documentation required in the financial services industry. While it is more targeted toward CYA with compliance documentation and other requirements, the basic premise of being clear, accurate, and intentional is a good one. At our company, we embraced this by adding to the process beyond what was expected from a compliance standpoint, because we were also viewing it from customer and internal effectiveness standpoints.

<u>Internal Communication:</u> Keeping everyone in the loop so no-one is caught off guard is a common complaint of employees that many companies are not doing very well. As I mentioned earlier, it can be easy to take communication for granted or assume that certain types of communication don't require continuous reinforcement. It is also too often assumed that only one form of communication is enough, be it meetings, memos, posters or bulletins scattered throughout the company walls. Not so. Time and time again, it has been proven to me how important it is to do a mix of communication on an ongoing basis in both written and spoken forms. Conducting our own corporate culture assessment made this abundantly clear while writing this book. I and my executive leadership were thrilled to see confirmed in the report provided to us that our employees were passionate about what they did in their jobs and looked forward to coming

to work each day. They also agreed that we operated based on a clear set of corporate values and that many of their personal values mirrored those of our corporate values.

For many executives, this would have felt like we had hit a home run in aligning our culture through communication. Not so again. We also discovered that in spite of understanding that we had core corporate values, newer employees weren't entirely clear about our mission and vision, while employees overall were unclear about some of our policies regarding hiring, family and work/life balance, and personal/professional development. Most alarming of all, a large percentage of employees were unclear of how decisions were made in the company and our expectations about customer satisfaction and employee performance. So basically we had an impassioned team that loved to come to work and felt that they were making a difference, but not totally clear how they were making a difference and what was ultimately expected about them in each of their roles.

This was a big "aha" for me, and the funny thing is, once this was brought to our attention, I could list without hesitation all the things we weren't doing and should be doing. This wasn't something to put in a memo and then be done with it. These concerns needed to be addressed and clarified in a multitude of ways to truly be understood. This was a team building and company awareness internal campaign opportunity that we embraced. And guess what? Those employees that were already passionate and loving what they were doing became even more impassioned and even more focused once they truly understood the "why."

External Communication: In our ideal culture, external communication means everything to us. And it should mean everything to any company desiring sustainability. What is being said and being felt outside of the company is your true barometer for tracking how effective you are operating as a company and a corporate culture. I am not just talking about the marketing messages and promotional communication being sent externally, but the "from the trenches" communication by our employees when outside of the company, as well as the "word-of-mouth" by customers, associates, and even suppliers or business partners. A company's reputation depends on external communication. A company's reputation can be irreparably damaged when external communication is affirming more of what the company isn't than what it is. For me, nothing gives me greater pride than to overhear an employee at a business function or marketplace event proudly talking about the company and the difference we make ... or receiving an unsolicited high-praise review on Yelp from a customer specifically naming one of our employees or the team who made their experience exceptional.

<u>Measuring Effectiveness:</u> If you are taking your communication protocol to the point of measuring its effectiveness, then you are truly embracing communication as the competitive advantage that it is. It is one thing to communicate and entirely another to know without a doubt that it is being heard, understood, and then embraced in powerful and empowering ways. One of the ways I have been able to measure the effectiveness and how genuinely our communication is received and accessible by engaged leaders is with what I call a "drop in." I literally will pop my head into a team meeting with a manager and instead seeing the look of "Oh my God, the boss is here," I will often get invited in it as a guest to sit in. I sit in and observe, not contribute, and everyone is comfortable enough to proceed and it is as if I am not in the room. Would the same thing happen if you dropped in on a meeting, or would the whole demeanor of the group change? My drop-ins help me know if things were being communicated effectively on a variety of levels. Sometimes, it helped me see that I have not communicated something effectively. I am a big believer that if people don't understand, it's not because the receiver is not understanding. It's because the person who is communicating is not doing it in a way in which the receiver can best learn or embrace the concepts or directives. Three people can be told the same exact thing, but hear or understand it in three different interpretations. Some people are audible, while others are visual and others are verbal. This is why communication in a variety of ways is so important.

Meetings for Momentum

If having a meeting in your company brings a sense of dread to you and others, then your meetings are contributing to the problem in your communication approach. Avoiding meetings altogether when your company has more than a handful of people isn't the solution either. Quite frankly, even a company of a couple of people needs to make productive meetings a part of how the company gets things done.

<u>Action Sessions versus Bitching Sessions:</u> If your staff meetings or an impromptu lunch with co-workers sounds more like the latter, then communication is a real problem within your organization. Of greater concern is if the bitching is occurring internally, then it is most certainly

occurring externally, and probably even more rampantly. The key to effective meetings and gatherings, whether planned or spontaneous, is that there is a well-defined purpose to getting together along with a desired outcome. As mundane as an agenda may seem, it has a valuable purpose in helping keep everyone focused, but more important is that there is a defined outcome. What will the meeting resolve, move forward, impact, etc? If the desired outcome is not defined, then the entire group will easily get side tracked, leave with no clear idea of what was accomplished, have more questions than answers, and yes, have more to complain about at the next lunch with co-workers. Even an impromptu lunch gathering, when communication is top of mind and top in practice, can result in ideas, energy and connectivity among employees. They can actually focus on getting to know one another or are sharing versus complaining about work.

<u>Pulse, Policy, Potential & Promise Sessions:</u> Let's face it. This is what bringing your leaders together should be all about and should also be what they should strive to do within the team of employees they are leading. Whether it is bringing the sales team, a department of people, the entire staff, or the leaders together on a regular basis, the idea of having meetings with momentum works when these four "P's" are consistently engaged and acted upon.

Pulse: The nurse practitioner may take your pulse during your annual physical check-up, but taking the pulse of your company should be a multi-faceted ongoing practice. It is essential to truly know without doubt how well you are doing what you have set out to do. Everyone in the company should be engaged in this process in order to share their own perspectives and insights according to what they are doing and how effective it is in meeting desired outcomes. Sharing "pulse points" through an open forum of communicating any concerns, high five's or anticipated problems, is part of this process. To avoid it turning into the "bitching session" described earlier, have a clear agenda of what the pulse points are in the company and the measures. For instance, if employee retention is important to your company, then reinforcing lower attrition with an update on the success or discussing effectiveness of a specific initiative to improve this would be shared.

Policy: When you first read this word, "policy," you were probably thinking it has red tape and bureaucracy written all over it. No. What I am talking about here are standards. Standards of service. Standards of quality. Standards of communication. Standards of delivery. Standards of performance. And this list goes on. As a part of taking your company's pulse, you need to set these standards so you can know whether you have a weak, barely there pulse or a strong heart-pumping exhilarating pulse in a particular area. Policy is not as much about policing or preaching as it is about preserving and improving. For instance, when an employee says, "Our policy is to always make our customers feel important," you begin to see what I mean by policies being empowering versus limiting.

Potential: I recall having a meeting full of discussion around a myriad of opportunities that each of my management team members felt strongly were the direction the company should go. While the fact that we were all discussing opportunities is positive and ideal, when everyone has their own agendas and reasons for disagreeing with one another's opportunities, then you know as the CEO that you have a huge communication disconnect. If management can't agree on opportunities, how can the company and its employees effectively pursue any of them? So it isn't just the opportunities, but the potential for each opportunity as it relates to what the company is ultimately trying to achieve in its vision and its mission. Which opportunities speak most wholly to the corporate values and your passion in serving customers or innovating offerings? When you have clear values, vision, mission, and core values, prioritizing really is easy and consensus around the priorities is too.

Promise: This is where action and accountability meet in order for the real momentum to be realized. How many times have you heard "all we do is talk about things, but never do anything about things." Ouch! Putting promise into the mix means there is a true commitment in moving forward as a result of decisions made during the meeting. Yes, decisions. Because when you go into a meeting focused on gauging pulse, reinforcing policy, and prioritizing potential, then your decisions enable you to take real action. You also have people ready and willing to step up to the action and be held accountable or to hold others accountable to see it through.

Not every session can focus on every pulse point or policy issue, so define in your overall internal communication plan some structure around when the pulse is to be taken and shared or a policy is to be reviewed throughout the year in various P4 meetings. Quite frankly, even if you are focused on one specific topic, using the four P's can work. Try it and you'll see what I mean.

Team Building & Celebration: A book that has shaped my approach to managing my company is The Great Game of Business. I embraced its principles so much that I gave our monthly team meetings the same name. The idea that the book's author, Jack Stack, shares of getting everyone in the company focused on how to help the company be successful resonated with me in a big way. Getting everyone on my team to think like owners also excited me. So we rallied everyone together for these monthly sessions that focused on sharing numbers, where we wanted to go, and what each person could do to make it a reality. We created sales incentives and rewards for achievement. I saw my team giving one another high fives as another successful closed piece of business was marked on our whiteboard. Our sales improved and it was exciting, except that into the third month, I realized that this momentum would be short lived if I did not quickly focus on ALL the ways our company was being successful. We were only focusing on the numbers, and based on some of the feedback from employees in the corporate culture assessment report, some other critical success factors were not being recognized, like customer satisfaction and rave reviews, team support and efficiencies necessary to help loan officers go into final closing, and a number of other successes that added up to the big record-breaking successes we were realizing. I was focusing on the home runs and not the safe singles and doubles plays critical to winning in our great game of business.

Communication should be focused on how it is going to make you stronger as a leader, your people stronger in working with one another and serving customers, and your company stronger as a competitor. If your communication is just focused solely on protecting interests, confirming policies and disclaimers, or promoting without personally engaging, then you don't truly understand the power of communication as a competitive advantage.

❖

The most effective corporate cultures embrace communication as essential to being exceptional. In Chapter 15 on Leadership Engagement and Chapter 16 on Employee Engagement, I share some best practices about communication in more detail.

CHAPTER 8
Ethics & Corporate Culture

Wooing clients in the world of high finance and investments has for decades included high priced outings, extravagant events, dinners at the finest restaurants, and, in many cases, special unique perks that would be described as something else on the expense report handed into the accounting department. Being young and ambitious when I first got into the industry, the wooing aspect was glamorous and appealing because it felt like a company benefit to go out to dinner and have the company pick up the tab. As an underling just getting into the business world, it can be intimidating as you begin to witness things happening that don't feel right, and yet are viewed as right and the right way business gets done by everyone around you. You tend to look the other way or keep your head down and focused on your own performance to avoid the inner conflict. Turmoil is felt by what your own gut is telling you that is the right thing to do, and yet, what is being done wrong, in your opinion, is being done by someone who is higher up or literally signs your paycheck.

One thing that I know for certain is that it's not just knowing right from wrong, but doing what is right. After all, not doing what was right for the long-term probably was what got us into this Great Recession and corporate upheaval in America in the first place. Now more than ever, ethics has been at the center of many business successes and failures. Ethics has become a requirement in undergrad business and MBA curriculums. What is concerning is that it needs to be taught in the first place, but this is the reality we live in.

For me, I define ethics to my family and employees as the gap between intentions and behaviors. Leadership, by example, is the way through which that gap is closed. In other words, everyone on your leadership team should be the stewards of turning your company's good intentions into right actions through being thought leaders and action leaders. If leaders don't practice what is preached, how can we expect our employees to do the same, or more important, know at all?

Someone asked me to explain what "doing what is right" means to me. The fact that I am a parent came to mind. I responded by saying that when I go home each night to be with my family, I want to feel proud of the choices that I made during the day. I want to be able to look in my daughter's or son's eyes and feel that they are benefiting from my choices in positive ways because my choices were right not just for me, but for everyone … my employees, customers, associates, business, and industry.

To my employees, I have also reinforced it in this way. Whatever action being taken by you, take a moment to consider if you would be proud of it or others would be positive about it. If there is even the slightest tinge of hoping someone does not find out or know what you are doing, then that is the answer loud and clear. It is not the right action.

How are you encouraging your management and employees to do what is right? How are you encouraging everyone in your life to do what is right? Most important, how are you demonstrating what is right in your actions?

Varying Degrees of Ethics

What also troubles me in the business climate today is that there appears to be varying degrees of ethics. How can this be? As I thought about this more, I realized that the variables exist because of varying beliefs, plain and simple. What one person believes to be right is different from another. Therefore, their intentions would be different, as well as their behavior, compared to another person in a similar circumstance. This is why alignment in a corporate culture is so important. It also is why communication about what is considered ethical and not ethical is essential to ensure a complete and undisputable understanding.

The idea of transparency has become the new word in vogue as a result of the financial crisis. As much as it is touted as being the way businesses need to operate, the reality is that it is uncomfortable to be transparent, which affirms its true weight and value. Being transparent means you must show your warts as well as your heart. My own transparency was challenged when I was in the midst of a David versus Goliath lawsuit, me being the David. During the period of discovery, I was reviewing all the documents requested by deposition and when I got to one particular document, I paused and scrutinized it from every possible theoretical angle. I became very uncomfortable as I grew concerned that this one document could be damaging to my case depending on how it was interpreted. I considered the option of shredding it as if it never existed. As uncomfortable as it was, however, I kept that document among the discovery items. I was steadfast in my belief that the bullying tactics of this behemoth company would not cause me to question my business conduct or the practices of my firm. From the time the lawsuit was first summoned, I felt it was a frivolous attempt to use might over right. I was not going to allow fear tactics to be the instigator of doubt or uncertainty.

Being steadfast in your ethics can be empowering and comforting, helping you quickly move beyond a twinge of discomfort once you remind yourself what is the right thing to do. The document I decided to keep among the deposition items ended up being the key document that helped me win the case. In hindsight, I realized that I was over-thinking while reviewing the document, literally allowing the stress of the lawsuit to get to me. By doing what was right, we prevailed. Interestingly, my Goliath opponent presented a document that was deemed to have been fabricated, which ultimately hurt their credibility, and their ability to win the case.

Ethics & Corporate Values

What we determined as we explored the varying corporate cultures described later in this book is that ethical conduct is reinforced by the corporate values of an organization. Many companies actually have "Integrity" as a corporate value because of the rampant ethical issues plaguing the business world. However, professing a value and then living up to it in action are two entirely different things. Right actions are more powerful than right intentions. But then, what are the right actions?

As mentioned in Chapter 4, our company's core values include two aspects that speak directly to ethical behavior: Integrity and High Trust. We felt these were necessary because the mortgage and financial services industries as a whole were being chastised in the media on a daily basis due to alleged unethical practices. Professing these values was not and is not enough. If they are only professed to look good on the corporate website, then they are meaningless and powerless. They must have intentional meaning backed by behavior that supports these values on a daily basis as being important.

For instance, with regard to Integrity as a value, we believe it completes us as an organization because it is the benchmark for knowing we are always doing our very best for our clients and everyone concerned. The dictionary definition of integrity includes: adherence to moral or ethical principles; a state of being whole, entire or undiminished; and being in unimpaired or perfect condition. I have a chilling analogy that occurred to me related to integrity that underscores the importance of each person, each process, and each function of a company as it pertains to integrity. I was in Palm Beach, Florida, in January of 1986 heading to baseball practice. While driving on the highway, everyone began to pull over, and you could literally hear everyone counting down. 3 – 2 – 1 and then blast off! Cheers quickly turned to an eerie silence that I will never forget. This was the day the Challenger exploded. I still get chills just thinking about it and have never forgotten it. I use it as an example with my leadership team. Integrity means that everyone plays an important role, and everything we do is focused on assuring that what we deliver to customers is our best work. When you read reports about the Challenger disaster, there were numerous delays and red flags from engineers citing a variety of concerns that were overruled by NASA officials. As managers and leaders, our integrity is most put to the test when our team brings issues or concerns to us. It is also when every other value is put to the test based on the decisions that are made.

In the culture assessment we conducted with our team, we gained insight about the importance of continual reinforcement of what High Trust and Integrity meant for us. While my leadership team members were unified in believing that ethical standards and conduct are an important aspect of our corporate values and we agreed that we conducted ourselves in an ethical manner, nearly 17% of our employees claimed that they did not know this to be the case in the assessment. Another area in which employees selected that they "did no know" included a whopping 43% of employees not knowing whether management treated poor performing employees in an appropriate and fair manner. While not knowing doesn't imply not doing, for me, the not knowing meant there was uncertainty, and it needed to be addressed.

This told me and my management team that we needed to address our values around High Trust and Integrity as each relates to our thoughts and behaviors. While our intentions were stated, what these intentions looked like, felt like and acted like needed reinforcement.

Intentional leadership is essential when it comes to reinforcing ethics because Integrity and High Trust are the most challenged of values in business. As sad as this is, a majority of the reasons why employees or leaders leave a company is because of integrity or trust issues. This is also why relationships, personal or professional, are irreparably severed. A person's integrity and ability to trust and be trusted places him or her at a higher level of confidence felt by others. This is accomplished through being intentional in actions and words. The same holds true in how a company is viewed as having high integrity and being trustworthy.

Immediately after the bottom fell out of the financial industry, and the bailout monies were being divvied-up in the millions to financial institutions, there were several instances where these same large financial institutions had planned extravagant retreats and meetings. These lavish multi-day extravaganzas came into question with public outrage. Companies led by intentional leaders made the conscientious decision to cancel the events, in spite of a great deal of the expenses already having been paid to hotels, caterers, travel agents, and others. For these leaders, the perception that would result from carrying on as if there was no crisis would have been much more costly in the long-run. They understood that doing what was right was much more important than doing what was already planned. Another example of capitalizing on the Integrity and High Trust factors was demonstrated by the handful of banks that did not accept bailout monies. To them, it was an admission of guilt or mishandling of funds that was not the case with them. You can bet they leveraged this to great advantages in marketing and communication for competitive advantage.

The Link Between Ethics and Morality

Morality is not a religious matter, it is a human matter and should be a business matter, as well. Look up the definition of "moral" in the dictionary and it states "principles or rules of right conduct or the distinction between right and wrong."

In Chapter 7, I shared the example of the sales manager I ultimately had to terminate due to his conduct that was deemed to be neither appropriate, nor in alignment with our corporate culture of valuing and respecting families and one another. Attempts to charge visits to Strip Clubs as client entertainment was not only unacceptable, but also degrading to what we were professing to be as a company that focused on family values. Even though this was a typical practice in our industry at conferences, it was not how we determined we wanted to conduct business.

At our firm, we have taken the idea of ethical behavior to deeper levels of understanding through being open and honest about what is viewed as internal guides to everyone in our company. We clarify and reinforce what is acceptable and ethical through helping everyone in our company better know how to assess a situation or circumstance. We challenge our people to gauge based on a "good for/bad for" or "private/public" basis.

- Are you considering what is in the best interest of everyone concerned about how you are proceeding with an action or decision? Would the decision be good for you, but bad for the company or a customer?
- Would the decision be good for the customer, but have negative repercussions for the company in the short-term or long-term? If short-term, is the value received in that the customer trust has been nurtured resulting in greater value to everyone concerned? If long term, is it really good for the customer in the long run?
- Ask yourself, am I taking action differently because it is in private rather than I would if it were being seen or heard publicly? Your actions should be consistent regardless of who sees or hears them or who doesn't. For us, personal conduct and professional conduct are on an equal plane. Oftentimes, we have found that it is personal conduct that causes professional conduct to be questioned. If both are coveted, then neither can be questioned.

Morals and the Ethical Leader

Is there a difference in one's morals professionally versus personally? Can someone with high morals in one area be trustworthy and credible if their morals are questionable in the other realm? My stance is that morals directly link to ethical leadership from both personal and professional standpoints. How someone leads others based on their moral fiber is no different than how someone leads himself or herself in the conscious decisions and choices being made every moment of the day. Our morals are the basis of the values we hold dearest and most sacred to whom we are as individuals, so it shouldn't matter whether we are in a personal or professional environment.

As observers and continuous students of humankind, a colleague and I identified a correlation between morals and ethical leadership. While we don't want to believe this is common, there are more instances than not of people who demonstrate higher morals professionally or personally, but not necessarily in both.

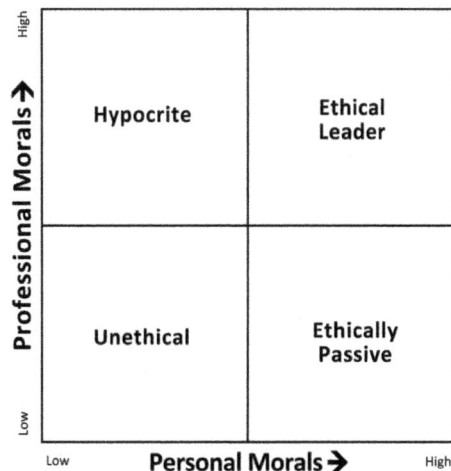

	Low ——— Personal Morals → ——— High
High ↑ Professional Morals	Hypocrite / Ethical Leader
Low	Unethical / Ethically Passive

High Professional Morals: The tricky thing about professional morals is knowing and believing whether the morals being professed are for real or for show. Especially when a person gains entry into a position of power or prominence, the appearance of ethics can be the real motivator for actually being ethical. This is especially true when a person behaves with high morals at work, but not personally. When leaders are adamant about moral behavior and conduct at work, but then are not moral in the way in which they live their personal lives, the perception of them is that they are hypocrites. Executives having mistresses come to mind, as well as having a strict drug-use policy in place and then abusing drugs themselves. The examples could go on and on. In most cases, these individuals are "acting" their morals versus actually believing and living them.

High Personal Morals: When it comes to a person with high personal morals, but low professional morals, it doesn't mean he or she is unethical. When it comes to their own personal conduct, they are highly ethical. The fine line is drawn for this individual by their confidence in how far they can take their moral beliefs into the workplace. While they have their moral code, they are not confident that they have the right to impose their beliefs on others. If the person is in a subordinate role, this can be even more difficult if leaders in the organization are conducting themselves against what the person believes to be moral. Nothing will be said. Nothing will be done. People with high personal morals without syncing their morals at the professional level will tolerate the environment and look the other way as long as it does not directly impact them. If it does, they will resign or look for another job, never sharing that the moral conduct was the real issue. Their passive handling of morals against their beliefs in the workplace typically results in a combination of being a victim and martyr in their way of justifying and thinking about what is happening around them at work.

Low in Both Morals: When a person is perceived to have no morals whatsoever, the perception is that the person is unethical. The difficulty lies in being able to always know whether a person is who they profess to be, or is a wolf dressed in a sheep's clothing. This person is different than the hypocrite in that they are consistent in their conduct personally and professionally. What exasperates people who work with these individuals is also what frustrates people who have personal relationships with them. The amoral person tends to have superficial relationships and if this person is a manager, they professionally will have a difficult time rallying support and productivity unless they strategically hire ethically passive team members.

About Culture

<u>High in Both Morals:</u> When you are high in both professional and personal morals, you have high convictions regarding your conduct and the conduct of others. There are no exceptions or special circumstances. Whether at work, at home or socializing, you have a core driving force within you that is your moral compass at all times. A whistleblower in a company is an example of someone who has high morals in both areas. They simply could not sit idly by and allow what they deemed wrong to continue to be the practice or policy. A person with high morals is an ethical self-leader, as well as an example to others, which is making them an excellent role model and leader of others. While it is ideal that those who are leading people in an organization are ethical, it is also valuable to have people who are self-actualized in their own moral basis to hold others accountable. In other words, those with high morals help keep us all honest when we may falter or lose faith due to others' actions or extenuating circumstances. It may be assumed by some reading this section that those with high morals are also judgmental or intolerant to the point of appearing self-righteous. A person placing themselves above others as a result of their moral beliefs is being driven by ego, not their morals. This is an entirely different character trait that speaks to aspects of ineffective leadership.

Ethics and Legality

I hesitated putting this section into this chapter because one would think that it is obvious that what is illegal would also be construed as unethical. But you only need to look at the cases of insider trading with the stock market or antitrust issues in price-setting schemes to know this is an issue that needs to be addressed. We will be introducing the different types of cultures in Chapter 9, but it warrants recognizing that the Mercenary Culture you will learn about has the highest risk of unethical behavior that can easily cross over into illegal behavior due to the key motivator and emphasis of that particular culture, which is money. When money is the motivator, greed has a way of being a driver of questionable choices. The most savvy unethical leaders are adept at insulating themselves from wrongdoing, not hesitating to redirect that attention to a scapegoat, or devising an intricate web of deceit that initially is impossible to untangle fact from fiction. The concept of a double set of books comes to mind when you consider the leader who takes his or her unethical behavior into illegal activity.

In a study conducted by the Hedge Fund Association completed in March of 2013, 35 percent of respondents reported feeling pressured by their compensation and bonus plan to violate the law or engage in unethical conduct. Additionally, 28 percent believed that if leaders of their firm learned that a top performer had engaged in insider trading, they would be unlikely to report the conduct to law enforcement or regulatory authorities. Insider trading appears to be an unethical issue that is not going to correct itself anytime soon. According to the study, it is likely due to a lack of confidence in the Securities Exchange Commission (SEC), with 54 percent of respondents citing that the SEC was ineffective in detecting, investigating and prosecuting securities violations, even though several high-profile insider trading cases had been recently prosecuted and won by the SEC. When enforcement and accountability are not in place, it is easy for certain people to rationalize that "it is okay because we won't get caught."

Building Trust through Vulnerability

Going back to the very personal example shared at the beginning of Chapter 7, I would be remiss if I didn't expand further upon the value and trust-building that occurs when you are comfortable with and capable of showing some of your vulnerability in your communication to others and your team. Internal and external communication or a lack thereof is the leading contributor either positively or negatively to how a company is viewed from an ethics and integrity standpoint.

Allowing yourself to be vulnerable is not showing weakness; it is showing a willingness to be open, to be honest, to be real, and to get to the issue at hand and beyond it. It is showing that you are human. As a result, communication can be honest and real, and solutions can be found or situations resolved in a manner that builds trust, confidence, camaraderie, and loyalty.

❖

No company is perfect and no individual is perfect. The true test of ethics comes down to how a company reconciles its imperfection and individuals handle theirs. More important than any other aspect of business, defining your ethics and developing your code of ethics should be parts of your orientation, ongoing communication, training, and development within the company.

About Culture

SECTION II

Defining the Culture

CHAPTER 9
Evolution of Corporate Culture

Our entire team of employees was gathered around the casket to say our goodbyes in our own unique way. This was a wake and an awakening all at the same time. We were saying goodbye in a teambuilding ritual to the way our company had been operating as a corporate culture. We were burying its dysfunction in place of the exciting corporate culture we had defined and determined we would embrace. Also with us were the management consultant associates, dressed as undertakers, with my executive coach conducting the last rites for everyone to listen, reflect and then release any of their anxiety, remorse or discourse. Inside the casket were pieces of paper with everyone's thoughts noted regarding aspects of the past corporate culture that needed to no longer be a part of our culture and be laid to rest. As our final goodbyes concluded, music from the Blues Brothers began to blast and a company-wide celebration ensued. As hokey as it may seem reading this at first glance, it was actually engaging, therapeutic, and a strong symbolism of everyone's commitment to what we wanted the company to be and what it would feel like, look like, and be like moving forward.

It was in 2001, when I began working with the management consulting company, that I was enlightened about the impact a corporate culture could have on a business. I had already been thinking in terms of values, vision, mission and a solid business plan driving the business' success, but not about how the company's overall culture could be the reason behind its success or failure to achieve desired performance measures. It was not until this time that I truly understood the strategic aspect of a corporate culture, as mentioned in Chapter Five. Quite honestly, initially, the idea of "corporate culture" seemed more like human resources and a management consultant jargon similar to "human capital" and "organizational change." To fully embrace it, I needed something tangible that would have real meaning to my business and to me.

The relationship between corporate culture and a company's performance has been a long-standing debate. A study conducted by Harvard, Kotter & Heskett and released in their book, *Corporate Culture and Performance* (1992), predicted that corporate culture would be "an even more important factor determining the success or failure of firms in the next decade." What was predicted more than 20 years ago has taken until now to finally sink in and be fully embraced.

While going through the work with the consultant and my leadership team in determining what we desired our corporate culture to be, we were introduced to a game-changing corporate culture model developed by Rob Goffee and Gareth Jones in 1996. It was later presented in their book, *The Character of a Corporation* (1998), which highlighted four quadrants based on two dimensions to describe a company's culture: Networked culture, Communal culture, Mercenary culture, and a Fragmented culture.

Two Dimensions

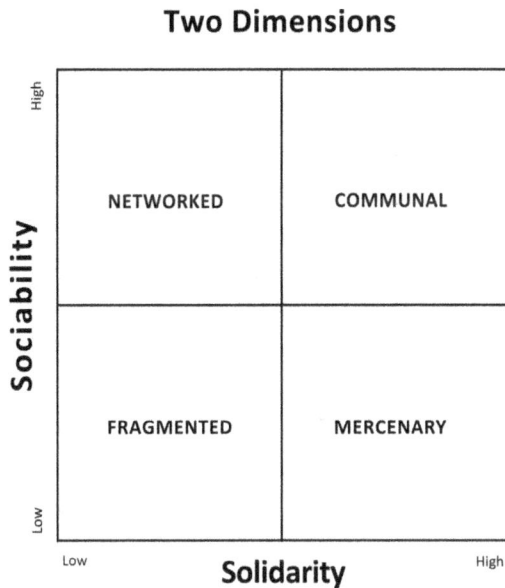

Credit: Rob Goffee/Gareth Jones

We embraced this model's concepts, focusing on the Communal Culture as our desired ideal. The ideal of High Sociability and High Solidarity made sense to me from a teambuilding standpoint. As we continued to build our Communal Culture over a decade, I realized that the two-dimensional focus on Sociability and Solidarity was not getting to the core of what we were trying to achieve in our corporate culture evolution. Performance needed to be more prominently in the mix. Additionally, we knew a level of commitment and unified understanding was critical to the culture sticking. If the culture we were striving for was going to be sustainable to help the company realize true endurance over time, everyone associated with the company needed to be engaged and feel engaged.

Three Dimensions, Not Two

As I explored this theory more intentionally, the culture model introduced by Goffee/Jones evolved as a result of my own experience and further validation from my research and development team. We conducted extensive secondary research defining the characteristics of companies viewed with strong corporate cultures that had also stood the test of time. This was qualified by looking at companies that had been in business for more than 50 years. We conducted primary research with small to mid-sized companies to gauge their people and performance factors in order to correlate this with the likelihood of endurance.

The result of our due diligence was a three-dimensional model versus a two dimensional model. The three dimensions are the connection between Sociability of People and their level of Engagement that is essential to fully realize desired operational results or Performance. When these three dimensions are operating at high levels, it is our premise that you are building a company of Endurance and long-term stability within your company.

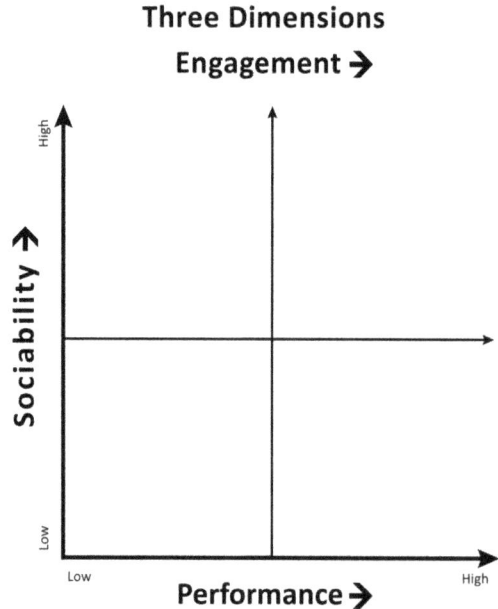

Sociability & Engagement: Where our 3-D model is partially in agreement with the Goffee/Jones Model is the aspect of a corporate culture where the interaction of people is measured on the left vertical axis. There is no disputing that people are essential to a business being able to operate. Goffee/Jones describe their focus on people as Sociability or "the degree of sincere friendliness experienced among members." According to Goffee/Jones, a culture with High Sociability is more likely to see people within the company socialize inside and outside of work. However, Goffee/Jones limits Sociability to this aspect of friendliness and personable attributes, not taking into consideration the full realm of what people represent within a company's corporate culture at multiple levels.

Defining the Culture

Engagement of the people to unify them is and should be a core focus of how people interact and transact within a company and with one another in working together. When values are shared along with a vision and mission for the company, the degree in which people will willingly and effectively interact and work together towards goals and objectives is measured better by their level of Engagement versus their level of Sociability. Additionally, while Goffee/Jones limited the Sociability factor to employees and how they interact with one another, Engagement in the 3-D model extends outward to customers, not just employees, as well as all relationships that directly or indirectly may impact the company. The way in which the company chooses to interact with people in general is an Engagement element. The impact of social media in business further validates the need to expand the definition of Sociability within a business.

Performance versus Solidarity: The Goffee/Jones Model places Solidarity on the horizontal axis, which is focused on the teamwork and unity of the people. Solidarity is described as "the degree in which people need to work together (whether they like each other or not) in order to get the job done." Solidarity was also described in a white paper released in 1996 by Goffee/Jones as the group's "ability to pursue shared objectives quickly and effectively." However, there are countless companies with goals and objectives and yet the performance is not happening and results are not realized. High Solidarity does not guarantee high performance. It is our premise that Solidarity is a trait aspect of engagement, but only a piece of the equation. If people within in a company are united in a common purpose or vision, they are more engaged in their work. Therefore, it was our hypothesis that to truly make a corporate culture relevant, Performance must be a measurement on the horizontal axis. This is where the leadership of the company, in my opinion, must drive the Performance of the organization. How Performance is defined, what is measured and how it is measured is directly influenced by the ability of the leadership to engage their team members. The leadership's approach to getting their people to produce and perform within the company also is a differentiator in the type of corporate culture that is dominating the organization.

Sociability + Engagement + Performance = Endurance: As a CEO and founder of my company, Endurance was the ultimate outcome I desired after the roller coaster ride of multiple setbacks. As my R&D team continued to research this aspect further, we determined this merited an evolution of the Goffee/Jones Model, as mentioned earlier, from the two-dimensional focus on Sociability with Solidarity to a 3-D model for corporate culture, demonstrating the relationship between Sociability, Engagement, and Performance in order to realize Endurance. By tying the Sociability of people to their level of Engagement, and then their level of Engagement to Performance, our theory of Endurance beckoned to be studied and analyzed further. Can High Sociability with High Engagement lead to High Performance that can also guarantee a company's Endurance over time? The answer is, "Yes!"

In a study released in 2012 entitled "A Study of Very Old Japanese Companies: Are There Common Survival Strategies?," it confirmed that 100+-year old companies' ability to sustain, in spite of economic, competitive or unanticipated conditions, can be tied to some of the corporate culture aspects our research and assessment beta test revealed as ideal in looking at High Sociability, High Engagement and High Performance indicators. The study confirmed that companies that still exist, since being established before 1911, scored significantly higher in emphasizing relationships with suppliers, customers, employees and local communities (Sociability), developing leaders and succession planning (Engagement), strategic focus on profitability over sales volume (Performance) and continuous improvement and measurement of their defined core strengths (Performance). The study was conducted by a team of professors, Vicki R. TenHaken, Professor of Management at Hope College in Michigan, and Makoto Kanda, Professor of Economics at Meiji Gakuin University in Japan. The team has conducted a study of Japanese and American companies exceeding 100 years in business and has documented many success factors tied to corporate culture. More about this study can be found in Chapter 21.

The Quadrants

The names of the four quadrants in the Goffee/ Jones Model (Networked, Communal, Mercenary, Fragmented) have stood the test of time, and still resonate to this day as logical and relevant with only one minor modification that we felt was necessary. In our evolved model, however, we changed the name of the Networked quadrant to Networking.

Due to the High Sociability factor of this quadrant, and based on our own experience as a High Engagement company, coupled with further research of other companies with High Sociability, the people represented in this quadrant were not just more connected or networked to one another on the friendly scale, but also on the relating and camaraderie scale. Their Sociability naturally compelled them to be a networking group of individuals inside and outside the organization in how they interacted with and related to people in general. Therefore, the word Networking made more sense as the name of this quadrant versus Networked. As we presented this within my management consulting firm, it also resonated with clients as well. Networking has become a business term that is all about relating and connecting with others.

The difference in the traits of each culture can be defined based on where they fall in the three dimensions.

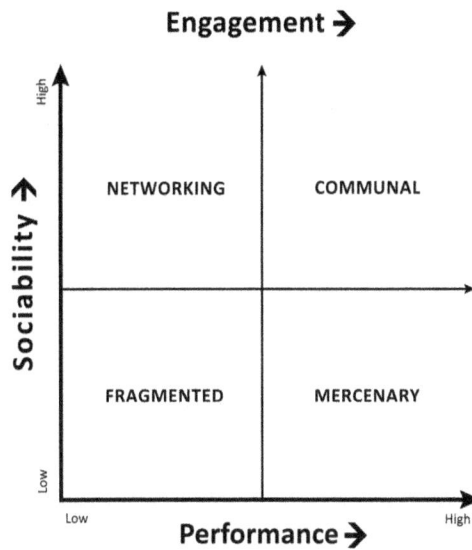

Networking Culture   =   High Sociability, Mid to High Engagement, Low to Mid Performance

Communal Culture   =   High Sociability, High Engagement, High Performance

Mercenary Culture   =   Low to Mid Sociability, Low to Mid Engagement, High Performance

Fragmented Culture   =   Low Sociability, Low Engagement, Low Performance

Another clarification that needs to be made as we explore the evolution of the culture model further is the aspect of community. Goffee/Jones placed corporate culture and community on the same plane, as interchangeable when referring to any one of the four quadrants. What we have found is that the dynamics of each quadrant can be classified based on different levels of engagement in how the company works effectively or ineffectively together, resulting in very specific descriptors based on engagement in combination with performance. Therefore, our premise is that the only quadrant that truly functions like a community is the Communal Culture. The Networking Culture takes on the characteristics of a country club, sorority or fraternity. The Mercenary Culture takes on the characteristics of an aristocracy or dictatorship. The Fragmented Culture takes on the characteristics of a bureaucracy. Interestingly, Networking, Communal and Mercenary can share aspects of feeling like a family, but with very different dynamics and values driving the way in which each of them operate under the guise of a family unit.

Finally, Goffee/Jones claimed that none of the four cultures are "the best," stating "… each is appropriate for different business environments. In other words, managers need not begin the hue and cry for one culture type over another."

❖

Based on our research and due diligence, a Communal Culture is ideal and is the only culture in which a company can realize endurance of decades and beyond. Additionally, the Networking and Mercenary Cultures can be effective and sustainable, just not as endurable over time as Communal. In the next chapters, you will gain more in-depth understanding about each of the four corporate cultures.

CHAPTER 10
Networking Culture

A teenage son of a restaurant owner climbed up to the roof of the family restaurant to discover several black label beer cans which had been tossed up and strewn across the roof by the restaurant's night manager, Charlie. The son really liked the night manager and thought to himself, "Daggumit, Charlie, why did you do that?" The son had known the night manager his entire life and was certain that Charlie would be fired. Instead, he learned from his father that he was going to support Charlie in getting some help. That night manager ended up retiring from the company years later.

The example above was a story shared by Dan T. Cathy, COO and President of Chick-fil-A Restaurants about the compassion he admired in his father and is proud that it is still prevalent in the way the multi-billion dollar family-owned enterprise operates today. In an interview regarding the company's success, Cathy emphasized, "It's not location, location, location. While that is important, for us it is more people, people, people ..." From engaging customers and team members to internally growing future operators and taking pride in long-term vendor relationships, Chick-fil-A has made building and nurturing strong relationships with people as the foundation and secret recipe for its success.

Relationships are everything in a Networking Culture. People are the focus. What is considered to be in the best interest of the company centers around taking care of its network of people every time. Leadership drives this aspect of the company in a variety of ways, inspiring through their actions and words the corporate values that are centered around what is best for the people working within the company, as well as those being served by the business.

The Social Butterfly

<u>High Sociability:</u> A Networking Culture is a fun, friendly and celebratory environment with lots of smiles and chit chat while working. Employees and leaders are personable and oftentimes their conversations are more

personal sharing than professional sharing. This makes it feel like they are one big happy family. They also feel connected as if they are part of a congregation or a country club, which results in the family aspect of it having some standards around inclusion and acceptance to fit in.

This is exemplified in Chick-fil-A with its stance on gays and same-sex marriages. The Networking Culture feels like one big happy family as long as everyone is in agreement with the focus on fun, relating and activity. This is true for both people inside and outside of the company. Friendships easily form within and extend outside of work. Celebrations at work are more focused on personal occasions such as birthdays, births, marriages, graduations, etc. Employee gatherings include picnics, social sporting events, parties around holidays, and will include customers in some of these special gatherings or social events. Customers will be included for the purpose of connecting with employees and one another in celebrating the relationship. The socialization extends beyond customers and employees into the communities where the company operates in charitable and engagement activities focused on celebrating or serving people. From 2010 through 2013, Chick-fil-A gave more than $68 million dollars to over 700 organizations in alignment with their core values through fundraising and community service events.

Low to Mid Performance: People or relationship-driven performance is the focus that can be effective. Under the right leadership, a relationship-driven focus can impact company growth, but only to a certain extent without other drivers. Making people happy, both inside and outside of the company, is the ultimate goal. For the customer, this is impressive and valued, but part of the reason business performance is not at the highest level is because decisions that are being made are motivated by relationships taking precedence over what may be financially prudent. What is in the best interest of the company's bottom line can be ignored over what is in the best interest of the employee or customer. Profits or even sales are not as much of a driving force for the company as is comfort and consideration of people.

Chick-fil-A's Cathy openly admits that the company could be making more money if opened on Sundays, but they determined that holding true to their values was more important to their culture and the way in which the company, as a family-owned business, desires to operate. Many lifestyle types of businesses fall into the Networking Culture quadrant because there is less of a focus on high-growth sales and profits, and more of a focus on relationships and the financial performance that keeps people living in a comfortable manner at the mid-level performance scale or a "getting by" manner at the lowest performance scale.

Achieving Endurance: Excellence in customer service and the intentional focus on the customer enables a Networking Culture company to be sustainable over time. The fun factor of doing business with the company and the friendliness when conducting transactions with the company are loyalty-builders for the customer. However, when performance measures are not put into place in relation to customer service or the delivery of products or services, an inconsistency can negatively impact the customer experience. Another factor impacting endurance is that fun and interaction among employees can distract them from doing their ultimate job for the customer.

Southwest Airlines, named among Fortune Magazine's 2013 Most Admired Companies, is another example of an ideal Networking Culture, proving that endurance is possible amidst regulations and an industry plagued with a reputation for poor customer service. According to its founder, Herb Kelleher, the key for building a company of endurance is its everyday focus on people in making work fun, knowing each and every employee personally, and paying personal attention to everyone they served. For Kelleher, this also translated into getting out of their people's way and letting them do their job. Everyone was impassioned by how Southwest was adamantly different, with no frills and plenty of thrills for passengers because of the fun experience. The company has never had a furlough or layoff, unprecedented in the airline industry, and has been described as "the greatest success story in American airline history in terms of turning intangibles into monetary value" as a company with a "decades-long dominance of its segment of the airline industry" through more efficient operations and removing the frills of travel, replacing them with fun, entertainment and genuine human care.

Networking Culture Defined

C	Common Beliefs
U	Unconditional Allegiance
L	Leadership Energizes & Motivates
T	Teammates Playing & Working Together
U	Unified Understanding
R	Reciprocal Respect
E	Expectations around Excellence

The Networking Culture is defined by common beliefs about relationships, including celebration, interaction, and how people should be treated. These are people who look forward to going to work mostly because of the people they are working with, rather than what they are doing at work. They have an unconditional allegiance because the leadership is well liked due to their chummy, friendly approach to working with the team that is energizing and motivating. However, the minute the fun is replaced with feeling like real work, allegiance can waver.

Having a good time while working is the hallmark of a Networking company. This company is more likely to be the one with ping pong tables, meditation rooms, company gyms and "fun" distractions for people when they want to take a break from work.

What will make the company more sustainable lies in how the foundational aspects of the Culture is supported and reinforced by leadership in the areas of unified understanding, reciprocal respect, and expectations around excellence. The Networking Culture with a vision and mission tied to their common values will be able to take their customer obsession to a level of impact in the area of performance as long as the expectations about what serving the customer means are defined.

Where a Networking company can fall short is in the area of accountability. Because of the chumminess and focus on personal relationships, professionalism can become a grey area. Team members who are not pulling their weight on the job may be covered by others on the team because the other team members are caring for them, versus holding them accountable. Leaders have a more difficult time firing or letting go of a team member because of their personal relationship, which sometimes is keeping someone on the team when another more qualified person would be better suited for the position.

I found myself caught up in a Networking Culture quandary when an employee who I initially thought had great promise was falling short on the performance side of expectations. This employee chose my company over big corporations because of the Sociability aspect of my company. I considered this person to be an excellent match for our Culture due to the mutual respect and loyalty this individual demonstrated in his previous employment and attitude. As time progressed, it was evident to me that this individual was more suited for strictly a Networking Culture and simply could not achieve the levels of performance that were expected from not just me, but all of our team members. Additionally, while this individual was personable and likable, he was not engaged in performing with the rest of the team. He became lazy in his job, relying on his likability and personality to carry him through. This worked for a while, and also made it more difficult for me to finally make the tough decision to let him go. Over an extensive period of time, I continued to try to rally this employee into performing, but it was causing more tension and friction than effectiveness. Conducting the Culture assessment helped make it easier for me to finally make the long-overdue decision. We parted friends and still have remained friends to this day.

Networking Team = TEAM x 2

The way in which a team is formed, interacts, and engages is the true differentiating factor for each type of Culture. For the Networking Team, the dynamics are around a feeling of togetherness, effort in support of one another, being accepted and liked, and having fun.

TEAM X 2 = Work & Play

T	=	Together & Timeless
E	=	Excellence & Effort
A	=	Acceptance & Altruism
M	=	Merriment & Making Do

T = Together & Timeless: Teams are formed more on a basis of who gets along the best in working together versus who may be the best combination of talents to work together for a particular goal or objective. People look forward to going to work because time seems to fly by and it is fun.

E = Excellence & Effort: Excellence is defined by the effort in serving one another and the customer. Going above and beyond for either the customer or each other is the focus of recognition and the reason for celebration with groups and others throughout the company. The idea of "A for Effort" is considered reward and recognition-worthy. Having happy employees and happy customers is the indicator of excellence in business.

A = Acceptance & Altruism: Being liked and accepted is important for members of the team, as well as managers of the team, which can sometimes cause challenges in effectively leading the group through challenges or changes. Altruism is a core value of unselfish giving and devotion for the welfare of others, which, as cited earlier, can also mean covering for a co-worker or team member beyond what may be in the best interest of the co-worker or the company.

<u>M = Merriment & Making Do:</u> Because fun is such a part of the Culture, making money is secondary and not the primary focus. Making enough money that enables everyone to continue to enjoy both their work and life is the benchmark.

A Networking Culture appears to be well-suited for a lifestyle or hospitality business. A bed and breakfast is a good example of a business that is both lifestyle and hospitality, many of which would operate in a Networking Culture mindset. Many country clubs, golf clubs, or fitness centers are also examples of a Networking Culture. Dot-coms were also in the Networking realm before the bubble burst and emerging technology firms thereafter added other measures and deliverables into the business operational strategy.

❖

For founder Kelleher, it went even beyond a corporate culture in what has made Southwest Airlines so successful. It was the fact that the company had a corporate soul with values that dictated that every decision being made must be centered on the people experience. When other airlines were making cost-cutting decisions that negatively impacted their cultures, Southwest Airlines invested more in its culture, guarding and protecting it, knowing that it was its people-driven culture, not its products, process or structure, that was empowering its competitive advantage.

CHAPTER 11

Communal Culture

My passion outside of business is baseball. In 2002, I established a competitive team of high school players supported by one-on-one coaching and training to supplement what they were already doing on their school sports teams. Soon after, other former baseball players who were businessmen with children the same age as my son were interested in starting competitive teams like mine. Showcase Baseball Academy was born. From the very beginning, we as parents determined the importance of balancing values such as respect, integrity, having fun, and continuous learning with performing to win. Developing players who were successful meant that they not only were top performers on the field and as a team, but top-notch individuals in academics, manners, consideration of others, and conduct. Our ability to bridge competitive spirit with human spirit has evolved into the fastest growing baseball academy in the Southeast, now hosting 30 competitive teams and serving more than 400 student athletes since 2010.

I am convinced that the fact that the Communal Culture was embraced from the very beginning is the underlying reason the academy has been so successful and valued by everyone involved. A lot of youth sports organizations profess to develop players, but they are doing the players a disservice by not teaching them the reality of winning and losing. To the other extreme, competitive youth sports organizations, where winning is their only focus, operate to the detriment of the youth involved in self-esteem, morale and development as individuals. We wanted to teach these athletes how to win, but also how to lose and grow from the experience. Our whole idea was based on the reality that one of these days these players would be adults. They would be competing for entrance into college, jobs, and a variety of other things. That's why we also focused on critical success factors for them to achieve better results academically, when communicating and presenting themselves, and in their life in general.

The Communal Culture immediately stood out to all of us on the leadership team at Ameritrust as the ideal corporate culture for our organization based on the values, vision, and mission we already had in place for our company when we began to explore being a corporate culture in 2001. To be able to build a company based on the Communal Culture from the very beginning when we were establishing the baseball academy was the only way, in our opinion, to assure its success. The feeling of "getting it right" and "doing it right the first time" was exciting for me and enthusiastically embraced by all my partners at the academy.

However, I would not have been able to truly embrace or appreciate the full impact a Communal Culture could have, if me and my team had not gone through the evolution we did in rebuilding Ameritrust. In the rebuilding process, our first step depended on my leadership team to define what being a Communal Culture meant to the company, our people, and our customers. We also needed to consider what it meant within an industry that was not in alignment with the culture we knew was right for us. As we embraced and built our foundation upon being Communal, it not only stuck, it worked.

I am not proposing that the Communal Culture is ideal because it is the one that worked best for us. It is the ideal culture because of the quantifiable relationships between Sociability, Performance and Sustainability. The Communal Culture brings the most desired aspects of engagement and results together that create a higher probability of sustainability.

Most Sustainable Over Time

The Communal Culture is sustainable because it balances people and results in a positive, empowering way with an emphasis on being the best while also doing what is in the best interests of and for everyone concerned. My R&D team was surprised to find it written by Goffee/Jones that the Communal Culture "is an unattainable ideal" to achieve in

Engagement →

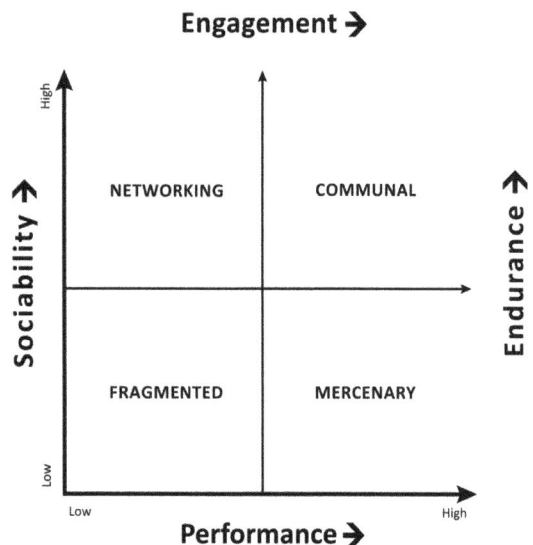

a commercial enterprise. Part of the reason for this is that Goffee/Jones defined their culture quadrants based on measuring Sociability with Solidarity. As mentioned in Chapter Nine, we determined that Solidarity is a characteristic within the Sociability axis. Therefore, a better measure of sustainability or of the company's endurance amidst challenges is in the relationship between Sociability and Engagement of the people in achieving High Performance.

High Sociability: In a Communal Culture, relationships inside and outside of the company are nurtured, appreciated and explored. Employees share on personal and professional levels in their discussions and interactions. Teamwork is a way of working and getting things done. Celebrations recognize both personal occasions and professional achievements. This extends to suppliers or business partner vendors, as well. Everyone is engaged in delivering the company's products and services in a unified manner because they feel connected and valued in the roles that they play in serving the customer. Relationships are important to the Communal Culture resulting in an obsession with serving the customer and not hesitating to lend a hand to help a team member. Customer relationships are developed on a personal level, as well as professional level, including socializing that encompasses personal occasions or interactions outside of the business.

High Engagement: What sets the Communal Culture apart from all the other cultures is the aspect of Engagement. It takes engagement to a level of loyalty and commitment that is often envied by those from the outside who are looking inside. What this means is that loyalty, passion and commitment among the management and team members for achieving the company's mission is thoroughly embraced and understood. This also extends outside the firm to the customers, vendors and suppliers. Everyone is on the same page focused on working together as effectively as possible to achieve the desired end results.

High Performance: Purpose-driven performance defines the Communal Culture with relationships keeping the team connected, engaged, focused, and accountable. Because the company's mission is purpose-driven, everyone in the company views the company as making a tangible difference. Because the purpose is also strongly connected to being customer focused, there is a company-wide obsession to perform in service of the customer. Measures in performance are multi-faceted in a Communal Culture with benchmarks for employee growth, employee advancement and retention, customer satisfaction, customer retention and loyalty, sales growth, profitability and innovation.

<u>Achieving Endurance:</u> With employees passionate about what they do and what the company is doing combined with a strong sense of pride in performance and productivity, the combination is a powerful stability factor for the company's longevity. What makes the Communal Culture more sustainable is how passion not only impacts the way in which the team works together, but also motivates why the team works together in a high-performance manner. The Communal Culture is the only culture in which a company would achieve multiple awards and recognition for Community Service, Best Place to Work, Best Customer Satisfaction, and Fast Growth or Top Growth all at the same time.

Communal Culture Defined

C	Communal Beliefs
U	Unwavering, Unconditional Allegiance
L	Leadership Inspires & Motivates
T	Team United & Motivates
U	Unified Understanding
R	Reciprocal Respect & Responsibility
E	Expectations around Excellence

The Communal Culture is the only culture in which beliefs and values are shared as true connectors at a core emotional level among employees and leadership. The values that an employee lives by are also what they work by. All values are shared, with none being in conflict. As a result, there is an unwavering and unconditional allegiance because work feels like a natural extension of the person. This is further reinforced by leadership that inspires and motivates employees to serve, grow and excel both personally and professionally. The communal beliefs also unite the team to trust and know that they can count on one another. The level of trust in a communal culture is more authentic, resulting in team members holding one another accountable and also being more willing to teach and advance one another for the greater good of the company, department or in serving the customer. Everyone takes responsibility for how the team and company achieve results.

Communal Team = TEAM^2

The Communal Team is able to take a company to higher levels of achievement and performance due to the way in which these teams work together and are put together. The exponential effects are what truly validate this culture as the most sustainable driver for a company.

TEAM^2 = Next Level Growth

T	=	Trust & Talent
E	=	Excellence & Execution
A	=	Attitude & Aptitude
M	=	Mind & Might

<u>T = Trust & Talent:</u> In the Communal Culture, having faith and confidence in one another as a team is at the heart of how people feel about one another and work together. There is a focus on working together to leverage the unique abilities of each individual for a synergistic effect in what can be accomplished as a result. Hiring talent is a combination of reaching out to family and friends, the company's professional network and also a recruiting process. The ultimate hire must be based on the best candidate with the combination of communal values and the specific talent and skill set desired.

<u>E = Excellence & Execution:</u> An obsession for serving their customer is what drives decisions, solutions and activities as customer satisfaction and loyalty are considered a measure of excellence. Standards and benchmarks are established throughout the company as a means of measuring and defining what excellence means in the services and products being provided. Processes, procedures and systems are in place to increase both productivity and the ability to best deliver to the customer and operate internally as a team. Excelling individually and as a team in the best interest of the team, the organization, and the customer is defined as what is necessary to achieve a high-performance outcome.

<u>A = Attitude & Aptitude:</u> A positive, proactive attitude prevails in a Communal Culture that means it is a win-win for the team, the customer and the company. Readiness and adeptness with a focus on ongoing learning and development is considered essential to success. Continuous learning for both professional and personal development is a benefit of working at a Communal company, believing that life and work must respect and nurture each other. A sense of pride prevails in each employee feeling

like an important part of the team and a contributor to the company's and each individual's success.

<u>M = Mind & Might:</u> Strategic thinking and critical thinking for long-term and short-term advantage is considered a role of everyone throughout the company. A Communal Company values employees' thinking and abilities by including them in the strategic planning process, in order to be agile and action-oriented in a strategic, unified way. Because team members are respected and valued, they put thoughtful and relevant action into their work, feeling empowered to do what is right and best for the company, team and customer. The concept of "all for one and one for all" is at the very core of proving that the strength in numbers is defined by the people first resulting in a strong bottom line, as well.

❖

With the Showcase Baseball Academy starting from the beginning as a Communal Culture, we have avoided a lot of heartaches, headaches and setbacks. It allowed us to stay strategically focused on our vision, mission, and the desired outcomes for our teams, the individual athletes, their families, and the organization as a whole. Making the shift to the Communal Culture in Ameritrust was painstaking because of all that was necessary to overcome, change, adjust, and then entrust to see it through. It was worth and is worth every bit of effort in the type of organization we represent today.

CHAPTER 12
Mercenary Culture

Back in 2005, greed was running rampant in Wall Street. I remember going from Wall Street firm to Wall Street firm reviewing various mortgage products. The push from the firms was always, "Johnny, you need to market this product to your audience." I would review the products and then get back to them the next day after my analysis and ask the questions, "Is this really good for the customers? Is this really good for the homeowners of America?" The surprising answer by some people within these firms, many of which are now out of business, was "It will make us money." Products were developed with a focus on the money to be made versus what would be of value and advantage in serving the customer.

Greed is most associated with the Mercenary Culture, but what is important to clarify is that there is greed with good intentions and greed with ulterior motives, which draws a razor-sharp line between a Mercenary Culture that works and is sustainable, compared to the one that does not work and ultimately meets its demise. The example above demonstrates what can happen when greed with ulterior motives is the driving force. It doesn't surprise me that most of these firms are out of business, because ulterior motives also tend to disregard integrity, compliance practices, and even policies to achieve the end financial gain. We only need to look at the robot-signed mortgage loans to know this to be true.

For the Mercenary Culture work is what life is all about and the money is what drives the work. Work is considered the primary focus and, in some cases, the only focus of those who are employed. The mentality of "leave your personal life at home" holds true for this culture, but hypocritically, taking work home is considered a sign of dedication and commitment to the company. In extreme cases, work can actually dictate what and how you are to act and even live outside of work.

Show Me the Money!

In the movie, Jerry McGuire, the famous line, "Show me the money!" by the lead character effectively summarizes the focus of a Mercenary Culture. Making money is what it is all about and what all decisions are ultimately based upon. The critical difference between the Mercenary Culture that succeeds and the one that will not stand the test of time is how the company approaches making the money.

Going back to the movie, Jerry McGuire, the main character, a successful sports agent, has a moment of realization in which he sees his clients as paychecks when a young son of one of his injured clients curses him out for his insensitivity. This is an example of a Mercenary mindset where clients are more about the money that will be made than that they are actual people.

Low to Mid Sociability: In the Mercenary Culture, the interaction among employees and their relationships are work focused entirely with personal sharing kept to a minimum, if shared at all. While there are still teams working together, it is driven by who needs to work together for the greatest productivity. This Culture can also tolerate and encourage lone stars as long as they reap financial gains for the company. Everyone in the company is a tool for making money for the company. Celebrations will occur in a Mercenary Culture, but they will be focused solely on work-related achievements and accolades, not personal occasions. Another characteristic of being on the lower Sociability scale is in how families of employees are viewed. In this environment, work is first and family comes second.

I remember one New Year's Eve when I was 22-years-old and still working at midnight at the finance company I was working for at the time. In fact, my bosses were still working because that was the culture. It was the end of the month and the numbers had to be put in on the last day of the month. I missed trick-or-treating nights with my children for the same reason, because it was always the last day of October. I saw first-hand the toll the culture took on my bosses, many of whom had crumbling marriages and were cheating on their wives or were already divorced. Some were alcoholics and openly disgruntled with the organization, but felt that they were "owned" by the company and, therefore, had to crack the whip relentlessly, not realizing the abuse they were inflicting on employees.

High Performance: Performance, primarily around profit, sales, and the bottom line is in overdrive in this culture. Being the best to the point of elitism is a source of pride and status. Being competitive and winning at all costs is also the hallmark of a Mercenary Culture. Squashing or crippling the competition is a performance measure, as opposed to being preferred or having more market share. The mindset of survival of the fittest ironically applies to this culture even within the company itself.

In a Mercenary Culture that is at the lowest scale of Sociability and the highest scale of Performance, you see people being used up and spit out emotionally and literally in the effort to meet sales and profits goals. This also plays sadly into the personal lives of the employees who have allowed the culture to run their lives. I recall when I was still working at the finance company I came into work one morning to find a co-worker and saw him sitting in his chair with his head down just staring into space. I asked him, "What's going on?" He replied, "My wife just left me." I said, "I'm sorry to hear that. What can I do to help?" He replied, "Let's talk about it later. I've got to get back to work." We never did talk about it later and I was immediately struck by the how the culture had totally screwed-up this man's priorities. He had children and, at one time, a happy marriage, but was beaten down so bad by the expectations of the culture that he did not feel he could take time away to rectify his marriage because of the demands at work.

Achieving Endurance: A look at the financial industry as a whole validates that a Mercenary Culture is less sustainable and it can be volatile to maintain over time due to its autocratic nature and aristocratic, above reproach attitude. However, a Mercenary Culture with values that include professional development, obsession about the customers, and rewarding employees for their achievements, while still only money-focused in nature, is likely to be more stable over time, but not as stable as a Communal Culture.

Mercenary CULTure Defined

C	Common & Coerced Beliefs
U	Unwavering, Unquestioned Allegiance
L	Leadership Coveted & Revered
T	Team Under Scrutiny & Tested
U	Unified Understanding
R	Respect & Responsibility
E	Expectations around Excellence

Elements of the destructive cult can creep into the Mercenary Culture dependent on the leadership and overall company mantra. While to succeed in the company, employees must share beliefs around work, money, competitiveness, and bottom-line performance, the culture is also adept at coercing and manipulating both employees and leaders to believe in exchange for reward, recognition or inclusion. An unwavering and unquestioned allegiance to the company and what it represents by the leadership, typically someone who is escalated to the point of reverence and being untouchable like a mafia godfather commanding respect or a horse's head may appear on your pillow. Nothing is ever good enough for the Mercenary Culture, with the team constantly under fire, on demand and call, and continuously being tested and pushed to the limit.

If it stops at what is described above, then you are hearing the failings of what I refer to as the Miser Mercenary Culture as opposed to a Maverick Mercenary Culture.

The Maverick Mercenary Culture is a more high-performance team focused on reinforcing a unified understanding of the leader's vision and the company's mission. The company and its leader demands respect, but divvies out responsibility across the organization with high expectations of excellence by everyone within the company. The company only works with the best of the best and, therefore, expects only the best results in the form of profits, sales, industry position, marketplace dominance, and economic leverage.

Mercenary Team = TEAM / 2

The Mercenary Team is of the mentality that to win the war, you must divide and conquer. The company is typically subsets of teams of one to a few, but not necessarily ever a team as an overriding whole.

Team/2 = Divide & Conquer

T	=	Talent & Tenacity
E	=	Excellence & Exclusivity
A	=	Acceleration & Activity
M	=	Money & Me First

T = Talent & Tenacity: Top-level talent who are considered to be the best of the best is what the Mercenary Culture expects in its people. They typically will work with recruiters and top placement firms, combined with a rigorous candidate screening process. Working for the company is considered having earned a badge of honor, therefore the long hours are accepted and embraced by any new hire with gusto. Tenacity when it comes to anything being strived for is how the company expects everyone to approach his or her work. Like a dog with a bone, a fervent attitude of conquering, winning and consuming the reward once attained is prevalent throughout the organization. Whatever needs to be done to accomplish goals is embraced with clearly understood consequences and a steadfast focus towards the expected result.

E = Excellence & Exclusivity: Excellence is about being the best at everything that is being done. It is a winner/loser mentality where the company must always be the one on top. In companies where innovation and intellectual property are involved, there is secrecy even within the company, where some individuals or teams have exclusive rights and the breach of confidences even within the company are grounds for dismissal. Success in the company equates to gaining more and more privileges as part of a more elite status within the company.

A = Acceleration & Activity: The work pace is fast and furious with continuous activity and an expectation of continuous short-term gains to mark success. Leaders are demanding and co-workers are demanding with one another in order to meet aggressive objectives and goals.

The key to effective dividing and conquering in a Mercenary Culture is in working as a team while understanding the division of labor and responsibility. Too often, it is chaotic because everyone is frantically trying to get work done, but not together and not cohesively. When there is a team effort associated with the activity, there is a high level of adrenaline running through the organization.

M = Money & Me First: Money is the driving force of the Mercenary Culture and is the measure of success at both the corporate level and the individual level. Individual success and advancement in the company is based solely on monetary measurements. This results in a highly competitive environment internally, as well as externally, where back slapping and back stabbing are considered the natural course of getting to the end prize or goal.

Going back to the movie, Jerry McGuire, after being cursed out by the son of the client, McGuire affirms to change his ways, with a focus on people first. His colleagues, being Mercenary on the side of greed at all costs, set it up to get him fired even though they were high-fiving him for his new-found sense of what is right to his face. They also steal all his clients, except one. The one client whom is left with him has a chip on his shoulder and an ego to match. While throughout the duo's relationship in the movie, the primary focus is on money, and there is a camaraderie and relationship that evolves in support of the other in achieving this ultimate goal, making the client a better player, and making McGuire a better person.

Near the end of the movie, Jerry negotiates a super-large contract demonstrating that big money can be made based on a client being valued and considered. His client achieved greatness during a Monday Night Football game after being contracted, resulting in a flurry of reporters wanting to talk to him as he came out of the locker room. His first request was, "Where's my agent?" and as Jerry approached, they hugged in celebration before the interviews could begin. Another agent, who was standing nearby said to his client, another player on the team, "How come we don't we have that relationship?" and proceeded to attempt to hug his client. The client pushed him away because it wasn't authentic.

❖

The key difference between the Maverick Mercenary Culture that works and the Miser Mercenary Culture that doesn't is in the focus on people in relation to money. Money is still the main focus in both, but where the Maverick Mercenary Culture sees how to make more money by being inspired by their customers and serving the customers, the Miser Mercenary Culture sees people, especially the customer, as merely a tool and means for making money.

CHAPTER 13
Fragmented Culture

A business unit focused on government energy audits was operating in many ways like the government itself, with regulations dictating its every move. The complacency of the operation was a comfortable fit for many members of its workforce who had been with the company for a long time. They were there to collect a paycheck without having to put in significant effort as long as they followed the rules and methodically did their jobs. There was no desire to achieve results. The motivation was more around doing what was necessary so "you wouldn't lose your job." With a large portion of its workforce soon to retire, a new generation was coming in to take their place. While the organization was doing just enough to stay in business, it wasn't doing enough to attract and retain good people to replace those leaving. A lack of sociability, especially important to the new generation, was making it difficult to retain new people and even attract the right people for positions in the first place. New employees would walk out because they would quickly realize that this was not the place they wanted to work for years or even months. Attrition was crippling the company, but it did not know how to fix it.

As one of my clients in my management consulting firm, the company described above was suffering from being a Fragmented Culture. Even though they were able to fill spots reasonably quickly, they would lose people just as quickly. The new generation had expectations of being in a work environment that was performance-driven and people-driven, and while people may have been nice in the interview process, neither of the expectations was realized by the new hires once they began their roles in the company. Everyone worked pretty much independently and there was no collaboration. There were no performance measures, with the only real directives focused on doing the jobs according to the regulations and policies. The lack of culture resulted in a void being felt by the new employees.

A lack of or confusion about the culture within a company basically means there is an absence of a specific culture. In describing a corporate culture that is Fragmented, I hesitated in calling it a culture at all, because it is void of a specific culture that unites its people within the organization. Therefore, I describe the Fragmented company as suffering from an unCulture. The company is fragmented because so many of the aspects that make a strong corporate culture are either undefined or non-existent.

In looking at the definitions of the word cult and the differences between a constructive and destructive cult described in Chapters One and Two, shared beliefs and values, whether being common, communal, or coerced, are not evident or defined to bring the people within the Fragmented organization together. In many cases, the organization does not have corporate values or even a vision or mission.

The foundational aspects that transform a cult into a culture described in Chapter Three - Unified Understanding, Respect & Recognition, and Expectations around Excellence - are also missing, primarily because of a lack of leadership. Without having leadership to reinforce a unified understanding or expectations around excellence, employees are left to use their own interpretations and personal beliefs to dictate what they understand and believe is expected. You typically will not see any form of employee recognition within a fragmented organization because there have been no expectations or standards to measure results needed to reward performance. Employees, if asked, will not be certain whether the work they do is valued or respected by their managers, only that they are expected to do what they were hired to do.

The unCulture Effect

With nothing really bonding or binding the group of people together, the company experiences low engagement of its people (Low Sociability) and low results (Low Performance).

Low Sociability: Low Sociability within the company is first evident by how employees relate to one another. These individuals are nameless, faceless drones as far as they are concerned. They may be working in the same place or even in the same space, but rarely interact. Discussions are reserved primarily for the purpose of doing their job when they must interact with someone else in the company to gain information, a resource, or direction. This employee is also more likely to have a "punch in/punch out" mentality. It is more of a job than a career, and more about getting a paycheck than bringing anything more of value to their existence. Leadership, or lack thereof, further alienates everyone by being missing in action for the most part, not highly visible, and often times referred to as "paper pushers."

Low Performance: The importance and relevance of employee, leadership and customer engagement is quantified by the lack of results realized in a fragmented "unculture" without engagement. Phrases such as "doing what I need to get by" and "putting my time in" are the language of a fragmented organization. Jobs are viewed as necessary, but not important or for making a real difference, just a means to an end product or service being delivered. It is not hard to see why a fragmented company can be one step away from going out of business.

Low Engagement: The people within the organization have their own belief systems. They are operating from their personal beliefs as their guide for how they do their work, why they are working for your company, and why they are earning their paycheck. The organization is operating with many silos indifferent to others. Everyone is showing up and doing their job, but they are not working together. If this is what your work environment sounds like, you have an assembly of people working at the same place, not an engaged team.

Enabled Endurance: We all know that there are organizations that have been around for a long time in spite of operating in a fragmented way. There is no better example than our federal government of this being true. It is broken, and yet is still in existence because it has been enabled by the support of other nations, regulations and policies, and procedures to keep it afloat. Even amidst mind-boggling deficit, it continues to churn because of its dependency. Any organization that is reliant on other organizations or on streams of support to survive can find themselves Fragmented as a result of its dependency and complacency. If it knows it will continue to get support, there is no reason to perform or be concerned as long as another bail out happens.

The Dependent vs. Independent Difference

Goffee/Jones claimed that a Fragmented Culture could be an effective culture, specifically for certain industries such as Universities and Educational institutions. Our Culture Model has been challenged based on the fact that there are several examples of organizations that would be perceived as always having been Fragmented, yet have been around for decades. We disagree. Chances are there are sub-cultures operating in the more ideal realms helping the organization survive, even though it has never thrived. The key differential between Fragmented organizations and companies operating with Communal, as well as Mercenary or Networking culture dynamics is that the latter three cultures are self-supporting. Companies or organizations operating in any three of these cultures are independent in achieving their performance measures versus being dependent. For instance, public universities are heavily reliant on state and government funding to be sustainable. Not-for-profits relying on other agencies' financial support or government funding sources are also more fragmented than not-for-profits with a stronger private funding focus. Without the supporting funding, these organizations would not survive. You can probably identify such organizations in your community or in the news that prove my point.

TEAM x 0 – No Team At All

When you multiply anything by zero, you get zero. That is the best way to describe the approach to teaming in a Fragmented organization. There isn't one. Teamwork is not a focus or a priority. Teams of people are not brought together to get work done. Everyone is responsible for what they were hired to do and that is what all the individuals entirely focus on from the time they walk through the door to the time they walk out. Doors are usually shut with each person's nose to the grindstone doing what they were hired to do. Companies with a large portion of their workforce telecommuting can easily fall into a fragmented state unless measures are taken on the corporate level to counteract the distance and virtual barriers.

When Yahoo's CEO Marissa Mayer ended the work-from-home policy, worldwide outrage was the initial reaction with the company being viewed as initiating an unfamily-friendly policy by a female leader who determined to go against the tech industry norm of flexible work policies. The reality is that Mayer was seeing fragmentation and as a new incoming CEO, determined key initiatives that would bring the group more together as a team. The work-from-work initiative was not the only transformation made. Other changes made included revamping the company's travel and expense policy manual "that humans could understand," distributing smart phones, and offering free food to staff, which were practices she knew well from her days with Google.

Bureaucracy Rules

A fragmented organization is also more likely to be viewed as bureaucratic. This is because of another form of dependency that exists – on policies, procedures, rules and regulations, some of which may be outdated or in place in order to serve a minority versus the majority. With no one taking a leadership role in the company to recognize the outdated ways of operating, they are just accepted as the way things are and have been done. Managers of employees are primarily focused on everyone following the rules by doing their specific jobs, and only their specific jobs. When rules and regulations are focused on serving a minority versus the majority, fragmentation continues to spread like a plague across the organization. Workers are disgruntled by what is perceived as unfair or preferential, but still do their jobs because that is what they are being paid to do. As long as they get paid, they accept that there is nothing they can do about a policy, fair or not. Another form of bureaucracy is in having too many levels of hierarchy within a company with no-one being accessible or available when decisions need to be made.

In an article entitled "The Scourge of Bureaucracy," an example includes a high-tech entrepreneurial company that grew quickly, becoming publicly traded when it had grown to 400 employees and $300 million dollars in sales, and resulting in merging with a larger company. The larger company was "a top-heavy organization with 17 divisions and layer upon layer of executives" where getting through to the CEO "was like getting through the Secret Service." The company was described as being "a highly political place with big egos, power struggles, finger pointing, sugarcoating, and everyone covering their "you-know-whats." Ironically, it is a lack of accountability that is the downfall when an organization allows its bureaucracy to take over. The policies, procedures and processes are more focused on safeguarding the company than serving its workforce or customer base. A lack of engagement results in people looking the other way or using the policies as a means of placing blame versus taking responsibility.

Departmentally Fragmented

Another way a company can be Fragmented is in having multiple sub-cultures that are opposing each other or not working effectively together. Oftentimes, this is the result of different departments within the company taking on the characteristics of differing cultures. For instance, the Finance department might be Mercenary, the Customer Service department could be Communal, the Marketing & Sales department is Networking. The managers of each of the departments are the drivers of these specific cultures within each department, which also can make the leadership or management team meetings fiascos.

In my consulting practice, I see a fragmentation mindset occurring specifically as it relates to departments when the culture model is first presented. At the surface level, top management will say, "Let's make our customer service department networking, our sales and marketing communal, and our accounting and finance departments mercenary." It also is something we discover as the issue after conducting the assessment and specific departments are operating in a particular culture quadrant counter to other departments or the company as a whole. For a company to realize its true potential as an enduring enterprise, it must commit to operating as one corporate culture and build its strategy around it as emphasized in Chapter 5.

❖

Recognizing fragmentation in your company is a first step towards moving it forward. Yahoo's Mayer recognized several practices that were either reinforcing or further fragmenting the company and they needed to be corrected. This is what being a leader is all about. The result of her initiatives toward "amplifying its greatness" through nurturing a corporate culture have proven the value of culture-driven initiatives. The company's release of its Yahoo! Weather app, which reached its goal for its first quarter in only four days, validates the power of knowing the type of culture that will help take a company to its next level. For Yahoo, eliminating telecommuting enhanced its ability to be a more collaborative, inventive, and engaged environment.

CHAPTER 14

Assessing Your Culture

An executive, who had just moved to the Carolinas from New York, was seeking to purchase two automobiles for himself and his family. They had not needed one for years since they were living in the heart of Manhattan, where the subway, taxies, walking, and trains were the natural modes of transportation to get anywhere they needed to go. Enjoying the beautiful sunny weather during a weekday, the executive walked first into a Mercedes dealership in flip flops, shorts and a tee shirt. He was greeted with the assumption that, based on his attire, he could only afford the lower end models on display. The sales associate, without any discovery or needs assessment, immediately took the executive to the lower end models and began talking price points. Feeling more like a transaction than a customer, the executive walked out and then proceeded to a BMW dealership. This experience was markedly different. The sales associate immediately greeted the executive and then proceeded to ask specific questions about his and his family's needs. From performance to the ease of putting a car seat into the vehicle, everyone was being considered before the first vehicle was shown. The executive ended up purchasing both vehicles from the dealership, one at the most expensive price-point, based on the trust built and the value explained as a result of a sales associate who first focused on understanding the needs of the customer. The executive has been a loyal customer since then and has referred countless others to the dealership based on his experience.

This example is what my CFO experienced when he moved here to join our firm. Corporate culture in a company is not just inside its walls. It is demonstrated on a daily basis by the experience of working with the company, whether the experience is by a customer, a vendor, an advisor, or the people in its employment. To truly know and assess your corporate culture, especially if you feel it needs to be aligned, shifted or rebirthed, as my company did, you need to see it first through the eyes of everyone else. Otherwise, you are operating a vacuum with blinders on that will result in a culture being dictated versus truly embraced and coming to life within your organization.

360 Degrees of Clarity

As we embarked on further solidifying and building processes around managing and maintaining our corporate culture, I could not find any assessment tool that helped a company gauge and identify its corporate culture that addressed both the people side and the performance side in relation to sustainability. That is why among my first initiatives within my newly established management consulting firm was to develop an assessment tool that could measure a company's current corporate culture state from a 360 degree perspective.

Leadership and Employee Perception vs. Reality: Understanding both the perception of the company's culture and what is desired is the critical first step to becoming an aligned and vibrant corporate culture. In a team meeting, we defined the four quadrants and their characteristics asking each person to mark an "X" next to the culture the company was currently operating within, and then a "•" to indicate which corporate culture was desired. We then developed a combination of statements that help leadership and team members select: 1) What is 100% true about the way the company operates, 2) What do they strongly agree are aspects of how the company approaches various aspects of operations, and 3) Comparing different corporate culture approaches to determine which one is the current approach the company takes in operating. (To learn more about the assessment, go to page 232 to The CURx^2 Assessment section.)

Customer Perception vs. Reality: The one thing I know for certain is that a successful corporate culture in a sustainable company must be obsessed with serving their customers. In examples later in this book, this is an underlying success factor that is clear and undisputable. That is why the example at the beginning of this chapter was the one that I chose to share. Both Mercedes and BMW autos are exceptionally engineered and highly branded automakers. I have actually heard similar stories from others where the exact opposite happened. It depended on the dealership and their approach. Yet, both Mercedes and BMW present strong corporate values, visions and missions about what sets their companies apart.

However, in the case of the dealerships, they are the first impression of each company's culture to the buyer. For my CFO, because the value of relationships, both personally and professionally, and caring about the customer, as it related to our business approach, were parts of his mindset, the value of the dealership being only about the money at the Mercedes dealership did not appeal to him and he walked out. When he was greeted with a sales associate at the BMW dealer, who genuinely wanted to find a vehicle to meet his specific needs, he experienced a relationship-focused interest versus a transaction-focused interest, and therefore ended up transacting business multiple times with the company that he felt had related best to him and his family's needs.

Supplier, Vendor, Contractor Perception vs. Reality: The true measure of an authentic corporate culture is in how the company treats its vendors, suppliers, and anyone with whom they outsource in order to operate or function as a company. In too many cases, you will find companies treating their customers like gold, but their vendors like dirt. While this may work for a while, the marketplace scuttlebutt will eventually come back around to bite the company in its pocketbook as vendors respond by not being as responsive or diligent in serving the company, opting to focus on where they are valued as a true vendor partner, and ultimately affecting the company's ability to serve its customer. Therefore, gaining insight from the perception of your company's culture from anyone you outsource to is valuable and validating either in positive ways or in need-for-shifting ways.

Culture Sub-quadrants

What we learned in conducting our internal assessment is that we were operating in the Communal quadrant, but in the least desirable sub-quadrant, which was Communal Fragmented. This indicated the trend toward becoming split between Networking and Mercenary if we did not

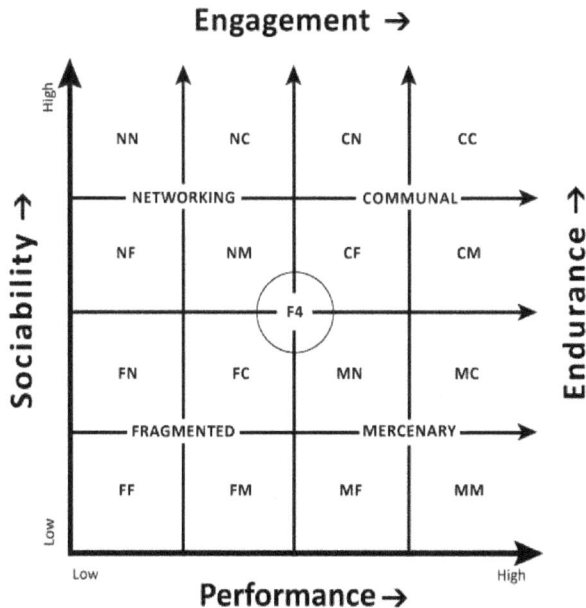

work on areas where the fragmentation was taking place.

Within each main quadrant, there can be aspects of another culture that impact a company's effectiveness in a particular culture as a result of characteristics from another culture being evident. This can cause a fragmentation different from the Fragmented unCulture described in Chapter 13, since your organization is fragmented because of what can best be described as a split personality.

In our case, we showed signs of extreme behaviors within our company on both the Networking side and the Mercenary side that were impacting our core desire to be Communal. In other words, we were not practicing what we preached in certain micro-areas that we needed to address and bring back into alignment based on the type of culture we wanted to exist inside and out. For instance, we would hold regular events under the guise of teambuilding that were highly social in nature outside of the office, including golf outings, cocktail hours, and parties. As management, we would pat ourselves on the back for giving employees time away from the paperwork, number crunching, and closing business, but then expect them to hit the ground running with higher sales expectations and profit performance because we had given them a little fun time. We basically thought to ourselves, "We let you have some fun, so now get back to work."

From Teambuilding to Team Nurturing Practices

What I described in the previous section is what too many companies do – surface-level teambuilding instead of team nurturing. If you are committed to building a corporate culture, you must be committed to nurturing your team on a variety of levels as an everyday practice in your business based on the culture you are striving to be. The key to building a performance-driven, engaged team culture is through practices that encourage interaction, input and celebration. The problem with most teambuilding events or training is that they create a good time, but camouflage or don't even address the real issues affecting team engagement or performance. Once we recognized that we had fallen victim to this way of teambuilding, we changed the dynamics of our events and ways in which we reinforced team engagement. Now our events are agenda-driven with employee input as the driving force behind how the events are being run. Our events are now collaboration and celebration driven to nurture development and engagement. We organize the events to encourage employee sharing and problem solving in a "safe zone" of open communication to better understand issues and ways to resolve as a collaborative team. Specific development activities are based on a combination of cross training education, as well as skill-based reinforcement determined from employee input and goals for advancing their skills and abilities within the company. We celebrate successes in a variety of realms, both personal and professional, and also through sharing and recognition inspiring the element of fun tied to desired results. What transpired as a result of these events is an overall openness to sharing and problem solving in everyday operations. The safe zone initiative created at our events ultimately reinforced that it existed within the company as a whole.

Actual Reality versus Desired Culture

In Chapter 7, I shared some of the findings we realized from our own assessment that indicated where some of the disparity in perception versus reality of our culture existed. When you determine that what you desire is what you really want your corporate culture to be, the communication that occurs in listening, hearing, comprehending, and disseminating on an ongoing basis during the transformation process cannot be under-stated.

As emphasized earlier in Chapter 6, this cannot be successful unless it is managed from the top down, while being inclusive of everyone within the company. For us, we took each area of concern to our hearts to more clearly define and improve understanding of what was expected based on the feedback. We identified issues in our processes, policies and attitudes that could be affecting employee, customer or supplier morale and perceptions. We reinforced our vision, mission, and core values through engaging in dialog at meetings by sharing examples, asking questions, and gaining perspectives from various areas of the company that continued to build upon and reinforce our compelling corporate culture story.

Chances are, after reading Chapters 10 through 13, you have a perception of which corporate culture quadrant you think your company is in right now. However, if you only operate based on your perception, you could potentially do more harm than good. We found in conducting the $CURx^2$ Assessment that typically the perception was worse than the actual reality. Why was this the case? The areas that were identified as the greatest issues were also the areas that were impacting people in negative ways, causing their perceptions to be more negative. The perception typically meant that is where the culture was heading if not managed and then nurtured properly.

❖

Managing and nurturing the corporate culture is and should be a priority of leadership. The next chapter on leadership engagement will help you know the best way to improve consensus and unification of leadership in order to build things the same company-wide.

SECTION III

Aligning Your Culture

CHAPTER 15
Leader Engagement

It is never easy to admit as an entrepreneur or a CEO that you may be a key part of the problem in your own company. Ego has a way of taking control when being in charge. When I first started my company, it was my ego that was running the company, not my spirit. I had started the company because of the behavior of my previous bosses, and yet I was not acting much better than they had been acting. I was guarded, micromanaging, inaccessible, and uncommunicative. Even though I was not as bad as those for whom I used to work, I was not as good as I needed to be to truly break the mold of a leader the financial industry had dictated was the only way to be. My example was dictating how others were acting, as well. Our teams were not being communicative and individuals were guarded just like I was behaving. Managers who I had hired began coming to me to hold me accountable for the type of organization I professed I wanted ours to be.

I am grateful to these managers and team leaders who trusted my vision more than feared my potential action. They not only saw potential in creating a financial company that was going to prove success without sacrifice and mayhem, they also saw potential in me as its leader. There are many things that contribute to how you behave as a leader. I know for me, I was destined to be someone who liked being in control of everything, which stemmed from being an athlete and a policeman's son. When you take being in control to an extreme, it shuts people off and shoots people down. They hesitate to question you due to the force by which you wield the control. They hesitate to perform to their full potential because they fear it might overstep some unspoken boundary or not be recognized for their contribution or effort.

Protecting and nurturing the culture within a company is under leadership's charge, but everyone has a role in its viability and sustainability. Before your entire organization can be engaged, your leadership must be engaged and passionate about what the desired corporate culture will look like, feel like, and be like. Leadership must establish the foundation for the corporate culture to take shape and then grow stronger.

In Chapter 3, I introduced three foundational elements as the "ure" of the CULTure. Without these three key elements in place, leadership cannot operate cohesively within the corporate culture. Defining each of these at the leadership level as it relates to your desired corporate culture is pivotal to being able to live the culture on a daily basis.

Unified Understanding: If leadership is not in alignment in understanding, it will be impossible for your organization to be aligned. As mentioned before, this is a top-down initiative that must be embraced by anyone in your organization defined as a leader or in a leader role. Some of the questions you need to be able to answer and agree upon include:

- What is our company vision - three years, five years, ten years, and twenty years from now?
- What is our mission and ultimate purpose as a company?
- What are our core corporate values and why are each of them essential to serving customers, one another, and the marketplace?
- How do we want to be perceived by employees, customers, the marketplace, and the industry?
- What are we passionate about in how we conduct our business compared to others in our industry?

Respect & Responsibility: Without mutual respect for everyone's role in the process with everyone taking responsibility for the corporate culture, it will just be something that looks good on paper with no heart and soul behind it. Some questions you need to be able to answer in order to reinforce the way your company operates and to ensure that your corporate culture continues to flourish include:

- How can and should we demonstrate our commitment to our values, vision, and mission on a daily operating basis?
- How do we reinforce what our mission and values mean to employees, customers, and the marketplace?
- How do we engage all employees in the process of nurturing our corporate culture so it continues to thrive?

Leader Engagement

- How do we assure that employees embrace and live the culture, which enables it to continue to flourish and be our competitive advantage?

Expectations around Excellence: Without expectations and standards around your idea of excellence, there is only confusion and assumptions that will ultimately fragment or divide your culture. Your leadership team must set these standards and then be willing and impassioned to uphold these standards in their own actions, as well as in their words and expectations of others.

- What will be our measure of excellence around customer satisfaction and loyalty?
- What will be our measurements of excellence around employee satisfaction and development?
- What will be our measurement of excellence around sales and profitability?
- What will be our measure of excellence around productivity and efficiency?
- What standards need to be put into place to ensure excellence?
- What policies need to be put into place to ensure consistency in delivery and understanding?
- How do we reward and measure our results with our employees at a variety of levels?

Different Cultures, Different Styles

Having an executive team that is truly in sync with what works best in your desired culture is essential to the corporate culture being maintained and effective over time. What we have determined in our research is that the highest level executive within each of the Corporate Cultures has a specific style and approach that works best and most effectively within that culture. As a result of the top-level executive's style, there are also ideal styles for his or her management team in order to work effectively together within the culture and to effectively manage and engage employees.

As I stated earlier, our research supports the Communal Culture as the ideal corporate culture. All aspects of this Culture are positive in how it synergizes the sociability of its people with the performance of the company for global sustainability. Because of this premise, we conclude that the Communal Culture is the only culture with a true leader at the helm supported by leaders. The Networking Culture's top-level executive we have defined as a Director, whereas the Mercenary Culture's top-level executive we have defined as a Dictator. As for the Fragmented unCulture, leadership engagement is non-existent with no one at the helm focused on corporate culture.

The Networking Director

The top executive of a Networking Culture can best be described as a Director because the focus is entirely on socially directing the company due to its high sociability nature. The satisfaction and delight of the people working in the company, as well as its customers, are the total focus. Any performance measures are connected to relationships with people.

This executive-in-charge wants to make sure everyone is happy – employees, customers, and anyone associated with the company. The Director is surrounded by a management team that serves as either connectors or ambassadors in order for everyone else to be willing and engaged players on the team. Making sure there is a happy ending to any challenge or problem a customer or employee may have is what is sought. Smiling faces are considered a measure of success.

Consider the popular series from the 70s and 80s, The Love Boat, and you can begin to visualize the approach of the Networking Director. Merrill Stuebing was the ship's happy-go-lucky, lovable Captain, supported by the very likable Gopher, Doc, Julie, and Isaac, each focused on being the consummate problem-solvers, relationship builders, and ultimate hosts and hostesses to passengers.

Director as a MOVER: The most effective Director possesses the characteristics of the MOVER described in Chapter 6 in the following ways:

DIRECTOR
MOVER
Connectors ⟷ Ambassadors
Players

- Being a motivator and manager of the culture focused on its overall impact on people;
- Embracing opportunities that will best serve the customers, people, or the relationships within the company;
- Being more values-driven than value-driven in decision-making pertaining to the company's growth;
- Achieving excellence through engagement of everyone being the solutions and drivers of customer and employee satisfaction and loyalty.

The MOVER Director will select his or her executive management team based on who will best support the culture and the company's focus on people. As a result of achieving excellence through engagement, positions within the company, including management positions, will be filled based on personal connections. Because the MOVER Director values people and what they contribute to the organization, this executive is more likely to fill positions by promoting from within the company.

Chick-fil-A's CEO Cathy, mentioned in Chapter 10, shared the importance of succession planning to the success of a company when speaking at an Institute of Leadership Development class at Terry College of Business in 2011. Reinforcing the longevity of his corporate leadership and that his best restaurant operators were individuals who moved up in the ranks within a restaurant or the company, Cathy shared that at the heart of knowing you are going in the right direction as a leader is knowing if you have followers. "That's when the magic happens because the next generation of leaders are today's followers. That's why you have to be intent about leadership development. Success is about succession and you have to start thinking about that day one ..."

Director as a SHAKER: Where the Networking Culture can take a wrong turn is if its Director is operating from a SHAKER mindset, also described in Chapter 6, versus the MOVER mindset. While on the surface, this Director is all about

DIRECTOR
SHAKER
Connected ⟷ Cheerleaders
Players

everyone getting along, this Director will also have a tendency to show preferential treatment leading to dysfunction within the organization. The executive team will more likely be the friends, family or personal connections of the top executive. While highly sociable and positive in working with the executive team and engaging with employees, there is an underlying sense of an inner circle of chumminess. Those who seek to advance into this inner circle are engaged in impressing and getting on the good side of the top-level executive and his or her executive team in order to be included. Because of the overall positive approach and focus on people, the hierarchy that exists is not as evident or viewed as a negative because it is a fun place to work. Important to note here is that the top-level executive can effectively bring on board family members or personal friends or contacts into the executive ranks and be a MOVER Director. The key difference is in the motivation behind the hire in the first place. The

MOVER Director will assure that the family or friend is capable and competent for the job or role needed within the company, whereas the SHAKER Director will allow their relationship to rule the hire versus what is perhaps in the best interest of the company, even creating a role within the company in order to include the family member or friend.

Connector versus Connected: The Connector Manager under the MOVER Director is truly focused on being a connector between the executive level management and the people working in the organization for reinforcing the corporate culture and what the company is setting out to do for the customer. In contrast, the Connected Manager is more focused on their connection to the SHAKER Director than connecting the people within the company to the corporate culture. As a result, there are subcultures within the SHAKER-led Networking Culture.

Ambassador versus Cheerleader: The Ambassadors under the MOVER Director, just like the Connectors, are touting the company as a whole. They may or may not be in a manager role, but are committed to being a positive internal and external representative for the company to other team members, out in the marketplace, and within the industry. They are the word-of-mouth generators. However, Cheerleaders, under the SHAKER Director and Connected Managers, are more likely focused on touting those in management positions within the company versus the culture of the company overall. They see their roles as getting everyone behind top management as a team. Cheerleaders are typically self-motivated in an effort to gain favor in order to ultimately be among the "Connected."

The Communal Leader

The Communal Culture is the only corporate culture where leaders exist at multiple levels. The World English dictionary definition of a leader is "a person who rules, guides or inspires others." The key word in this definition is "inspires." The Communal Leader inspires and then takes it to the level of empowerment through everyone embracing the guiding principles of the corporate culture. The focus of this executive-in-charge is to make sure everyone operates as a high-performance team united and focused upon achieving excellence in fulfilling the company's higher purpose.

The character Captain James T. Kirk of the Star Trek Enterprise original television series is an example of a Communal Leader. Besides being caring, considerate, and passionate, he was also focused and purpose-driven in his expectations of excellence. There was mutual respect and admiration for his diverse managing team including Second-in-command Mr. Spock, Chief Engineer Scotty, Chief Medical Officer Dr. "Bones" McCoy, Pilot Lieutenant Sulu, and Communications Officer Lieutenant Uhura.

The MOVER Leader: The Communal Leader is the most effective MOVER because each of the foundational characteristics is embraced from both a people engagement and a company performance standpoint.

COMMUNAL MOVER

Leaders ←——→ Promoters

Partners

- Being a motivator and manager of the culture focused on its impact on people in combination with achieving high-performance;
- Embracing opportunities that will ultimately advance the company's higher purpose with consideration to the customers, employees, and the company's performance goals;
- Being equally values-driven and value-driven in decision-making pertaining to the company's growth and its role in the global marketplace;
- Achieving excellence through engagement of everyone involved in the company to be true solutions-driven partners in order to achieve desired outcomes, including being engaged in the process.

Named among Harvard Business School's "Great American Business Leaders of the Twentieth Century," SAS CEO James Goodnight is the epitome of leading by example as a Communal leader. Founded by Goodnight in 1976, SAS is still privately-held due to his insistence on what was best for its people, the company's ability to maintain excellence in software development, and in serving customers. In the midst of the dot com bubble in 2000, Goodnight turned down going public believing staying private would keep the focus on realizing profits through exceptional execution by its people. While it would have made him richer faster, his motivation in building his company has always considered people in tandem with performance initiatives. He has described his company's culture as "egalitarian" in its approach to decisions. The outcome must benefit everyone associated with the company and not just a select subset group.

<u>Leaders and Promoters:</u> The Communal Leader does not allow his or her ego to get in the way, and realizes the importance of bench strength within the organization. Because the Communal Leader appreciates and demonstrates in both actions and words what can take place with strong leadership, this top-level executive seeks to have Leaders beyond himself or herself within the organization. The Communal Leader also knows the impact a community of leaders can have within the company, both at the management level and among team members, to empower higher levels of achievement and problem-solving in impactful ways for the company.

Promoters can be found at both the management level and among team members. They share a passion for the vision and mission of the company to the extent that they will publicly share the advantages of the company openly and proudly. Promoters are essential and valuable because they are the voice of the company outside of the executive level. They validate that the company really is as it professes to be and, therefore, is a great place to work, as well as the best place to purchase services and products.

In Chapter 3, I shared the example of the pride I felt overhearing my employees touting what a great place our company was to work and do business with at an awards event. At Chobani Yogurt, their culture inspires all of its team members to be Raving Fans sharing the Chobani story and creating raving fans wherever they go. This is a top-down inspired concept that was nurtured by Kyle O'Brien, the company's Executive Vice President of Sales. Whether it's a future or existing customer, employee, vendor, supplier, or a complete stranger, each Raving Fan's energy, passion, sense of belonging and making a difference is so engaging that the attitude becomes contagious and continues to draw more and more opportunities, people and customers into the folds of the organization as a result.

<u>Employees as Partners:</u> What is most powerful about the Communal Culture is that even the employees take leadership in themselves and with respect to others and are also promoters inside and outside of the organization. Because of the equal attention paid to the values and value within the organization, decisions are made in collaboration and partnership with the best interests of the people, the company, the community, and the global marketplace. This not only adds value and leadership depth within the organization, but also company-wide ownership at all levels in initiatives that are determined important to success. The pride and passion that exists within a Communal Culture is

impressive and attractive to anyone outside looking in or inside looking outside.

You understand the true power behind having employees feeling like true partners in the business' success when adversity occurs. Instead of retreating, these "partners" rally to whatever needs to be done to bring the company out of adversity in a "we're in this together" mentality "so let's get it done."

When the wholesale securer of our mortgage loans pulled the rug out from underneath us and companies across the United States in 2008, I witnessed this partnership mentality first hand. In spite of this forcing me to lay off employees, these same employees were insistent on working with me to determine our next steps and opportunities. I came into the office the next day with employees who had been laid off still showing up to work to help with the transition and wanting to help in developing the strategy to move us beyond this setback. Every day I saw how powerful this was as I would witness the Mortgage Lender Implode O Meter continuing to count down the casualties of companies no longer in existence. Nearly 390 mortgage lenders between 2006 and 2013 have gone out of business, yet Ameritrust Mortgage still stands, stronger and better than ever.

The Mercenary Dictator

The top executives of Mercenary Cultures are best described as Dictators because their approach involves a high level of control combined with an intense focus on achieving financial gain, profitability and competitive advantage for the company. The focus of this executive-in-charge is to make sure everyone is doing their jobs in order to achieve the highest return on investment for the company with no exceptions.

While monetarily focused, Mercenary Dictators can be effective or ineffective based on the way in which they dictate that the organization is to operate and the extent to which their own underlying personal motivations influence their decision making and leadership approach. A Dictator MOVER is the key to the effective Maverick Mercenary Culture introduced in Chapter 12; Whereas the Dictator SHAKER results in an ineffective Miser Mercenary Culture.

The Dictator as MOVER: Yes, there can be an effective leader as a Dictator. The most effective Dictator possesses the characteristics of a MOVER in the following ways:

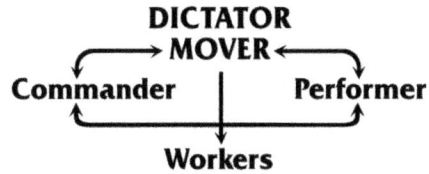

DICTATOR
MOVER
Commander | **Performer**
Workers

- Being a motivator and micro-manager of the culture focused on how the people effectively help the company realize bottom-line results;
- Embracing opportunities that will ultimately advance the company's bottom-line profitability, value, and sales growth;
- Being more value-driven than values-driven in decision-making pertaining to the company's growth;
- Achieving excellence through engagement of everyone involved in the company according to skills, competency and perceived value with a unified and intense focus on the company's bottom-line.

This leadership style, while relentless, domineering, and demanding, is motivated to inspire everyone in the company to be obsessed about serving their customers and being the very best at it, knowing the money that can be made and the potential for growth if this is done effectively. The Maverick Dictator leverages people as human capital committed to elevating the company's profits through shared communal beliefs. As a result of seeing people as assets, the Maverick Dictator crosses slightly into Communal thinking by recognizing their value and contribution to the end results. The Maverick Dictator is coveted and revered by the people within the company, as well as its customers and industry, in spite of having a reputation for sometimes being difficult to please or work with. Steven Jobs, late CEO and founder of Apple, is an example of a Maverick Dictator, and is featured in Chapter 32.

The Dictator as Shaker: The Dictator as a SHAKER is ego-driven to the point of no one crossing or challenging his or her decisions, expectations, or motives. A relentless

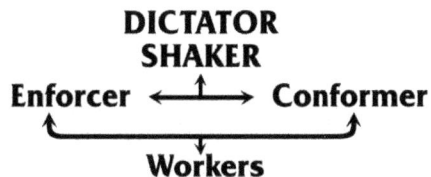

DICTATOR
SHAKER
Enforcer ⟷ **Conformer**
Workers

hard-driver, this Dictator expects action and results without fail, and won't hesitate to demean or demote in order to achieve desired results. Workers and suppliers alike are expected to put work first and be available on-call without fail. This Dictator is a Miser emotionally and fiscally in how decisions are approached, is focused ultimately on material gain at the expense of people, and feels no remorse.

The most classic example of the Miser Dictator is Charles Dickens' Ebenezer Scrooge. Greed and disregard for people has been the demise of many CEOs and companies throughout history. What ultimately occurs is the Miser Dictator becomes distracted by his or her own greed and personal agenda, to a point of a blinded obsession that ultimately leads to self-destruction or carelessness. I witnessed a Miser Dictator destroy a very good business in the baseball community because he became so obsessed with a competitor to the point of emulating, versus innovating or serving, the customer. His focus on doing what the competitor was doing to compete, versus differentiating in order to have advantage, resulted in losing customers and market share. He was continually harassing employees and members in search of what the competition was doing and saying instead of focusing on his own clients' needs and following his own "authentic" vision. This is a very common mistake many business leaders make. They keep their eyes on everyone else's ball instead of their own.

Commander versus Enforcer: The Commander is effective under the MOVER Dictator because he or she is an extension of the top-level executive in shared values, convictions and bottom-line performance for the organization. These managers are effective because of their ability to command respect and results through motivating workers in the right ways to achieve the end results. The Commander is hard charging, just like the Maverick Dictator, but is also powerful in how employees are rallied to be productive and effective in their work. The Enforcer, on the other hand, is an extension of the SHAKER Dictator in using threats and ultimatums as a means of getting workers to do what they are to do in order to impact the bottom line. While the Commander is respected, the Enforcer is detested and feared by employees for potential repercussions if their performance is not as expected.

Performer versus Conformer: The Performer has elevated in the ranks of the company as a result of being a top-performer in the company. Sales and big deals are the prerequisites for advancement and the Performer has proven their worthiness as a result. Becoming a Senior Vice President or making Partner are two examples of the Performer title in a company where performance and performance alone is the reason one is promoted within the company. The difference between the Performer and the Conformer is that the Conformer is a "yes" person on the job who achieves what is dictated by doing exactly what is expected of them, even if it goes against their personal beliefs or values. They reach a manager level because they followed the rules, produced what was expected, and are good examples to other workers of what it takes to advance in the company. However, in most cases the Conformer gets to a certain point in the company and cannot get any further because they don't possess the skills, thick skin or confidence necessary to move to the executive level.

The Fragmented – Leaders Missing In Action (MIA)

The Fragmented unCulture, just as it suffers from a lack of a team, also suffers from a lack of leadership. In a fragmented unCulture, the statement, "Our organization doesn't have leaders, only managers." is oftentimes what is agreed among employees, as well as by management. In many cases, managers may be not seen and only heard when something needs to be addressed. They are missing in action, causing employees to wonder what they actually do since it feels like the only work getting done is that by the employees.

❖

To determine which type of leader best fits your personality, core values and style, you will learn more in Chapters 22 through 24.

CHAPTER 16
Employee Engagement

I was making my rounds at Ameritrust and noticed one of my employees out of the corner of my eye in a slumped over the position in her cubicle, deep in thought with a distraught look on her face. I leaned in to say, "Is everything ok?" and she shot straight up, almost embarrassed to have been caught not working and said, "Oh, yes, everything is fine." and she fidgeted with some papers on her desk to begin getting back to work. I paused, and then said, "Are you sure everything is okay? Because you seem to be upset about something and maybe I can help." Tears welled in her eyes as she shared that her father had suffered a stroke, and she really wanted to be by his side as his only child and his only living family member, but could not afford to take off work. I told her to go to be by her father's side, and that her job was secure.

Engaging employees is more than teambuilding exercises and motivational events. Too many leaders underestimate the importance and impact of genuine caring in fostering strong relationships and allegiance of employees. The relief and gratitude on the young lady's face described above validated to me, like so many other similar situations with employees, how powerful the simple act of caring and empathy plays in being an effective leader. From that moment on, this employee viewed not just me, but our entire team as her extended family. She and her father were not alone, and as his health continued to improve, she came back stronger and more dedicated to our mission because she experienced the authenticity of our values first-hand.

When one of my leadership team member's father passed away, the entire leadership team attended the funeral in support of that team member. While that may seem extreme to you as you read this, the relationships we had forged as a leadership team went beyond the walls of where we worked. We truly cared about one another, including our immediate and extended families. We were there for each other, on the job, and as a support system outside of our jobs.

Employee engagement is first and foremost about relationship building. Like any relationship that is important to you, it requires continuous nurturing and reinforcement. When an employee first comes on board, like a romantic relationship, you are in the courtship phase. The employee has joined your ranks with great expectations, just as you have great expectations of him or her. Nothing but positive attributes are seen from both sides initially. Ideally, however, what is being viewed is from a basis of authenticity and not through rose colored glasses with blinders on.

To better understand what it takes on a daily basis to engage employees one-to-one, and one with each other, let's look at the digression of an employee who becomes disengaged over time.

The Disengaged Employee

Consider for a moment your first ideal job or position in a company and how you felt. You felt hopeful and excited, didn't you? You couldn't wait to get started and go in each day to make your mark. You had every reason to believe this was a great place to work because you accepted the position based on that belief and most likely many other positive and reaffirming factors.

Are you still with the same company where you had that first great job today? Most likely, the answer is "No." And also most likely, you left for another "hopeful" position because you weren't realizing all that you had hoped would materialize in the job. Moving to another opportunity was in your best interest, as well as in the company's best interest.

Why do we lose that hope? Why do we find ourselves beginning to change in our viewpoint of what seemed so great and perfect when we initially began our job? The answer is actually quite simple. The corporate culture and its inconsistency, misrepresentation, or direct conflict with who you are is the reason you begin to become disengaged.

Levels of Engagement

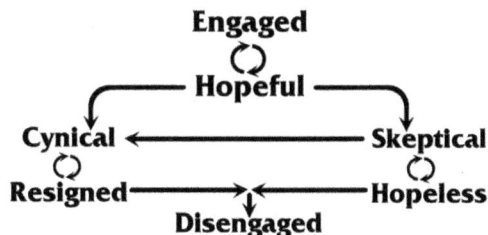

Circumstances, experiences and the environment can all play a role in why a once engaged and valuable employee becomes disenchanted and disengaged.

From Hopeful to Skeptical: Once hope is replaced with doubt, employees tend to move to the "skeptical" level of engagement. They become skeptical when they begin to witness or experience situations that go against what they believed they were going to experience at work. Some of the biggest contributors to skepticism are lack of communication, inconsistent directives, unexpected bureaucracy, limited opportunities, and lack of appreciation.

Lack of Communication: As mentioned in Chapter 7, lack of communication with an employee is one of the quickest ways to instill unrest and doubt. Once left to imagining what is going on, since communication about what is going on is lacking, the natural human tendency is to assume the worst. The employee then naturally assumes he or she will be negatively impacted, even though they are uncertain how or why. The integrity in which information is communicated is also of key importance. According to a study by MSW Research and Dale Carnegie Training, an emphasis on "positive managerial relationships built on trust and honest communication" with employees was a critical success factor for engagement. Go back to Chapter 7 and consider what you are not doing effectively so you can eliminate this as a reason for disengagement.

Inconsistent Directives: An employee can begin to have doubt when leadership is inconsistent in how the company is being managed, based on their actions. This is most often the case in a company without a clear vision or mission, resulting in a continuous change of direction or focus that causes confusion and frustration among employees and management. This also can occur if values are not clearly defined. In our corporate culture assessment profiler, an individual can rate their perception of how fairly employees are treated, how effectively decisions are being made, and the degree in which the strategic direction and purpose of the company is clear. When any of these, among other indicators, are poorly rated, there is a higher likelihood that employees are not engaged.

Unexpected Bureaucracy: The presence of bureaucracy is inevitable in some businesses operating within highly regulated industries.

Therefore, the fact that bureaucracy exists is not a deterrent to employee engagement unless it was not expected by the employee when hired. Too often, companies hide their bureaucratic ways to lure an ideal employee in, and then wonder why this employee is not able to effectively adapt when the bureaucracy is uncovered and realized.

Limited Opportunities: High achievement-oriented employees expect opportunities for advancement and growth within a company, whether it is or is not clearly identified in the hiring phase. When an employee realizes that opportunities are limited or not being treated as expected, and no effort is being made to demonstrate this as important for the leadership, then the employee begins to doubt that real opportunities exist, as was perceived initially.

Lack of Appreciation: Showing appreciation for employees is another area where leadership in companies fails to understand how powerful and simple practicing it can be for solidifying engagement. According to a U.S. Department of Labor, the #1 reason people leave their jobs is because they "do not feel appreciated." In a 2012 study of 1,700 employees conducted by the American Psychology Association, more than half of all these employees intended to search for new jobs because they felt underappreciated and undervalued. An attitude of gratitude that prevails throughout an organization builds camaraderie that reinforces respect of one another and values the role that each individual plays on the team.

From Skeptical to Cynical: When doubt is replaced with dissension or contempt, the employee has moved to the 'cynical" level of engagement. This typically occurs because the employee perceives a level of hypocrisy occurring within the company based on the actions of management, in addition to not experiencing what he or she had truly expected when hired.

Actions vs. Words: Walking your talk as a leader can never be overemphasized when it comes to employee engagement. Your actions speak louder than anything that is said or documented in an employee manual. Part of how we demonstrate that we truly care about our employees' families was in hosting family-focused events. During the holiday season, we learned that several employees with young children were feeling stressed about taking their child to see Santa amidst all the demands of the holidays. To alleviate that stress, we brought Santa to our employees during a holiday party, which included spouses, significant others and, of course, children. The most important aspect of this was not just providing Santa and accommodating employees and their children. It was that management, including me as CEO, was actively a part of this event, and we were actively interacting, engaging and enjoying. Many leaders in companies can misstep when they only talk it and don't walk it, which sends a mixed message to employees. Company-wide events can be hosted, and the management or key leaders never make an appearance. What is this telling your people?

Not Upholding Your Core Values: Nothing is going to create cynicism faster than when employees perceive that you are not upholding the company's professed core values. Your core values are bold statements professing what is important to you as a corporate culture. This isn't just an employee issue; it is also a customer issue. Too many companies break their own rules of engagement when it comes to both pursuing and retaining customers, which sends a contradictory message to employees and other customers about what the company really does stand for. I was personally challenged when a baseball team was considering joining our baseball academy. In explaining how we charge, operate, and work with the players, I shared that we say a prayer as a group before each game. One of the adult leaders of the prospective team stated that he had a problem with this practice and would not participate in that particular aspect of the program. This was a large team representing a significant income to the academy, but the Christian-based approach to working with our players was at the core of our values. My response to the adult was, "Then this is probably not the program for you." That particular adult walked out of the room, and I fully expected all other players, parents and coaches of this team to follow suit. But they didn't. They stayed because it was only one person's sentiment, not the team's sentiment. By staying true to our core values, I actually elevated the level of respect, commitment and engagement of this team in becoming a part of our academy.

Unkept Promises: Too often, leaders and managers fail to understand the reality that employees also have expectations. It is not just one-sided in what the company expects from an employee being hired. When employees choose to join your company, their decision was made on what the job entails in relation to their skills, as well as how good the company qualified as an ideal employer based on their personal set of criteria. In hiring an employee, especially for a highly competitive position, to gain the best candidate companies provide promises of compensation and advancement among other things that are offered to entice the individual to choose your organization over another. If these promises are not kept, then hope very quickly turns into bitterness and regret.

Limited by Bureaucracy: Bureaucracy within a company can lead to cynicism in an employee when the bureaucracy is having a direct impact on the employee in limiting his or her ability to do a good job or advance within the organization. A top-in-class graduate with a Masters degree in accounting secured a coveted position in an energy company's finance department. His initial year was rewarding, including the company supporting his studies to earn his CPA designation, in which he passed every phase of the exams the first time. While he was verbally recognized as a star in his department by his managers, the company's policies on pay increases and promotions were limiting the employee's opportunities to advance. Promotions were based on years of service, not just merit, and pay increases were capped with no employee receiving more than a small percentage on average. While he knew bureaucracy was inevitable due to the nature of the business and industry regulations, he did not expect the bureaucracy to impact his ability to advance or earn. When the employee was asked to take on the responsibility of a manager, without the pay or title associated with the position because it could not be approved until the employee worked an additional three years, the employee's resume was pulled out and polished for new employer opportunities to be sought. Although the employee remained dedicated to his work and doing an excellent job because of his own personal values, he also had lost faith in a leadership team that could so easily succumb to and hide behind company policies that were not valuing and rewarding the performance excellence of employees.

Lack of Recognition: Beyond feeling unappreciated, when an employee is not recognized for his or her contributions and efforts, over time this begins to wear on their loyalty and confidence about the company and its leadership. Especially when leadership takes credit without specifically recognizing an individual's effort and contribution, the employee disengages seeing themselves as being viewed as a means to an end versus a valued part of a team. In a study conducted by WorldatWork that was released in 2013, companies were realizing the value of company-wide recognition with a shift in how and why individuals are being recognized. Whereas sales performance was among the top three reasons companies in the study recognized individuals or teams in 2005, in 2013 sales performance fell to sixth in importance with length of service, above-and-beyond performance (in areas other than sales), peer-to-peer recognition, programs to motivate specific behaviors, and retirement being more prevalent among the companies that participated in the study.

From Hopeful to Cynical: A hopeful employee can bypass being skeptical and become immediately cynical when hypocrisy, unkept promises, disregarded values, or a lack of recognition occurs, which directly affects the employee. Feeling as if he or she has been taken advantage of or misled, the employee's doubt becomes discontent with everyone and everything at the company.

Whether the employee became cynical over an extended period of time or immediately as a result of what is viewed as a personal affront, this level of disengagement potentially can cause a great deal of discord throughout the organization if this employee is allowed to verbalize and influence others. However, some cynics, who are more introverted, may never verbalize what they are thinking. Instead, they will offer the occasional negative comment to themselves under their breaths to alleviate their own irritation or frustration with their working situation. These employees may also indicate their cynicism through body language, including rolling their eyes at comments or having tightly crossed arms while sitting in meetings. The cynical employee's quality of work begins to suffer because of a tendency to only do what he or she feels is necessary to get by. Cynicism brings out the insecurity in a person. This employee will become defensive when questioned about his or her productivity, and be quick to point blame elsewhere regarding the lack of performance.

Resigned versus Hopeless: The bottom rung of the engagement digression will result by employees either being more disenchanted with the company and its leadership, or being more disenchanted with their situation, or even themselves.

The "resigned" employee has lost faith in the leadership within the company and has determined that the company is no longer a good fit. This employee is more likely to be putting his or her resume back into circulation and only doing what is the absolute minimum activity to get by in their current position until a better opportunity comes along. These employees have resigned themselves to remain with the company on a temporary basis and direct their hope outward toward more appealing opportunities. While not impossible, it is difficult to re-engage this employee unless drastic measures are taken to rectify the perceived problematic issues within the organization.

The "hopeless" employee is a different story entirely. He or she, because of internalizing the situation more, believes to be stuck with no way out. Because their abilities to perform are in question within their own minds, they feel they must just do what they must, grin and bear it, get through the next day and then the future days until the weekend comes to give them a reprieve. These employees have lost faith in themselves or in the possibility that the situation will get any better.

The SHAKEN Employee

Looking deeper into the psyche of the "resigned" or "hopeless" employee can help you begin to see the spiraling effect each one can have on your overall organization with one feeding the other's misery and undermining even the best attempts to resurrect morale. Once employees reach these lowest levels, your organization, at least in their eyes, is on shaky ground. It is literally crumbling all around them in their eyes and it is up to you to reinforce it from the foundation to regain any inkling of hope. The organization is shaken, making the employee shaken.

The SHAKEN employee is oftentimes the result of a SHAKER leader described in Chapter 15 who has lost complete touch with the workforce he or she is leading as a result of being consumed by his or her own agenda and expectations.

S	=	Sad/Sorry	(Hopeless)
H	=	Helpless	(Hopeless)
A	=	Anxious/Angry	(Hopeless/Resigned)
K	=	Killjoy	(Resigned)
E	=	Exhauster	(Hopeless/Resigned)
N	=	Negative ROI – In the Red	

Shaken & Hopeless: Employees who are Shaken and Hopeless are unhappy, feel helpless, and are completely drained of interest in their work and what they are doing in their job. They have started shutting down and have become numb to what is going on around them as a measure of self defense. They are mentally exhausted, due to the turmoil they feel and/or witness, and do not believe there is anything that they can do. Many of these employees will stay in their positions as long as they can get by or they have acquired such low self-esteem that they believe they are lucky to still have their job, anxious by the likelihood they will be fired or laid off. Even though they dread going into work, they remain at the company because they feel paralyzed in their ability to do anything about the situation for the company and specifically for themselves.

What can be frightening as a CEO is when you are the one who feels hopeless. This happened to me in 1998, during my first setback with my company. I felt numb and helpless in how the market had impacted my business. I became disengaged with my employees, which made them feel detached and frustrated. If it had not been for my wife slapping me into reality, I could have literally been the reason for the demise of my company. This was a time when I had to make an adjustment in my own mental state to snap out of my hopelessness. I felt weak and almost paralyzed physically, and that's when I realized that part of this was because I had forgotten about my own well being. I had forgotten what a stress reliever and mental nurturer exercising had been for me, because I had slipped out of the habit. Instead of waking up and dreading the day, I decided to wake up and get moving, physically. I got back to running and it was liberating for me mentally and physically. I was running distances I had not run before, and the creative juices were flowing again in my thinking.

> **Shaken & Resigned:** Employees who are Shaken and Resigned are unhappy, but anger and resentment are the underlying reasons for their unhappiness due to their cynicism. They have reached this point due to feeling slighted, unfairly treated, taken advantage of, unappreciated, unrecognized, or all of these emotions related to their contributions. This employee is more likely to bring negativity into the workplace, being a killjoy through comments, behavior and communication when they are sharing their discontent and dissatisfaction with co-workers. This is all occurring while the employee is most likely in the process of seeking employment elsewhere, but damage can be catastrophic if action is not taken. Worse yet, oftentimes the dissension being caused by the employee is not even on the radar of leadership.

A Disengaged Employee Is A Fragmenting Employee

In essence, when an employee is shaken, the employee is fragmented and has the power and potential to influence and impact fragmentation throughout your organization either intentionally or unknowingly. For

Shaken and Hopeless employees, their lack of interest and tendency to do their job just to "get by" becomes a source of frustration and contention for co-workers.

For Shaken and Resigned employees, their negativity can get to the point of distraction for co-workers or become a weapon in rallying co-workers against the company, causing further disengagement and fragmentation with a domino effect of people leaving the company or new hires not staying long. These employees are focused on building evidence that will help them conclude that it's not them that is the problem, but it's everything and everyone else in the company.

Technology can become among the biggest excuses used by Shaken and Resigned employees for why things are not getting done, whether it is a lack of technology or technology issues. These employees will also point to the people right above them or below them if not getting answers needed or not getting support, anything to throw the responsibility away from them.

<u>To Keep or Let Go:</u> As a leader, you need to determine if the Shaken employee's morale is or is not salvageable. It would be easy to believe that either a Hopeless or a Resigned employee must go, but this is not always true. The key is to understand the underlying reasons for the hopelessness or resigned attitude.

A supervisor who had been with a company for several years was identified in our corporate culture assessment as resigned. Upon interviewing the supervisor further, he shared that he had stopped caring for quite some time because he did not feel that his input was being clearly heard, or that he was being included in decisions affecting his department. In his words, his "suggestions fell on deaf ears, and he was too tired to fight and deal with the confrontation that would inevitably occur," based on his experience with current leadership. He still cared about the people that worked for him, and took pride in his work, but he was exhausted and his health had also declined under the stress of the work environment. His years of experience and knowledge had good value, according to the consultant, who became an advocate for leadership in sharing suggestions from the supervisor that merited consideration. Some of the suggestions were put into practice, which was viewed positively by the supervisor and his department. However, the previous negative work environment had taken its toll, and shortly after improvements were beginning to be initiated, the supervisor suffered a heart attack. Recovering for several weeks, his department rallied together in order to continue to move forward the initiatives his suggestions had made possible.

Re-engaging: The best time to re-engage an employee is before he or she gets to the point of Resigned or Hopeless. However, it is not impossible to re-engage this employee if a mutually valuable transition can occur. The mistake managers and leaders will make in an attempt to re-engage employees is in focusing too much on "big vision" communication, thinking it will inspire and motivate all the employees. However, when employees are Shaken and Hopeless or Resigned, each employee is viewing everything with a foggy, near-sighted lens. They simply cannot see the big picture because they are only able to focus on what is right in front of them. The astute manager will acknowledge why the employee may be feeling hopeless or resigned and then establish a plan of action that will celebrate small successes so that the employee can begin to feel effective, useful or valued again. This is not about lowering standards, but about recognizing people achieving standards so that they can progress into a mode of exceeding standards.

The Danger of Cliques

While cliques can appear to be positive with teams of people banding together, the danger in cliques is their natural tendency to exclude or show preference, as well as influence behavior that could diminish company-wide team building and engagement efforts. Both the Mercenary and the Networking cultures are more likely to see the formation of cliques, which undermine the culture in overall engagement and performance effectiveness. In a 2013 CareerBuilder survey, 43 percent of employees surveyed stated "their offices were populated by cliques." Additionally, over half of those identifying cliques as an issue stated that "their boss is part of one." In the same survey, 20 percent also admitted to having done something they're not interested in doing or didn't want to do to fit in with a particular group. Consider the pressure to "fit in" when a manager or one of the top leaders is a part of the clique and most likely the ring leader of the clique.

While joining a clique can give an employee a false sense of security or a feeling of being on the inside track to special privileges, it causes dissension with those who are not included and an overall lack of cohesiveness within the organization. When you start having cliques within your company, this should be a danger, and a warning sign to you as a leader to take immediate action to make the entire organization "one big clique." What I mean is everyone is engaged and feeling connected with each other and with the organization as a whole. You need to get to the bottom of why the cliques have formed and what underlying agenda had motivated the cliques to form in the first place. Typically there is a leader of the pack, and this is where the re-alignment focus needs to begin in order to shift.

Table Touches: A good technique that I have put into practice is the concept of table touches, which I learned from an attorney who turned into a restaurateur. He wanted his restaurant to be the place where business executives could feel comfortable in conducting highly confidential meetings, while also feeling they were being taken care of with exceptional service and attention to the details during their dining experience. One of the biggest pet peeves he had as an attorney was attempting to conduct business over lunch or dinner, and continuously being interrupted by the server who was inquiring if everything was okay. Instead, the protocol was that the wait team would announce their dedication and commitment to an exceptional experience, and that they would check useful table touches as a means of weighing in with the table. If the members of the table were deep in discussion, the tapping would go unnoticed. But patrons knew that if anything was needed, the wait team was just minutes away from accommodating their every need, when needed.

For me, the idea of table touches was incorporated into my check-ins when making my rounds on an informal basis throughout the office. As I would go through the halls and pass by cubicles, the informality and friendly nature in which I would shout out to some folks and allow others to keep focused and working gave everyone the knowledge that if they had a question or needed something, they could feel comfortable and confident in connecting directly with me during one of my rounds. These rounds also helped me see if anyone was out of sorts or in a state of mind that could be of concern, simply by observing their demeanor, body language, and even their interaction with others.

One Big Clique

What makes an employee ideal and, therefore, the most likely one to be engaged and to succeed within your organization depends on the type of corporate culture you have defined that works best based on your goals, values, vision and mission. An engaged employee is one who buys into the cult-like aspects of your culture because you, as the leadership, have built a solid foundation to reinforce its value and validity as it relates to the employee on both the personal and professional levels.

Peer-To-Peer Recognition: In highly competitive industries, cliques can form within departments, almost appearing to pit a department against a department. This can be especially evident in Mercenary Cultures, where there is a level of hierarchy also dictating cliques. We put into practice a Peer-To-Peer Recognition Ceremony at the end of each monthly team meeting. It was to serve as a means of our team members recognizing the efforts and support of others. Our stipulation was that the peer being recognized would be in another area of the company versus strictly within their immediate team. This helped employees gain a higher level of awareness and appreciation for the roles others played in supporting one another' jobs. What began as a ten-minute exercise grew to be a 30 or 45-minute love-fest among team members sharing legitimate and inspiring appreciation and kudos with one another. The level of engagement that resulted from this regular practice was awe-inspiring to witness as a leader.

The Ideal Networking Employee

The ideal employee for a Networking Culture is a people-oriented person who enjoys interacting and serving people in their role within the company. Regardless of the position, the person shares the priority of people as the focus on the company and embraces relationship-building as an asset. The Networking-oriented employee is most likely to select the following statements as elements of an ideal working environment.

- Celebrations at work focus on recognizing people's special occasions, including birthdays, marriages, births, anniversaries and other personal milestones.

- The company believes that a job can be an enhancement to your lifestyle.

- The work pace is steady, but seems to fly by because everyone is having so much fun.

- I view my role within a company as a part of a team that cares about what it is doing for others.

- Mistakes are viewed as aspects of being human, and therefore, are accepted and dismissed.

- The hiring practice is to reach out to family, friends, and professional connections to fill positions.

- Personal development opportunities are a benefit of working here.

- Decisions are based on what are the best interests of the employees and our customers.
- Leaders in the company are friendly, fun, and personable.

The Ideal Communal Employee

The ideal employee for a Communal Culture is equally conscious of how people and performance work in tandem for their own personal success and the success of the company. Therefore, they value the role that relationships play in achieving performance measures within the company. The Communal-oriented employee is most likely to select the following statements as elements of an ideal working environment.

- Celebrations at work are a combination of recognizing personal special occasions, professional achievements, and company successes.
- The company believes that work/life balance creates happier and more productive workers.
- The work pace can be steady, or fast and furious, depending on demands, but is rewarding and enjoyable.
- I view my role within a company as a part of a high-performance team focused on a higher purpose.
- Mistakes are viewed as a part of learning and growing as an employee, a manager or in business.
- The hiring practice is a combination of reaching out to family, friends and professional connections, as well as a competitive recruitment process developed to find the best candidate.
- Professional and personal development opportunities are benefits of working at the company.
- Decisions are based on considering what is mutually in the best interest of employees, customers and the company.
- Leaders in the company are inspiring, motivating and empowering.

The Ideal Mercenary Employee

The ideal employee for a Mercenary Culture is high-driving and performance oriented, and focused on monetary gain for themselves and monetary growth for the company. These individuals are not as focused on relationship building, but on how relationships can help them achieve their goals. The Mercenary-oriented employee is most likely to select the following statements as elements of an ideal working environment.

- Celebrations at work focus on employees' professional achievements, as well as company successes.

- My job is a priority because it provides me the lifestyle and status that I enjoy.

- The work pace is fast and furious, which is exhilarating, in spite of the demands.

- Mistakes are not an option and should be avoided through a focus on performance and excellence.

- The hiring practice is highly competitive and formalized to retain the highest performance candidates for the position.

- Professional development opportunities are a benefit of working at the company.

- Decisions are based on what will positively impact the bottom line most effectively.

- Leaders in the company are successful, demanding, and have high expectations of me.

❖

If you thought that employee engagement was simply a matter of conducting a few teambuilding activities and providing a decent array of benefits, I hope that you now see that engagement begins and ends with you and your leadership team, underscored by the corporate culture you are nurturing. Once you identify and embrace your ideal corporate culture as a leadership team, you can better know the employees who are the most ideal to engage in sustaining that culture.

CHAPTER 17

Culture Shock

It was 2002, just a few days after firing the Sales Manager who was behaving with conduct that was not in alignment with our culture. I walked into our office and discovered that fifteen employees had cleaned out their desks and left overnight. Later I learned that these employees decided to leave without notice to work with the Sales Manager I had just fired. I walked around in disbelief, literally in shock that this could happen. I was dumbfounded by the total lack of consideration and felt personally devastated by this abrupt reaction by employees that I considered a part of a team. Some of the people that had gone I had thought were totally on board with our commitment to our corporate culture, while others who had left, quite frankly, I was not surprised. Then it hit me that the real issue wasn't who had left, but who was left behind and still working with us. How I managed myself and communicated to the team was going to be pivotal to how our commitment to being a truly Communal Culture would transpire.

The true test of how committed you are to your culture is in how you take action to align, adapt and make your desired culture a critical success factor in your organization. If truly embraced, it should be having a direct impact on all decisions, interactions, and the way in which you and everyone else operates within the company from that point forward. No exceptions! No wavering!

You also will be tested by unexpected actions of others, like the example I shared at the beginning of this chapter. The challenge as a leader, especially if the desired culture requires an evolution of you in your style and approach as the leader of the culture, is understanding what internally impacts your own behavior and motivations. The authenticity of your behavior and motivations are paramount to others, especially those left behind, in order to continue to embrace the desired culture so that it can flourish.

Programmed Self versus Authentic Self

A consultant I worked with in my own coaching brought to light the impact of how I was reacting to and processing situations based on my programmed self versus my authentic self. Whenever confronted with challenges, the programmed self is what kicks in based on a lifetime of experiences, influences and impressions that have shaped you in ways that are not actually true about who you are internally or even who you want to be. It is in many ways your defense mode of reacting to a given situation.

As I mentioned earlier in this book, I was the son of a cop and a college athlete. The combined experiences gave me a mentality of "my way or the highway" and thinking that "as long as I had the ball, I could control the outcome." As a result, whenever challenges occurred or a ball got dropped on a particular assignment, my programmed self would kick in and I would dictate to my team how "I would do it" or "it must be done" and in many cases, I would just decide to do it myself because then "I knew it would be done right." Not being very team focused or engaging, was it? The most frustrating part of all of this was that my deep-down intuition and my core values supported the concept that a team effort was so much more powerful than a solo effort, and yet, there I was sabotaging and going against what I genuinely believed, because of what I had been taught to believe. Big difference!

Understanding and recognizing the difference between your Programmed Self and Authentic Self begins with how you approach a situation when an unexpected event occurs that requires your action.

Programmed Self: When an unexpected event occurs, your Programmed Self will be more reactive, potentially assuming the worse concept based on past experiences or instilled thinking that may have influenced your beliefs about your self or a similar situation. Your attitude will be more suspicious, defeating or skeptical, seeing problems more than solutions. As a result, your behavior will be more negatively influenced.

Employee A is given an assignment. He turns in the assignment and it is returned with several questions and a request for more information and detail. Based on past experiences of being the son of a highly critical parent, this employee immediately views the feedback as his work being not good enough and having flaws. The demeanor of this employee is defensive when he attempts to understand what his manager wants, or he chooses to complain to co-workers that the assignment was not clear to begin with. With so much energy being put into complaining and being annoyed at what is viewed as doing it all over again, this employee misses the fact that his initial thoroughness actually raised valid concerns that warranted further investigation. His second-round report only scratches the surface of what was desired. Even though the first attempt was initially impressive to his manager, he loses future opportunities.

Authentic Self: When an unexpected event occurs, the Authentic Self does a gut check with your core values as the basis for how to take action. Therefore, instead of being reactive, you are proactive in seeking how to better understand more about what was unexpected. You may be asking clarifying questions to yourself or anyone else involved in the event. Your attitude is more positively influenced, seeing the unexpected challenge as an opportunity, and approaching it with curiosity, enthusiasm and a solutions-mindedness.

Employee B is given the same assignment as Employee A, and his report is also returned with questions and a request for more details. This employee knows that the work provided was his best work because it was prepared based on his core work values. When he receives the returned report with more questions and the request for details, he immediately seeks to gain additional insight and clarity from his manager by asking specific questions related to the feedback. Through the process of additional discovery, he learned that his manager was impressed with the initial work because it raised some valid questions of concern that would not have been raised otherwise. With the additional feedback, he explores the necessary resources to finalize the report as requested, and feels confident to offer recommendations based on the much more in-depth findings. The report is not only well received by his manager, but the recommendation is also embraced, which positions the employee for opportunities previously not available to him.

AUTHENTIC SELF

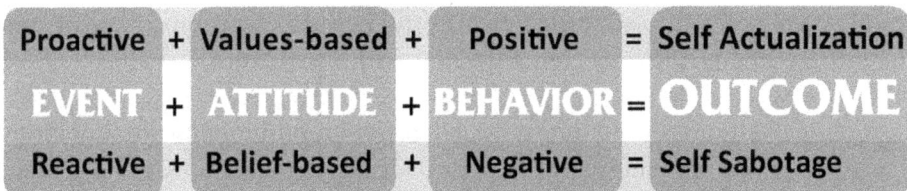

Proactive	+	Values-based	+	Positive	=	Self Actualization
EVENT	**+**	**ATTITUDE**	**+**	**BEHAVIOR**	**=**	**OUTCOME**
Reactive	+	Belief-based	+	Negative	=	Self Sabotage

PROGRAMMED SELF

What is important to note is that Employee A and Employee B could be the same person who either succumbed to his Programmed Self, or who confidently embraced his Authentic Self. Can you begin to see how powerful this concept is to enable someone to be not just an effective employee, but also an effective leader?

When People Leave or Must Go

Whenever you are going through an organizational shift, there will be attrition that cannot be avoided, both in regard to people voluntarily leaving, as well as those that must be let go because they don't fit the culture. Important to understand is that this is not just regarding employees, but all relationships associated with your business, including customers, vendors, suppliers, and other external business relationships. How you manage all of these relationships during the culture shift will have a direct impact on how those who remain will continue to embrace and will have confidence in the direction the culture is going.

Employee Relations: When it comes to employee relations, you will always be faced with tough decisions. When an employee screws-up or is not performing to their best ability, you must remember first that they are human. When you realize that an employee is not a good fit with your culture, even though you had high hopes, it is best to be respectful and yet clearly state why it is not working.

Zappos is so committed to a corporate culture fitting with employees that they offer a $2,000 bonus that employees can take and then leave after their initial orientation period. Very few recruits have taken the bonus offering, but those who have did so because they did not feel that they fit within the culture.

When you are broadsided by an employee unexpectedly leaving, how you conduct yourself with those remaining is pivotal to nurturing your corporate culture. Being angry and derogatory is not only distracting to your employees, but also destructive to the culture. Nine times out of ten, the person who has left was not a good fit with the culture.

Customer Relations: As counterproductive from a profitability standpoint as it may seem on the surface to lose customers, it actually does help align your culture and your business strategically. Confirming the desired culture also should confirm the ideal customers that will also embrace the culture and be most profitable and rewarding to serve within your culture. If your culture is built on quality and customer service with a focus on long relationships, then a customer that is price-focused in making the least expensive transactions would not be a fit.

Business Relations: Who your company utilizes as resources, support or for additional expertise also should be reviewed for how well they are in alignment with your vision, mission, values and culture. When we experienced the setback in our wholesale mortgage business, in hindsight, I can now see that the company that provided our credit lines was not in alignment with our values, vision or mission. Washington Mutual was, from their perspective, all about closing the deals and quantities of transactions. In essence, there wasn't a relationship at all, just a bottom line expectation. When we initially began our courtship, it was all about offering the lowest price points in order to close the deals. When we determined to go back into retail mortgages, we also determined the vendors with whom we would and would not do business based on our shared values and philosophies in serving customers.

The People Left Behind

Referring back to the example I shared at the beginning of this chapter, how I conducted myself and handled the mass exodus was either going to reinforce the evolution of our culture or make it fall apart before my eyes. As the visionary and driver of the desired corporate culture, it was essential that every action and reaction was handled with the utmost care and consideration in order for those remaining to continue to be committed to its realization.

Rallying Leadership: After the discovery of the entire team of people leaving overnight, my leadership team met immediately to discuss the next steps of engagement with everyone remaining in the company. This was even more therapeutic for me than I realized at the time because I was feeling personally beaten by the departure of so many team members. My confidence in myself as a leader was wavering even though my commitment to the culture was steadfast. This is where surrounding yourself with values-driven leaders on your executive team makes the difference. My leadership team was pivotal to steering me away from feeling hurt and moving me toward the reality of how it was a blessing in disguise. By doing this, we were able to focus on the present and moving forward, versus belaboring the whys of each person's departure. They were gone and our focus needed to be on the team we had now and how to empower them even more.

<u>Validating with Employees:</u> We met with the employees as a group to openly discuss what had happened. The focus was not on bashing and belittling those who had left, but on acceptance and being grateful for the opportunities that were ahead of us. What was evident to me is that no-one was taking the exodus as hard as I was taking it. As we rallied in support of each other, it was clear that those who remained in the firm believed it was for the best because those who had left didn't fit the desired culture anyway. When these employees witnessed my confidence in them as we moved forward, it also reinforced that prior to this, there were people within the organization who were violating our core values, which was a violation to everyone on the team who held them to be critical to our success and differentiation.

<u>Nurturing Customers:</u> With the size of group that left, it necessitated reaching out to customers immediately to assure them they would be taken care of as seamlessly as possible to curtail any worries or rumors since we could not control what may have been or would be communicated to customers by those who had left. It was essential that we focused on the positive support and serving of our customers and not criticizing or appearing to be disgruntled by the departures. This takes a great deal of humility and focus, because it is human nature to be negative in situations like these.

❖

Whether you are in the midst of defining and aligning your culture, or your organization is on a growth track where the corporate culture may be challenging to maintain, part of growing is effectively navigating through the inevitable turmoil that will arise in the process. The key is to stay steadfast as a leader guiding your organization forward, with confidence, humility and authenticity every step of the way.

CHAPTER 18
Shifting Cultures

The corporate culture assessment results were released to my client confirming that the sales department was operating in an entirely different quadrant than the rest of the company. This reinforced the dissension that employees felt whenever dealing with the sales team. Interaction was strained with the sales team literally barking orders to move products so they could meet their sales goals. While the company professed that teamwork and collaboration were parts of its core values, internally, the company was divided and disengaged due to what appeared to be preferential treatment and bias toward anyone in sales by top management. Even though sales were happening, quality issues were increasingly becoming a problem. Finger pointing became a regular occurrence as the sales team blamed other departments for the problems that were occurring and the other departments were blaming the sales team for improperly pushing what was not fully ready to be released. Instead of pulling themselves together to resolve issues and effectively address customer concerns, the company was literally beginning to fall apart at the seams. Top management knew something needed to be done. With the assessment to guide them, they began to better understand what it was going to take to pull everyone together again.

The scenario described above isn't unusual in a company. Certain departments can have a tendency to favor a particular quadrant over another. Accounting, finance and sales can be more mercenary in nature. Customer service and marketing can be more networking focused. The key is to determine which culture quadrant and sub-quadrant you desire to be in based on your core values, vision, mission and priorities as a company.

When you look at your organization as a whole, and then assess its current corporate culture dynamics compared to the one you ultimately would like to operate within, you will find silos that need to align, as well as areas that need to drastically shift. Before specific areas can be addressed, the overall organization and the top-down alignment and shifting need to be addressed.

As with any corporate initiative, for it to be successful it must start from the top down. If executive management is not committed to building the corporate culture, it won't happen. Before individuals within the whole company can be assessed, the executive team needs to be assessed and then reach a consensus of what will be the ideal corporate culture for the company

Aligning Leadership

When a company feels as though it is falling apart at the seams, the management within the company is most likely wholly disengaged themselves. Managers responsible for each area of the company lead their direct reports according to their own ideals of what will achieve success. With nothing to bring cohesion to the organization as a whole, it is just an assemblage of many moving parts with none of them in sync. Reasons for this have already been described including a lack of values, vision, mission, communication, and ethics. Before any of these aspects can be addressed, the lack of leadership and direction must first be addressed.

Who are the leaders within your company from an infrastructural basis? This is important to identify so that you are assessing the entire leadership funnel within the company and engaging them in the corporate culture building process. Those who will be the most likely to influence the rest of the company's team members need to have buy-in to the desired culture or it will never come to fruition.

This became particularly evident when we were beta testing the corporate culture assessment tool that we developed. Out of curiosity, we segmented the results of the executive level, supervisory level, and the project or team leaders within the beta company to reveal each segment's perception of where the company currently was compared to where they

Executive Management

NETWORKING   COMMUNAL

FRAGMENTED   MERCENARY

Illustration 1a

desired the company to be. A look at these three segments revealed that significant work was necessary among the leaders and managers within the company before a company-wide effort could commence.

The "x" symbol was plotted to indicate the respondent's perception of where the current corporate culture was within the company. If an individual felt that their particular department was in a different quadrant or sub-quadrant than the company as a whole, this was to be plotted with a solid square symbol (■).

As you can see by comparing Illustration 1a and 1b, the two levels of management had drastically different perceptions of where the company was as a whole. Interestingly, the project and team leaders' plotting was more in alignment with the perception of executive level management. (See Illustration 1c)

When facilitating discussion about the disparity, Middle Managers and Supervisors revealed that there was immense pressure from the

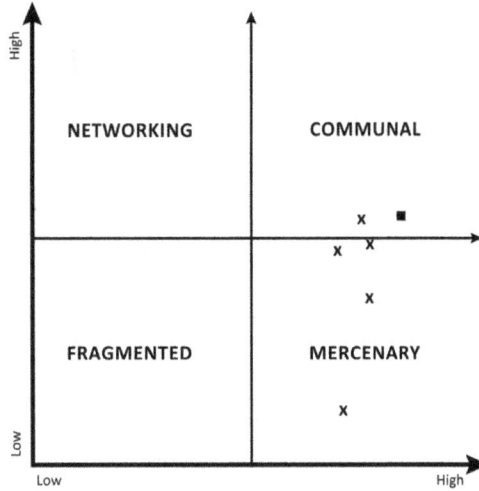
Supervisory / Mid Level

Illustration 1b

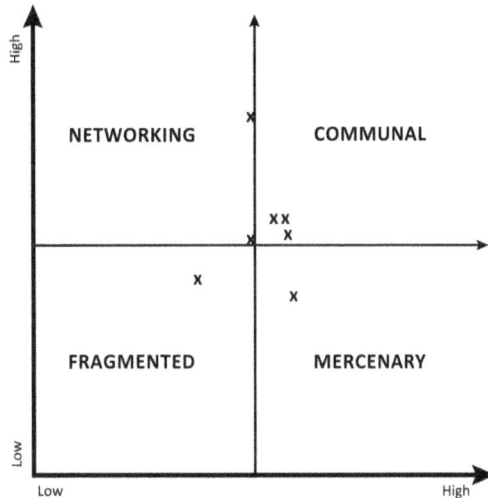
Project / Team Leaders

Illustration 1c

executive level to reach performance numbers, explaining their viewpoint of the company being more Mercenary. Because Executive Management wasn't seeing performance results, they viewed the company as more Fragmented. Project and Team Leaders viewed the company as more Fragmented because the dissension between the top and middle management levels was evident, causing confusion and frustration in attempting to lead their teams.

If the executive team had only viewed their results and then moved forward into looking at overall company results, they would have overlooked the disparity with the middle management level. The importance of multi-level management buy-in cannot be emphasized enough. Gaining buy-in and leadership consensus around the desired culture is paramount, and begins with clearly understanding the current perception of the organization's culture at the management levels.

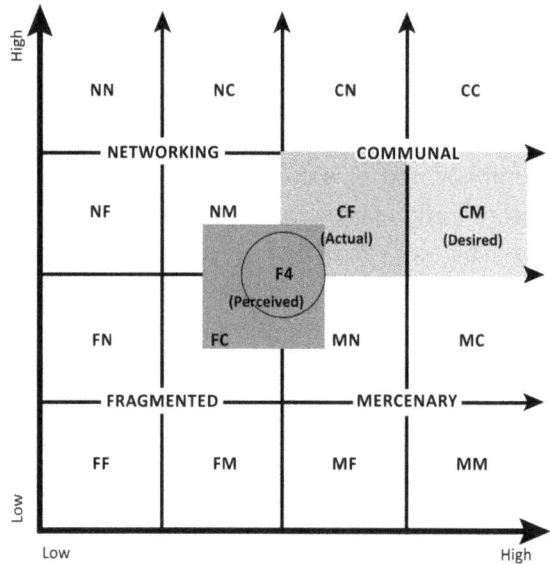

Illustration 1d

What was encouraging, with further disclosure of the assessment results, the desired culture of all team members was complimentary to what was ultimately desired by management. Additionally, the actual reality of where the company was as a whole was not as dire as the perception. (See Illustration 1d)

Determining Where to Shift

The process for determining which corporate culture is the ideal culture for your company begins with reviewing the basic differences and priorities of each of the culture quadrants. The following overviews the top ten differentiating aspects of each of the corporate culture quadrants.

Communal	Management is highly visible, accessible and engaged with employees.
	Company exists for a higher purpose that makes a difference.
	Purpose and profits drive strategy and decision-making.

Aligning Your Culture

	Communication is open and encouraged through regular written and verbal processes, standards, and initiatives.
	Celebrations at work focus on recognizing special personal occasions, as well as professional and company achievements.
	Our company believes work/life balance creates happier, more productive employees.
	The work pace here is steady, or fast and furious, depending on demands and needs.
	Everyone at the company views their role as being part of a high-performance team focused on a higher purpose.
	The hiring practice of our company is to reach out to family, friends, and professional contacts, as well as use a competitive recruitment process to fill positions.
	Professional and personal development opportunities are benefits of working here.

Networking	Management is highly visible, available and involved with employees.
	Company exists to make people feel included, appreciated and happy.
	Relationships drive strategy and decision making.
	Communication is free-flowing with no formal approach.
	Celebrations at work focus primarily on recognizing special personal occasions.
	Our company believes a job can be an enhancement to an employee's lifestyle.
	The work pace here is steady, but seems to fly by because we are having so much fun.
	Everyone here views their role as a part of a team that cares about what we are doing for others.
	The hiring practice of our company is to reach out to family, friends and professional contacts to fill positions.
	Personal development opportunities and lifestyle perks are benefits of working here.

Mercenary	Managers are accessible in varying degrees with employees as necessary related to performance initiatives.
	Company exists to make a profit.
	Bottom line and profits drive strategy and decision-making.
	Communication is formal and must be done in accordance with proper procedures and compliance internally and externally.
	Celebrations at work focus solely on professional and company achievements.
	Our company believes that a job is the reason for employees' lifestyles and should be their priority.
	The work pace here is fast and furious with high demands and long hours.
	Everyone here views their role as a critical part of achieving the company's high performance.
	The hiring practice of our company is a competitive, formalized recruitment process.
	Professional development opportunities are a benefit of working here.

Determining How to Shift

By analyzing the reasons behind the perception and actual reality of your corporate culture compared to where you desire your corporate culture to be, you can begin to define the action and activities that will aid in aligning the culture according to its desired outcome. Start by looking at the top ten differentiators and note the ones that currently are not a practice or focus of your current culture.

If you talk to the CEO or leadership of companies known for using their corporate culture as a differentiating factor of the company, they will say that their corporate culture cannot be replicated. There is a truth to this, because a corporate culture is the personality and psychology of the company that is made of by the sum of its unique parts. The most critical pieces of the corporate culture puzzle for you is your mission and the desired outcome that you hope to realize as a company layered with your core values and what each means to how you operate your company.

Don't attempt to mimic or replicate another company's culture. You will fail miserably. Don't simply adopt a listing of values that you believe you should have as your core values. Explore and confirm your core values for the critical success factors that they are and should be. I have had companies that I have consulted consider simply adopting our CHIPP values, and while complimented, I challenge it every time. Some of our CHIPP may survive and be incorporated into the company's core values statements. Their values breath a life all their own, even those that appear similar to some of ours, with a well-defined basis according to what is most important to their desired corporate culture.

Co-Existing Subcultures

Certain departmental functions naturally lend themselves to one quadrant over another. The key is to make sure that the desired culture is dominant and allowing the subculture to reinforce the company through its specific directives within the corresponding sub-quadrant of the dominating quadrant.

Sales & Marketing: Often times, Sales and Marketing departments are not in sync in an organization and may not even be engaged with one another. When this happens, the Sales department focus tends to be more Mercenary, while Marketing tends to be more Networking. If they are working collaboratively, they are more likely to be Communal.

Desired Quadrant	Ideal Sub-quadrant
Networking	Networking Communal
Communal	Communal Communal
	Communal Mercenary
Mercenary	Mercenary Communal

Customer Service & Support: Serving your customers isn't about being touchy feely anymore. It is about fulfilling and exceeding customer needs with a focus on retention and satisfaction versus pursuing and transacting. Customer service is becoming more measurable and a true differentiator for many companies. Whether it is through customer reviews or awards like J.D. Powers, companies with a strong corporate culture are putting customers at the center of their operational effectiveness. Even successful hard-driving Mercenary cultures recognize that a highly satisfied customer is a profitable and loyal one who is ready to buy, even at a higher price point if they feel valued and connected in some way.

Desired Quadrant	Ideal Sub-quadrant
Networking	Networking Communal
Communal	Networking Communal
	Communal Communal
Mercenary	Mercenary Communal

<u>Finance & Accounting:</u>   The very nature of Finance and Accounting departments lend themselves to a more Mercenary mindset about fiscal management with a focus on profitability and expense control. The fine line is in embracing the fiscal function away from a short-term gain and aligning it with a long-term growth mentality. This is where the overall core values of the company being effectively translated and communicated is essential. Oftentimes, the purchasing arm of the Finance department may send mixed messages to vendors, in being more transactional than relationship focused, even though the culture is professing a relationship priority. In my company, we actually redesigned our Finance department to embrace innovation and resourcefulness as a measure of effectiveness in turning expenses into profit centers. This resulted in engaging other parts of the company for perspective and insights that would otherwise not been involved.

Desired Quadrant	Ideal Sub-quadrant
Networking	Networking Communal
Communal	Communal Communal
	Communal Mercenary
Mercenary	Mercenary Communal

<u>Operations & Production:</u> The people on your team overseeing Operations and Production are the engines behind the ability to effectively serve and deliver to the customers. In many respects, these people are internal customers, as are all employees, who must feel appreciated, valued and respected for their contributions. When you have Operations and Production in alignment with the messages being sent out from Marketing, Sales and Customer Service, you have a well-oiled machine that is operating on all cylinders. This extends out to the supply chain, depending on your type of business in being a seamless operation.

Desired Quadrant	Ideal Sub-quadrant
Networking	Networking Communal
Communal	Communal Communal
Mercenary	Mercenary Communal

The most profound thing you can do within your company as you cultivate your corporate culture is to create a universal sense of worth and value across all company disciplines among your team members. This is part of the reason Zappos has every new recruit work in all areas of the company, beginning with customer service before settling into their hired role. Another best practice is to allow team members to shift gears in working with another team of people on a special project outside of their area of competency to gain added knowledge, insight and perspective.

❖

The more you encourage and foster interaction and collaboration among your people, with a well defined purpose, vision and set of core values to guide them, the more you will reap the rewards of a corporate culture building a company of endurance.

CHAPTER 19

Mergers & Acquisitions

The merging of two management companies had taken place physically months prior to the financial arrangement for a principal buyout being finalized and signed. The initial excitement perceived by the employees of the shared values and vision of the two owners was beginning to wane as reality was setting in with confusion regarding who was in charge, how the firm was going to ultimately grow, and what the future held for everyone who had come together and were now working together. Knowing that the firm was ultimately going to be bought out from the principal nearing retirement, employees were deluging the younger principal with endless questions, concerns and frustrations. Months had passed with no real momentum or strategy being realized causing some doubt by everyone, including the younger principal, if the merger was such a good idea.

The consultant working with this management company sensed the growing tension among the team members during strategic planning sessions, which included the principals themselves. It was deemed that the corporate culture assessment needed to be conducted with the two principals as a means of helping them see what has gone awry and how to get back on course and in alignment. The results were all telling with the perception of the firm from the younger principal having drastically wavered unfavorably at the dawn of signing the buy-out agreement. The silver lining, however, is that both principals still desired the same culture and shared many values. Lack of communication and engagement with team members, customers and referring partners had caused many assumptions to be made and concerns to be raised regarding the future of the firm. The assessment results were used as a basis for a facilitated discussion by the consultant with the principals who were able to share their perspectives regarding all the concerns, assumptions and misconceptions that were revealed in the results. The following day, the buy-out agreement was finalized with confidence and clarity.

The scenario cited above is not all that unusual. In many cases, the employees are the last to know about an impending merger, and then after the merger they are often left in the dark as to what it really is going to mean for their futures. While confidentiality is necessary when deals are being struck, a company so stealth in its actions that directly impact employees is a company to which few employees remain loyal or trusting as it relates to their stability and future. The most successful mergers and acquisitions are strategically orchestrated by having all stakeholders involved feeling valued, engaged and heard as the transition unfolds and continues to evolve.

Corporate Culture – A Basis for Elimination?

At the height of my company's recognition as an Inc. 500 growth company in 2005 and 2006, acquisition offers were coming in from all angles for me to consider. Offers were ranging from $20 million to $25 million for buying my mortgage company from national and international interests. It was overwhelming and also ego-stroking at the same time. As I looked at the three firms vying to buy my company, my options included a super regional bank, a national insurance company and an investment bank based in Europe. I declined all three offers for two reasons. The first and foremost reason was because I did not see a culture fit with any of the three firms. The second reason was that I believed my company could grow beyond where it was at the time and I knew I had the team to make it happen.

Is corporate culture a valid basis for elimination? Absolutely! In my evaluation, none of the banks were in alignment because our business was counter culture to the industry as a whole. Selling out to any one of these companies would have been the equivalent of throwing my employees and customers into a pack of wolves. The European bank was highly Mercenary, all about the money being made and could care less about its employees, based on its turnover and attrition track record. The super regional bank was a cross between Mercenary and Fragmented with a regulatory mentality combined with doing whatever it takes to make profits. The national insurance outfit was looking at the company as strictly an investment versus a strategic expansion. As I consider what transpired in the following years starting in 2007 and 2008 in the mortgage industry, all three of these institutions would have most likely shut the business down and most of my team would have been downsized or replaced. Culture didn't matter to these companies because it was all about the bottom line opportunity.

I discuss the challenges of building a corporate culture counter to what is practiced in an industry in Chapter 25. However, you can be in an industry where the culture standard is in alignment, but still does not find a good fit from an M&A perspective due to corporate culture variances or mismanagement.

Too Many Top Level Assumptions

Just as a company should do due diligence on income statements, financial reports, customer base, capital assets, and the list goes on, conducting an assessment on the company's corporate culture could help predict a great deal in how smoothly or disruptive the transition will be from both sides of the equation. Since most M&As are based on the numbers, too much is left to assumption from the top-down regarding the intangibles that impact the success and performance within a company. This is where the engagement of the people is pivotal to a successful M&A. And yet, so often, this is an afterthought once the merger papers are signed, sealed and delivered.

My research team studied records of successful and unsuccessful M&As and it only further validated the importance of considering corporate culture as a critical success factor criteria.

M&A Success - Cultures in Sync

There will always be challenges when it comes to merging cultures, but the likelihood of successfully syncing the two cultures is dramatically increased if the core basis of the cultures are understood and considered from the onset. Two companies that seemed to get this right are Wells Fargo and Cisco.

Wells Fargo/Wachovia: Wells Fargo has acquired many firms over the years and has made corporate culture one of its determinants with strategic-minded consideration every step of the way. When the merger between Wells Fargo and Wachovia was underway, among the statements included: "Management made 'culture' a number one priority. They focused on merging the cultures as much as they focused on merging technology."

Some of the culture-driven initiatives that Wells Fargo practices to effectively transition cultures when acquiring a firm include:

- Creating a "culture group" to assess and review the two cultures to make specific decisions on how to effectively foster the culture merger.

- Conducting "stay interviews" with employees to gather their concerns and to identify any issues before key people leave.

- Business unit heads going out of way with regular check-ins and gestures of appreciation to employees so they can keep them engaged and emotionally invested.

- Identifying weaknesses in the acquired culture in order to strategically address and nurture them throughout the transition.

- Taking its time to properly combine and transition technology, clients and markets for infrastructure building and faith-building.

- Showing customer-centric agility during roll outs including reverting back to accepting legacy Wachovia cards until expiration dates to accommodate convenience of transition to customers.

- Making IT decisions based on what would be least disruptive to customers and keep their best interests in mind.

- Giving charitable contributions of more than $2.8 million to non-profits in converting marketplaces based on customer and team member preferences.

Since the merger, Wells Fargo has continued to realize unprecedented profitability and performance as the fourth largest banking institution and largest SBA business loan generator. It doesn't surprise me that they are over 100 years old. After all, they are operating in the Communal quadrant, validating its worthiness and effectiveness to be the culture of endurance against the Miserly Mercenary industry that caused the financial tsunami in 2008 and made many companies casualties of the war on Wall Street.

Cisco Systems/Cerent: While the initial view of the companies' cultures was that they were not a fit, how Cisco manages cultural change and learns from previous acquisitions was paramount to the success of the acquisition of Cerent.

- Communicating "early, often and honestly."

- Exploring how its vision and that of the acquired company can complement each other;

- Implementing a mentoring program matching a Cisco veteran with an acquired manager to more seamlessly integrate core values within the company.

- Establishing a "buddy system" so that every team member in the acquired company had someone to go to with questions and concerns.

- Forming integration teams early in the process with leaders being approachable, actively engaged and involving team members in the process.

- A participatory style of leadership overall to facilitate employee citizenship and commitment.

In the acquisition examples of Wells Fargo and Cisco Systems, the proactive and intentional focus on engagement of people internally and externally is evident. More than 20 years ago, a study by Feldman and Murata cited, "Many acquirers need to understand that in an acquisition, it is not the assets, technology, or infrastructure that is difficult to assess and integrate before, during, and after the takeover, but it is more the people." The MSW Research and Dale Carnegie Training study mentioned in Chapter 16 further validated the importance of leadership engagement with employees, including senior leadership's ability to lead the company, communicate goals and vision, and to demonstrate social responsibility. The necessity and effective ability to evaluate the critical success factor of people engagement is what inspired my team to develop the CURx^2 corporate culture assessment process.

M&As - Culture Chaos

When cultures are not a fit and/or the acquirer is not a strong and cohesive culture, it is no wonder a merger becomes a nightmare for everyone concerned. Two examples of M&As that are viewed to have been unsuccessful ventures include Bank of America's acquisition of Merrill Lynch and Daimler Benz's acquisition of Chrysler.

Bank of America/Merrill Lynch: With claims that the merger was the equivalent of a "shotgun wedding" and the continuous litigation that has plagued Bank of America since the merger, the aftermath reinforces what can happen when short-term Mercenary greed takes precedence over engagement and long-term value creation and trust building. Some of the missteps that speak to the lack of a cohesive corporate culture that considers the best interests of its people and their engagement in alignment with performance include:

- Misleading shareholders in soliciting their votes for the merger by not fully disclosing Merrill's deteriorating financial condition at the time of the vote, resulting in approving a high-than-actual-value price to acquire.
- Approving more than $5.8 million in bonuses to executives disregarding performance problems.
- Demanding excessive long hours of junior-level workers in investment banking divisions, which took the public outcry of the death of a young prodigy to force review of policies.

Daimler-Benz/Chrysler: Well documented as a corporate culture worst practice, the Daimler-Benz and Chrysler merger failure validates the intangible value of people engagement tied to performance when considering acquisition opportunities. Key missteps made by Daimler-Benz are in being a poorly matched culture fit from the onset including:

- Being a Mercenary hierarchical company with a clear chain of command and centralized decision-making compared to Chrysler's Communal, more team-oriented and egalitarian approach.
- Differing values and management styles between German and American managers in serving clients and developing products.
- Little effort for trust-building resulting in key executives resigning or being replaced by German counterparts.
- Drastically different pay structures with Daimler disliking huge pay disparities compared to the American practice of rewarding CEOs handsomely.
- Unwillingness by management teams on both sides to compromise in an effort to effectively merge cultures.

When Daimler-Benz sold Chrysler in 2007, it was no surprise. The merger has been a case study in the paramount importance of corporate culture to success in a merger and acquisition.

❖

The examples shared within this chapter make it abundantly clear. Corporate culture alignment is critical to the successful acquisition or a more seamless merging of two companies. Another important note is that the company with the strongest, most defined and aligned culture wins in the end in the battle of cultures.

CHAPTER 20

Empowering Performance

Being a big fan of Jack Stack's book, The Great Game of Business, I established a monthly Big Game of Business rally event at my company with all my team members. My CFO reinforced our vision and mission and shared the numbers on how we were doing pertaining to sales goals. I was the ultimate high-energy cheerleader welcoming everyone in for the half-day of "go team go" and "way to go" celebration. In my Communal mind, I was doing all the right things in reinforcing our focus and values, conducting engagement activities, and recognizing achievement. Thanks to the consultant I was working with, I was quickly brought down to reality in the fact that I was still being Mercenary disguised as Communal. We were only focused on the sales and profitability numbers and only recognizing the big Million Dollar Producers, leaving everyone else out who was pivotal to those producers achieving this coveted mark of distinction. The consultant's observation was the cold splash of water I needed to realize that I wasn't truly recognizing and empowering performance in all areas of the company.

When you are focusing only on the numbers in your business, you can quickly only give the kudos to those people bringing in those numbers. While that "frontline" person is getting all the glory, the reality is that it takes a team to make the cash register ring, contracts to be signed and sales to be made. In the example above, I fell victim to what most companies are guilty of doing. I was only rewarding the sales people, ignoring everyone else. Are you doing the same thing?

Enterprise-wide Performance

As I pondered what my management team and I had been doing, we took a step back to reconfigure what our Great Game of Business team meetings should evolve into based on recognizing all areas of performance.

The following list and descriptions should be a strong basis for analyzing your own performance measures and criteria within your company.

<u>Core Values-based Criteria:</u> Upholding the core corporate values is oftentimes taken for granted that it is being done. However, by putting performance-based emphasis in support of your values, you also will be reinforcing reasons why the values are so important to the success of the company. Take a look at the core values you have defined for your company. Then consider how you can recognize values-based activity, behaviors and conduct.

For instance, as introduced in Chapter 4, our core corporate values at Ameritrust are Customer Obsession, High Trust, Integrity, Passion, and Personal Growth (CHIPP). Therefore, putting best practices into place to reinforce the values as well as recognizing team members in these areas was deemed important to demonstrate why our core values were pivotal to our success as a company.

> **Customer Obsession:** For Ameritrust, this is about making everyone feel important.
>
> - A best practice of managers making a personal call to a customer based on any review that was below a certain rating scale.
> - Conducting surveys to confirm both customer and employee satisfaction, since each co-worker is viewed as an internal customer to one another.
> - Recognizing positive reviews and comments made by customers to specific team members.
> - Recognition of a team member going above and beyond in assisting a customer by a peer or manager.
> - Recognition of team members jointly exceeding customer obsession expectations.
>
> **High Trust:** To us, high trust is earned when everyone can be proud of the choices they make for themselves, co-workers, customers, and the company.
>
> - Communication standards to help team members respond better, collaborate well, and serve one another and customers.

- Trust in team members to share any concerns about a particular vendor or supplier that does not appear to be operating with the same core values.
- Recognizing decisions that demonstrate respect, consideration and trust-building among team members or with customers.

Integrity: At Ameritrust, integrity means completion in every facet of the products and services we provide. It is honest and conscientious effort, attention to the essential details, following through with commitments, excellence in execution, and seeing everything completely through to a satisfying end.

- Putting systems into place above and beyond industry standards to assure integrity is maintained at all levels.
- Recognizing quality of work and attention to accuracy, details and deadlines.

Passion: For the Ameritrust team, having that burn in the belly is about being the best at what we do. We are competitive, especially since we have a passionate focus on living and working our values as our definitive advantage over competitors.

- Everyone telling the accurate story behind why we take pride in being different based on our founding philosophy.
- Recognition of team members touting Ameritrust at public events.

Personal Growth: Recognizing that each person is an individual with their own personal desires and life outside of work is important to Ameritrust, because it reinforces that we appreciate the whole person.

- Sharing one another's personal goals and aspirations so the team can facilitate and support the individual.
- Recognition of a team member's successful completion of a licensing requirement or other professional goal that was a personal growth initiative.
- Recognition of a team member's successful marathon run or other personal goal.

Consider your values and how you can instill good practices and reward your team members when seeing them being practiced in action.

<u>Support-based Criteria:</u> Too many companies fail to acknowledge and recognize the people behind the scenes making things happen. For the mortgage division in Ameritrust, we were remiss in not giving due credit to the underwriters and processers supporting our loan officers. After coming to this realization, we identified specific acknowledgements for excellence in turnaround time of mortgage documents, shortening of closing cycles, submittal to underwriting (S.T.U) and clear to close (C.T.C).

Consider the different roles directly supporting your sales people or operations. Identify specific success factors that contribute to making sales or the final delivery of your offerings happen.

<u>Team-based Criteria:</u> Identifying Peer Recognition opportunities is an excellent way of getting team members to recognize one another for a job well done. Creating competitive, yet collaborative recognition of teams within your company fosters relationships among the individuals within a team while also rallying the entire company to take efforts to the next level. Important is to have more than just sales performance measured, but also recognize efforts and successes in quality of work, customer satisfaction, quantity of work, individual or team milestones, personal and professional achievements.

<u>Sales-based Criteria:</u> Celebrating the achievement of overall company sales goals should be supported by individual and team-based sales achievements. For instance, in addition to recognizing new and re-occurring team members who get into our coveted Million Dollar Club, we also began recognizing milestones and individual improvements for sales team members.

<u>Profitability-based Criteria</u>: Being profitable is key to becoming a company of endurance because it means you will continually be in a strong position to invest in improvements, reward employees, take care of customers, and expand on an asset basis versus debt basis. Establishing performance measures around profitability and then rewarding its achievement could mean anything from profit-sharing to granting bonuses to all team members. Additionally, sales people who are more successful at closing higher profit sales should be recognized, even if they aren't the top producers overall.

<u>Efficiency-based Criteria:</u> Another area in which many companies fail to give due credit is related to the areas of the company that have a direct impact on efficiencies within the company. This could mean anything from

accounting to operational initiatives that associates undertake to improve efficiencies through implementing procedures, new systems, software, or project management practices that improve the company's overall effectiveness.

<u>Service-based Criteria:</u> Whether or not your core value includes a customer service component, outstanding service to customers has become one of the most powerful differentiators for companies today. Recognizing exceptional service results within your company reinforces best practices and underscores how service achievement ties to sales achievement.

Personal Growth & Professional Performance

Measuring performance when it comes to truly engaging your people should also consider the individual. When the individual is considered, versus dictated to, about their direct impact on each person's dedication and passion toward helping the company achieve its goals is exponentially increased. Critical for achieving success, however, is involving the individual in the process of setting individual goals and milestones to measure success.

In my company, we consider the whole person when our managers sit down with each team member to confirm goals. We encourage each employee to share life goals, as well as career, job and professional goals. Then we collaboratively discuss action steps and target dates of achievement to create immediate accountability and momentum. As stated throughout this book, we are operating as a Communal Culture, therefore looking at both personal and professional performance measures is important to nurturing the culture and practicing what we preach. To better understand how performance measures can be approached in Communal, as well as the ideal quadrants within the Mercenary and Networking Cultures, I recommend implementing a Performance Playbook into your performance management process.

Performance Playbook

As a means of holding myself and my management team accountable for effectively motivating and managing team members, we developed a Performance Playbook to be used in the initial orientation for each employee, and then thereafter to monitor their progress. The Playbook's main purpose was to reinforce understanding of the company's operations and market differentiation, while also serving as the basis for a preparing a scorecard for team members based on their individualized business plan.

Every Playbook should contain:

- Updated history of the company
- Mission and Purpose Statement
- Vision Statement
- Values & Philosophy of Operations
- Company's Unique Advantages
- Being a Successful Team Member
- Team Member Success Plan

The Team Member Success Plan is a worksheet section of the Playbook for the team member and the direct report manager to review for input with goals specific to the individual based on a discussion around goals in a variety of areas. This is why it is important for your company to identify all the areas the company seeks to measure so that you can effectively mentor and inspire each team member to support and grow with the company.

The key differences between the Communal, Networking, and Mercenary cultures are in the types of performance considered priority to monitor and measure.

Communal Playbook = People & Company Success: The Communal Culture is the only culture to place equal priority to measuring corporate, professional and personal achievements. The Communal Culture will have the widest range of measurement focuses in order to holistically look at the company's performance, as well as individuals' performance.

Corporate

- Financial Goals
- Profitability Goals
- Customer Service Goals
- Customer Engagement Goals
- Process Improvement Goals
- Best Place to Work Goals
- Employee Retention Goals
- Employee Recruitment Goals

Individual – Professional/Personal

- Career Advancement Goals
- Job Effectiveness Goals
- Professional Learning Goals
- Lifestyle & Living Goals
- Family/Relationship Goals
- Leisure Goals
- Luxury Goals
- Health/Fitness Goals

Networking Playbook = People-based Success: The Networking Culture is more focused on the People aspect in identifying areas to measure for performance. While sales and profits will be benchmarked and monitored in the ideal Networking Communal Culture, a greater emphasis is placed on measuring employee and customer satisfaction, loyalty and engagement. Additionally, personal growth, as well as professional growth, are nurtured and supported. This results in measurements that include:

Corporate	Individual – Professional/Personal
• Customer Service Goals	• Professional Learning Goals
• Customer Engagement Goals	• Lifestyle & Living Goals
• Process Improvement Goals	• Family/Relationship Goals
• Best Place to Work Goals	• Leisure Goals
• Employee Retention Goals	• Luxury Goals

<u>Mercenary Playbook = Professional & Company Success</u>: In a Mercenary Culture, the focus on making money is what entirely drives the performance measures. However, to be a successful Mercenary Culture (Mercenary Communal), acknowledging other corporate performance measures will result in a more engaged overall team.

Corporate	Individual – Professional/Personal
• Financial Goals	• Career Advancement Goals
• Profitability Goals	• Job Effectiveness Goals
• Customer Engagement Goals	• Professional Learning Goals
• Process Improvement Goals	• Luxury Goals
• Employee Recruitment Goals	

❖

The bottom line is when it comes to measuring performance, the more effective you are at recognizing and properly acknowledging the individual and his or her contribution to the company's ability to meet its goals, the greater commitment, passion and purpose-driven focus you will realize from each team member.

CHAPTER 21

Building Endurance

It was 1886, and modern health care was in its infancy with most standards and technologies that we take for granted today not in existence. Two brothers set out to make surgery more sterile with the introduction of mass produced, ready-to-use sterile dressings and sutures that were introduced in 1887 and followed by a how-to surgery manual provided in 1888. They also introduced the first commercial first-aid kits in 1888 and maternity kits to make childbirths safer in 1894. These products were pioneered in collaboration with doctors, surgeons and consumer feedback supported by free information to the public on prenatal and infant care, disease prevention and more. Saving lives and preventing suffering was the driving force behind the items manufactured "irrespective of any consideration of profit" according to a documented 1910 quote about one of the founders of the company.

The company described above is Johnson & Johnson, which to this day is still driven by the difference it can make in the health and safety of lives through its products. Johnson & Johnson has validated that its priorities are sound by giving shareholders a higher return than the aggregate return in the S&P Pharmaceutical or S&P Healthcare Equipment categories, 29 consecutive years of adjusted earnings increases, and 51 consecutive years of dividend increases.

What is a company of endurance? It is a company that can stand the test of time against competitive turmoil, economic chaos, or any other calamity that is thrown in its path. While evolving the Corporate Culture assessment model and determining that the ultimate goal was to build a company of endurance, we embarked on conducting secondary research to determine if this was a viable theory. We were alarmed to learn a startling statistic regarding what has occurred with American businesses over the last century, making our conviction to our theory on companies building endurance into their business model even more steadfast.

Fact #1: In 1957, the average life of a company in the S&P 500 Index was 75 years.

Fact #2: In 2013, the average life of a company in the S&P 500 is 15 years.

Are we creating a disposable business economy? Think about this for a moment. In a 57-year time span, the average age of a company in the Standards & Poor Index has reduced in life span by 60 years! Clearly, Johnson & Johnson is an exception to this trend. This beckoned to be studied further for several reasons. The first reason was to determine if having a company of endurance and longevity means anything any more. If it didn't, then perhaps building a company of endurance isn't as much of a goal as we believed it should be. The second reason was to understand why this has happened and understand the value of building a company that truly can navigate and stand the test of time profitably and sustainably.

We began identifying companies to analyze that had been in business for 50 years or more and discovered a study about the success factors of companies reaching 100+ years in longevity in the U.S. and Japan. The study was conducted by Professors Vicki TenHaken of Hope College in Michigan, U.S.A. and Makoto Kanda of Meiji Gakuin University in Tokyo, Japan. The study first looked at companies in Japan, some of which had been started prior to the year 1000, which ranged in annual sales of 100 million yen ($1 million) to 100 billion yen ($1 billion) with the average company over 100 years old equaling 5 billion yen ($50 million) in annual sales. The study began in Japan as a basis of comparison to U.S. companies, since the oldest known companies in the world are based in Japan.

According to Census data, only one percent of companies in the United States are over 100 years old. TenHaken and Kanda's study sought to confirm how these companies operated similarly to Japanese companies, as well as defining the key managerial behaviors and culturally specific behaviors that contributed to the company's longevity. Their findings reinforced our premise of the importance of engagement when it comes to people and performance for a company's endurance.

Managing Corporate Culture

Among the top findings in the TenHaken/Kanda study was "the existence and deliberate transmittal of certain values and beliefs" which were "described as a key survival factor in the case study companies." These values and beliefs "function as the fundamental business guidelines for the firm and provide core ideas" about which members of the company can identify and embrace. Often, these core values were established by the founders of the company and then passed down through generations. Leaders of these companies consistently "confirmed the importance of their corporate creed or values as a primary factor in the success of their business." Furthermore, the study revealed, "These values and beliefs form the fundamental culture of the company and are used to enhance employee identification with the business."

In Chapter Three, I stated the importance of the top level management, and specifically the CEO being a steward of the culture within the company. TenHaken/Kanda's study reinforced this by reporting, "Managers clearly see themselves as stewards and custodians of the business and feel an obligation to manage it in a way that ensures survival into the future."

Johnson & Johnson was founded on values and beliefs that were formalized into a company Credo in 1943 by General Robert Wood Johnson, which still drives the company's operations today. Entitled "Our Credo," the document priorities include an emphasis on relationships. First priority is to its customers and suppliers. Second priority is to its employees. Third priority is to its communities. And then the forth priority is to its shareholders. The underlying belief is that if customers, suppliers, employees, and communities are taken care of fairly and thoughtfully, the company will prosper and shareholders will ultimately benefit. Core values cited in Our Credo include: high quality products, reasonable prices, service promptness, fair profit for suppliers, respect of individuality, recognition of merit, fair compensation, work/life balance, ethical conduct, good citizenship, health and education, protecting the environment and natural resources, innovation, and making a sound profit with fair return. Ranked among the best places to work, the most respected brands, and among companies with the best reputations, Johnson & Johnson is proof that purpose-driven management guided by clear values and beliefs leads to endurance.

Managing Business Relationships

Another finding of the study is that century-old companies consider relationships at the core of operations. "These firms regard the maintenance of relationships with customers and the development of their suppliers from generation to generation as very important to long-term success." Older companies believe that cooperation of others is essential to their success over a long period of time. Establishing long-term relationships contributes to a company's "ability to weather environmental challenges, as well as their ability to learn and adapt over time." Because these relationships are viewed as important, these companies put a "premium on actions that will retain suppliers and customers from generation to generation." They view maintaining relationships as a sacred duty to the overall well being of the company.

Older companies view suppliers, team members and customers as more than people being involved in mere transactions or exchanges of goods or services for financial gain. As a result, they are willing and interested in sharing ideas and technologies and mutual learning as a value-added basis of the relationships.

As a major event during IBM's centennial year celebration, THINK: A Forum on the Future of Leadership brought together leaders from government, business, academia and science, along with an audience of up-and-coming leaders from across the globe, "to deepen a collective understanding of the keys to success on a smarter planet." The Forum sought to unearth new answers to important questions, examining the deep, structural changes confronting world systems. Forum participants were encouraged to take a "forward look at how information and technology is reshaping the modern world and how institutions can reinvent themselves in the next decade and beyond to meet these challenges." IBM's fortitude as a technology company to reach the 100-year mark is testimony to its ability to adapt, learn, grow, and know how to respond and proactively seek and leverage solutions and alternatives amidst lightning-speed global change. Its openness and leadership in ideas exchanges, such as the Forum, demonstrate the power of respecting and nurturing collective intelligence through valuing business relationships.

Managing Leadership Succession

Promoting from within is a common success factor of 100+-year-old companies. These companies consider long-term relationships with employees another keystone factor to their success. Therefore, these companies invest heavily in the training and development of employees with a very deliberate focus on teaching the history of the company in conjunction with advancing skills needed within the company. These companies see their investment in their employees as a proactive means of building retention of lifelong, loyal members within the organization. As a result of this dedication, these companies also emphasize development of future leaders within the ranks of the company versus hiring leadership from outside of the company, "resulting in a systematic process for leadership succession." When an employee is identified as a high potential leader, a career plan is defined for developing the potential leader, including having hands-on experience in the company operations to learn the business from the inside out.

IBM's leadership succession approach is considered exemplary and among the best in the world through a corporate culture that seeks out potential CEO candidates, as well as other leaders, from within the ranks and spends years preparing them for the moment they will be appointed to a top slot. The company identifies candidates based on the individuals who demonstrate their ability to manage the breadth of IBM's businesses, are successful in the jobs they are given, and can build consensus among team members. Leadership succession is considered critical to successfully serving customers for the long haul. According to the company philosophy, predictability in such an unpredictable world can be an advantage when it comes to nurturing and developing strong leadership within the company. Bench strength translates into customer confidence and overall corporate competency. When Virginia Rometty took over as CEO of IBM in 2012, the appointment was met with positive feedback and further testimony to IBM's historically strong succession planning, according to analysts. IBM's successful ability to develop leaders from within is further validated when compared to a leading rival, Hewlett Packard, which experienced the unprecedented CEO turnover of four executives in the position over a ten year period, including three replacements within a one-year span, all coincidently hired from outside the ranks of the company.

Managing Social Relationships

Building relationships with their local communities was also a hallmark of companies older than 100 years. "A close connection with their community, including social as well as business relationships," was identified as an important longevity factor in the case studies. These companies are active participants in their local communities, investing time and resources into projects that will benefit the local community. They are also active in promoting the community and developing local networks for mutual learning and benefits. They understand the value of these relationships as a positive influence on the company's reputation and view their role in contributing to the local community's good reputation a reflection of them as a corporate citizen.

Wells Fargo, established in 1852, has considered corporate stewardship a foundational aspect of its successful engagement within the communities it serves, claiming that its success comes from the time-tested formula of "local people making local decisions because they know what their communities need." Its philanthropic initiatives are far reaching across all markets it serves, as well as with great depth in the areas of giving that it focuses upon. From homeownership, community development, and financial literacy, education programs to supplier diversity, environmental initiatives and team member giving, Well Fargo combines monetary giving with volunteer hours to make measurable impact in every community it serves. From being named Number One in giving worldwide by the United Way to supporting more than 1.5 million team member volunteer hours annually, Wells Fargo has also gained credibility with accolades that include being named among Barron's Most Respected Companies and among Fortune Magazine's Most Admired Companies.

Managing Fiscal Responsibility

Leadership and managers of older companies were more fiscally conservative and strategic in how the company leveraged its financial resources and invested in future growth. They are less likely "to go into debt as a means of financing their business even if this means slower growth. They operate with a level of leanness and efficiency that enables them to set aside money in prosperous times to weather the lean years with the ability to fund new opportunities when they arise without depending on external sources of financing." I suspect that a part of the reason these companies operate more efficiently is because of the buy-in and collective engagement of everyone on all levels in the company focused on a unified mission and purpose based on the company's guiding principles. Everyone within the company holds themselves accountable for being fiscally responsible.

When John Bilbrey was hired into his position as Hershey Co.'s CEO, Wall Street proclaimed that he was a good, steady bet for a safe, conservative company. Established in 1894, Hershey Co. is another example of the Communal value of considering the people, the company, its customers, and the marketplace as a whole when it comes to making money and building a company of endurance. Demonstrating every facet of the Communal Culture in how the company treats employees, engages in the community, and strives to make a difference beyond delighting chocolate-lovers' taste buds, Hershey Co. has not only realized steady growth, but also impressive growth over recent years.

When you consider the Standards & Poor's 500 Index trend shared at the beginning of this chapter, it is not only alarming, but also telling about the need to focus on endurance in conjunction with performance in a company. In many ways, the S&P 500 statistic is a sad, but real indicator of what Corporate America has done to itself. While mergers and acquisitions may be partially to blame, in my opinion, the loss of traditional values and ethics has been mostly to blame. Also important to note, the companies that have stood the test of time, such as Wells Fargo, IBM, Johnson & Johnson, and Hershey Co., when they are involved in M&A they are the acquirers with no intention of changing the company's name, culture or founding principles. Seems to me that corporate culture plays a much more important role in a company's worth and value than it has been given credit.

❖

Perhaps in the future, endurance will be the true measure of a company's worth, both in marketplace trust and in stock market value. Endurance does matter and corporate culture is the critical success factor to building a company of endurance. The key is to define and nurture the corporate culture that best suits your company's value, beliefs, philosophy and vision. I encourage you to go back to Chapters 10, 11, 12 and 14 to gain insight to the different corporate culture quadrants to successfully balance people, performance and engagement for optimal endurance. Then confirm what will work best for you as a leader in your company by continuing on to read Chapters 22, 23, and 24 that are focused on the leaders best suited for each culture type.

SECTION IV

Leading the Culture

CHAPTER 22

The Networking Director

A fledgling airline was experiencing cash flow problems in its first year of operations. The CEO and management team were faced with the dilemma of either selling planes or laying off people to save cash so the company could meet its short-term obligations. Instead, the management team, after crunching some numbers and analyzing operations, decided to put a challenge before the ground service people. The CEO posed the idea that if the turnaround time at the airport gate could be reduced from 55 minutes to 15 minutes, it would improve the revenue producing capability of the planes thereby reducing the likelihood that people would need to be laid off. The personnel agreed and met this goal. This level of confidence in its people has been a key differentiator of the airline from this pivotal game-changing initiative in the 1970s to how it operates today. When incidents of September 11, 2001, severely decreased airline traffic, this airline was the only airline not to lay off people due to reduced air traffic as a result of loyal team members being willing to take a pay-cut, rather than being laid off, because of their enjoyment and belief in the company in which they were employed. Today, these team members, ground and flight crews in tandem, accomplish a 20-minute gate turnaround against the industry average of more than an hour. This airline has also never had a plane crash, proving that safety and efficiency can go hand in hand.

Most of the time, a corporate culture evolves and becomes dominant over time. This was the case of Southwest Airlines. The emphasis on people did not really kick into high gear until the early 1980s, according to its co-founder, Herb Kelleher. But the dedication and determination of its people to meet that first challenge certainly set the wheels in motion from that point forward. The company's people-focus has made it the most enduring and profitable airline to-date, and its corporate culture is deemed its greatest secret weapon against competitors.

Networking Director – Strengths to Leverage

Herb Kelleher is an example of an effective Networking Director in every sense. The best part of being a CEO or executive manager in a Networking Culture is how much fun it is to work with the people, many of whom end up being friends with one another outside of work, as well inside as team members. The camaraderie is openly evident in day-to-day interaction, which is inspiring and reassuring to witness and build upon if done effectively.

The key to being effective in directing a Networking Culture-driven organization is through understanding the fine line between sociability and engagement to the point of inspiring solidarity that is more than about likability, but also about productivity.

For purposes of identifying the ideal characteristics of a Networking Director, we focused our analysis in studying CEOs, like Kelleher, who managed effectively in the Networking Communal sub-quadrant, as well as the Communal Networking sub-quadrant, since these are the sub-quadrants we deem have the potential to produce a company that can endure over time with characteristics of a Networking Culture.

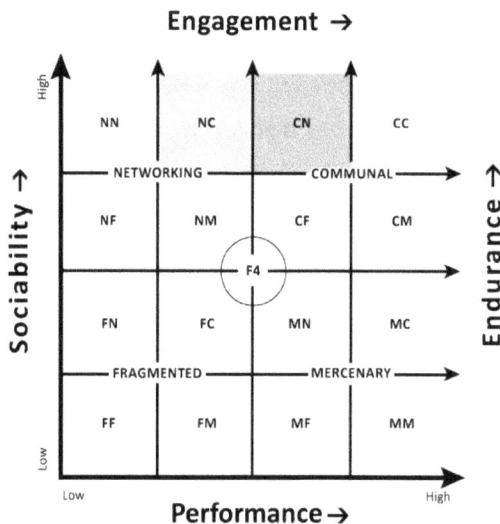

The Ideal Networking Director:

> **Is Fun & Focused:** There is a clear understanding that fun at work is inspired by the company's vision, mission, and values as they relate to enjoyment for the employee and customers alike. Management encourages fun activities within the workplace that have a positive and memorable impact in their focus on serving customers and being effective team members. For instance, the humor and liberties taken by Southwest flight attendants when providing safety instructions to passengers actually gets passengers to listen because they are so entertaining, versus tuning the attendants out, which is what typically

happens on other flights. The humor and entertainment actually results in passengers comprehending and remembering the instructions being given more effectively.

Is Engaging & Stimulating: Management is engaging and actively involved with team members on a regular basis. The open line of communication, even with the CEO, is free of any screening, with all top level management openly communicating and accessible to employees. Management encourages participation with ideas and feedback from all levels of the company and openly invites input and feedback on a regular basis, oftentimes through less formal means of gathering and receiving.

Inspires Camaraderie & Consideration: Being considerate of the work team and individuals on each team is important for management. The organizational behavior as a whole is less formal and more personal, which can result in more one-on-one interaction. Managers and employees will tend to get to know one another on a personal level because of the informal environment. As a result, managers are more considerate of personal issues or situations that then affect work-related decisions or policies. Chick-fil-A's policy to be closed on Sundays as a day of religious respect and as a rest for employees is an example of this level of consideration.

Golden Rule Ethics: Because people are at the focal point, the Golden Rule of "treating others as you would like to be treated" is the basis of ethical conduct and expectation within the company in the ideal environment. There is not necessarily a written creed or guidelines, as the Golden Rule seems clear enough to the Networking Director and management team to be expected of everyone. Policies will be put into place to help manage this expectation as it relates to customers, employees, and vendors in how everyone is to be treated and respected.

Celebrates & Recognizes: Effective management in a Networking culture celebrates both special personal occasions and professional individual achievements. They also will celebrate team-related accomplishments, as well as customer-related milestones. The key is that all celebrating is people-centric in the focus. Management takes time to recognize individuals and team members as people and professionals within the company. So while you take time to celebrate birthdays, holidays, births, marriages, and other personal highlights for employees, you are also celebrating professional and team successes, customer service excellence, and professional growth achievements. Where Networking cultures miss the mark is when they only celebrate personal occasions. While it feels all warm and fuzzy to recognize births, birthdays, and personal successes and milestone, if you are not also recognizing the efforts of your people doing their jobs, you won't get the best from them at their jobs.

Inspires Customer-Driven Performance: The Networking CEO and management team is steadfast in their belief that customers are to be more than served, but taken care of beyond their expectation or anticipation. Interestingly, this does not necessarily mean that the customer is the first priority. Probably the key difference between the Networking Communal sub-quadrant and the Communal Networking sub-quadrant is in the priority between employees and customers. For the Networking dominant sub-quadrant, employees are viewed by the CEO as the first priority because if they are taken care of then the customers will naturally be taken care of by happy employees. When Communal is dominant over Networking, the customer is considered the number one priority, and team members are valued for the special roles they play in serving customers, and, therefore, are impassioned to serve customers.

Founder of Costco, Jim Sinegal, proved that caring and focusing more on employees and customers than company profits in company decision-making actually was the reason the company realized impressive profits and growth, and an even more impressive 12 percent turnover rate spanning three decades in an industry sector where the average annual turnover rate exceeds 70 percent. In spite of paying workers significantly higher than minimum wage, covering a majority of healthcare insurance costs to both full-timers and part-timers, and rewarding employees with bonuses and incentives, by promoting from within among countless other people-centric benefits the company grew by 70 percent during what as economically challenging times for other retailers. When Sinegal retired in December, 2011, its co-founder Craig Jelinek took the CEO reigns, with no intentions of changing how the company operated in its employee-first priorities. Since Jelinek took leadership in January 1, 2012, Costco's share price has continued to increase at a 30 percent gain and the company has continued realizing double digit growth. The Networking Director – Derailing Factors

Where Networking Culture management can become derailed is when they are operating primarily from the Networking Networking or Networking Mercenary quadrant in how they are managing and guiding the company.

Fun & Frivolous: Fun without an underlying purpose is just a distraction. This is where many Networking Directors go awry when the fun incorporated into the workplace is not purpose-driven, but becomes an excuse for not getting work done. I cannot help but think of the character Michael Scott in the sitcom series The Office. His "fire drill" meetings in the conference room at Dundar Mifflin have zero substance and are designed more like a "recess" break for employees than a productive gathering. When an employee actually confronts him with a work-related issue, he gets perturbed that people actually want to think about or focus on their work. An example in my own company includes a manager who was more in the Networking realm in this fun and frivolous mentality. He came into my office claiming that we needed to make more money so that we could put in a foosball table and pop-a-shot machines. He also wanted to relax the dress code. His focus on fun was overriding decisions around the best place to invest profit. When it is more about play than work, the bottom line suffers and the business cannot be sustained for long. I realized this when I began to analyze results from sales conferences my team would attend. Everyone would come back with a pile of business cards as evidence of "connecting" with people. The problem was, there was no engagement. The conferences were viewed as play time versus work time, a typical Networking mentality. My team would spend more time hanging out with one another than building relationships with potential or existing clients. I pulled my team together to discuss the primary purpose of these conferences when I saw a trend that we were not getting any new business out of this investment. It would have been easy for me to pull the plug on investing in conferences, but instead, I attended a conference and demonstrated how to engage and build relationships so my team could model what I was doing. Leading by example is the most powerful way to get your point across.

Celebrates Like Family: While this may seem like a wonderful characteristic, what is meant here is that only personal occasions are reasons to celebrate as a team. Birthdays, marriages, engagements, births, anniversaries, or even successful marathon runs are reasons to kick back and have a party at work. Professional accomplishments of an individual are not as focused upon as a reason for team celebrations by management, while these accomplishments may still get a private pat on the back or high five by management or team members. The personal relationship building is emphasized with a lesser focus on the professional side of the individual.

People Over Performance: When relationships with people are too heavily prioritized over performance, issues with performance are not always effectively addressed. Employees will cover for other employees because of their relationships, and in some cases the management will also look the other way due to concern over the employee's well being, including how losing their job would affect their family or other team members who are friends. If performance and disciplinary protocol has been established, it may still be developed to favor of the person over the profession. For instance, a company policy of one of my client managers includes waiting until Monday to discipline employees if a performance issue occurs towards the end of the week, so that they can enjoy their personal time on the weekend, versus it ruining their weekend. Another manager prefers to wait to discipline on Friday, so that the employee has time over the weekend to process and decompress. While each manager is being considerate in regard to timing, the delivery of the discipline is really what matters. If delivered in a constructive and empowering way, the timing becomes irrelevant. Another danger in the Networking Culture atmosphere is when a manager spends an inordinate amount of time moving people from department to department in an attempt to "find the right fit" for these individuals who were not performing in their previous roles. The amount of time, money, and loss of production that occurs by not confronting and dealing with the employee's performance issue costs far more than that employee's salary to a company.

Personal Over Professional: Personal issues among employees are more prevalent and vocalized in a Networking Culture. Because of the friendships that are formed, the friendship can be viewed as taking precedence over effective leadership when tough decisions must be made. I can personally relate to this. In 2002, an employee I had to terminate during our culture shift was a personal friend. As a result of our close friendship, our behavior during conferences was more like being on Spring Break versus executives doing business. When I realized that this behavior was not setting a good example or was balancing the focus on people and performance, I determined that this behavior was not serving anyone or the company well. As a result of making this declaration, my personal relationship with my friend suffered because we weren't "partying" and "palling around" any more. In many ways, this behavior was cliquish, as described in Chapter 16, which also was not a good example for engaging the rest of the company. As the CEO, I had to be intentional in not just declaring, but also demonstrating what was considered professional behavior when representing the company. It is important to set boundaries of expectation on personal and professional conduct within the workplace. It doesn't have to be regimental and impersonal, but it does need to be clearly understood by everyone.

Preferential Treatment: Even though the corporate values may profess the Golden Rule of treating everyone as you would want to be treated, the personal nature of relationships that develop within a Networking Culture can easily lead to a perception of preferential treatment by employees of other employees who seem to have a greater personal connection or ties to the management. With friends and family often being brought in as employees or managers, versus using a formal recruitment process, there can also be a natural tendency for non-related employees to perceive potential preferential treatment due to the personal ties with friends and family. This also can be viewed as cliquish from the outsider looking in.

Feast or Famine: Because money is not a driver for the Networking Culture as a whole, it can be easy for the company to be managed in extremes. When times are good, money is thrown into areas that may be fun and festive to everyone's enjoyment, but not necessarily strategic regarding how it can reinforce replication of the success for the long haul. When times are tough, cut backs will be all inclusive as a means of rallying the team together, including the top level executives demonstrating their integrity by sacrificing first as a measure of engagement. The challenge with this is that the roller coaster impact of a feast or famine mode of operation causes the same roller coaster effect in morale. While employees will remain loyal, they will be more stressed and worried about losing a great thing during the famine times.

❖

As indicated by the ideal characteristics and the derailing characteristics of the Networking Culture cited in this chapter, the leadership and management priorities are pivotal to whether the ideal Networking environment exists or the less ideal environment persists. In the special section concluding the book, Four Companies, Four Cultures, in Chapter 26, you will read about how Facebook has effectively moved from the potentially derailing aspects of Networking Networking and Networking Mercenary into the ideal sector of Networking Communal.

CHAPTER 23

The Communal Leader

A young programmer and statistician working for a NASA subcontractor witnessed first-hand the negative impact of what he called "working in cubicle farms" and an environment that contributed to a turnover rate of more than 50 percent annually. When he co-founded his software development company in 1976, he vowed to build a company contrary to the norm in the industry – a place where people would enjoy coming into work. He believed that happy employees equaled happy customers and high performance can be realized in a 35-hour work week with childcare and healthcare facilities on premises. More than 30 years later, the leadership who founded the company has stayed true to its purpose internally and externally, building steady growth and profitability in the billions.

James Goodnight, co-founder and CEO of SAS, admits that he didn't have any grand vision of how being an employee-friendly workplace would be a value driver for business. He simply wanted to create a company where he would want to work, different from what he had experienced working elsewhere. It was over the years that he learned how his employee loyalty led to customer loyalty, stronger innovation, higher-quality software, and building a business of endurance against industry odds. Goodnight's leadership has been pivotal to making strategic decisions for the good of SAS employees, customers and the company for a true win-win-win.

You have probably figured out by now that I believe the Communal Culture is the ideal culture to strive for in a business. That being said, I also believe the Communal Leader is the only true leader among the corporate culture options. There are countless books on the market about the essentials of a great leader, and the cliff notes always seem to point to characteristics that describe the Communal Leader

Communal Leader – Strengths to Leverage

Why are Communal Leaders so effective? Because they understand how engaging people directly ties to performance for the long haul. They possess a people-consciousness balanced with performance-mindedness that realizes consistent and sustainable results.

Based on studying Communal Leaders along with my own journey in evolving into one, these characteristics are key to effectively leading a Communal Culture.

Practicing Ethics versus Preaching Ethics: Communal Leaders model and reinforce the core values of the company and what is believed to be appropriate and ethical. They walk their talk in all aspects of how they conduct themselves within the company. Their perception of fairness is exemplified in the actions they take and the policies they make for standards within the organization. Voted among the ten most ethical CEOs in Corporate America in 2012, Aflac's Dan Amos demonstrated his sense of fairness and valuing of everyone's contributions to the company by how he approached his own compensation. Under his leadership, the company's profitability had grown ten-fold over a 30-year period. While 99 out of 100 CEOs would have used the growth as justification for their salaries to also grow ten-fold, Amos insisted that the shareholders approve executive compensation plans via their vote, making Aflac the first major U.S. corporation to ever set this as a policy.

Balancing Confidence with Humility: Communal Leaders are not just about being right, they are always about doing what is right. Confidence is not ego driven, it is purpose driven. Their willingness to take risks is tempered with an acceptance that employees may make mistakes with learning and growing being the expectation. They exercise authenticity through being intentional, genuine and transparent in their own mannerisms and ways of interacting with everyone. My first boss came across to both me and others working for him as being someone who never failed or did anything wrong, not because he was perfect, but because he would not be accountable. Instead, he would be shifting the blame to others or making excuses when something did not work out as planned. This behavior quickly became his demise, as employees emulated his behavior. I recall coming into the office and being approached by four different people who were blaming other departments for the poor results we were experiencing. As the direct manager of these individuals, I had to guide them in pointing their fingers back upon themselves to identify what they controlled or could have controlled, reminding them that placing blame serves no value within a team, but problem-solving, learning and growing from the experience does provide team value. Communal Leaders hold themselves accountable and create an atmosphere through their own example of team members taking accountability in their actions. Being accountable means you are willing to openly and genuinely share and communicate your own shortcomings or missteps that may have contributed to a less-than-desired situation. As a leader who is willing to do this, you open up the same level of trusted sharing in others. The end result? A focus on solutions and learning, instead of blaming and back-peddling.

Enforcing Power with Compassion: Communal Leaders speak with authority and caring concern for those being led. This is a fine line as a Communal Leader because sometimes you can care so much that you can feel as though you have failed when you must relay unpleasant news or developments that have occurred. This is especially true when you must let an employee go for performance reasons, even though you really like him or her as a person. Compassion for the Communal Leader is the secret ingredient when enforcing policies, a decision, or a termination through demonstrating an understanding about the employee's perspective while also being consistent in your authority as the leader. I recently heard an example of a company leader who shared that the employees she had fired later came back and thanked her because of how she handled the termination process. She leveled with them and also provided clear guidance on what these employees could do to overcome their shortcomings in their future employment. She empowered these employees instead of deflating them, while also doing what she knew needed to be done.

Engaging & Empowering Others: Communal Leaders encourage participation and inclusion at all levels. They naturally attract and hire team members who are personally aligned with corporate core values because they exemplify these values, leading by example. Their ability to intellectually stimulate, motivate and inspire employees creates a desire in them to achieve higher levels of performance. Tony Hseih, CEO and founder of the online shoe phenomenon, Zappos, has made inclusion an integral part of how the company orients employees into the folds of the company from the very beginning. Every employee, no matter what role they were hired to fill, starts with training in the call center serving customers, and then spends hands-on time in all facets of the company before settling into their hired positions. Not only does this engage new employees, but also reinforces the importance of everyone's critical roles in "delivering happiness" to customers. The practice also gives employees intricate understanding of how the company operates through the collective effort of all team members.

<u>Managing Perceptions & Behaviors:</u> For Communal Leaders, outward success should reflect inner substance. They understand that they are role models and believe that good leaders understand that leadership is a social activity that is also dependent upon interaction with others. They are charismatic, while also acknowledging the importance of being fiscally responsible and strategically focused. Kyle O'Brien, as Executive VP of Sales for Chobani, instilled the importance of protecting the Chobani Greek Yogurt brand by helping every employee understand the ramifications of their personal conduct, decisions, and behavior while representing the company on and off the clock. He reinforced this understanding on a daily basis through communication and continuous discussion among team members regarding perception versus reality in the eyes of fellow employees, customers, brokers, and the industry as a whole. The end result was creating employees who were passionate about protecting the company's good name and reputation in everything that they did and said, because of his example and substance as a leader.

<u>Equal Commitment to People and Profits:</u> Communal leaders view the people in the company as valuable assets instrumental in the company's ability to effectively deliver what is being offered and to generate profits. Therefore, decisions around profitability and the bottom-line take into consideration what is in the best interest of the people associated with the business, including employees, customers and suppliers. James Goodnight's dual commitment to the well-being of employees and being profitable is the reason that SAS is still a privately-owned entity with no plans to go public. For Goodnight, going public would have been selling out his culture and the company's distinct advantages on many levels. While he courted the idea of an IPO in the early 2000s, he determined it was not in the best interest of his company and opted to safeguard the SAS culture, which was solidified when a company-wide survey indicated that 87 percent of employees were against the IPO. While Wall Street questioned the ability for the company to continue to scale-up without going public, Goodnight has proven his stubbornness and commitment has paid off. At the time that an IPO offering was being considered, the company's sales revenue was exceeding $1 billion. With the company nearing the $3 billion mark in sales, experiencing year-over-year profitability since inception, and

being valued at over $7 billion as of the writing of this book, Goodnight has proven that protecting a culture is most certainly good for a business' bottom line.

❖

To be a Communal Leader is to be a leader who embraces the trilogy of High Sociability, High Engagement, and High Performance in order to build a company of enduring value and long-term stability against all odds. Google, featured in Chapter 27, and its leadership, have been successful because of an exceptional ability to embrace the trilogy with gusto.

CHAPTER 24

The Mercenary Dictator

In 2008, an impassioned and dissatisfied company founder took action with the simultaneous closing of 7,100 U.S. stores for a period of four-hours to retrain baristas in the art of pulling good espresso shots and steaming milk. This action came only a month after he successfully regained his CEO position, when he determined that the acting CEO had "watered down" the intended experience, and viewing the actions as commoditizing the brand. Aggressive growth plans had backfired to a certain extent in the eyes of this founder, who took responsibility for allowing the focus on shareholder return to take precedence over the intended customer experience. While performance meant everything to this world-renowned entrepreneur, he also believed that "There's no long-term shareholder value if it isn't linked to building long-term value for your people."

When Howard Schultz, founder of Starbucks, took what some folks considered drastic measures in closing thousands of stores across the country for a few hours, to him it was absolutely an essential initiative to bring the company's standards of excellence back into alignment. It is a relentless passion for excellence that distinguishes successful Mercenary Dictators from the unsuccessful ones. The passion is focused on excellence in the customer experience or innovation, not the ownership or empire. For Schultz, and other CEOs like him, to be involved in key decisions of the day-to-day operations of Starbucks assures that excellence is top-of-mind every day. His taking back control was driven by being highly intentioned when it comes to the excellence of the end product and serving the customer. In a memo Schultz sent to Starbuck's then CEO in 2007, he cited a laundry list of decisions that he felt created a "dilution of the experience" for the customers. He also held himself accountable for agreeing to these decisions, but in hindsight, he determined that the company had gone off-course and needed to be re-navigated back towards its foundation of coffee heritage, customer experience, and competitive advantage.

The most appealing part of being at the top of a successful Mercenary Culture is the exhilaration that comes from the fast pace and high stakes that are an everyday aspect of doing business. Everyone is focused on high performance and total consistency in delivery for achieving the desired excellence and bottom-line numbers. Being the best at what they do in their industry with a competitive spirit that effectively balances mutual respect with an undisputable demand for excellence is at the core of the culture. Because of the high performance expectation, Mercenary executives are more likely to come under fire as a result of performance and excellence being a no-exceptions mindset, making it the most stressful of the leadership positions from a corporate culture standpoint.

For purposes of identifying ideas and not ideal characteristics of executive leadership in a Mercenary Culture, we focused our analysis on studying founders and executives who manage effectively in the Communal Mercenary sub-quadrant, as well as in the Mercenary Communal sub-quadrant, since these are the sub-quadrants we deem have the potential to produce a company that can endure over time with Mercenary Culture characteristics. Starbucks is best identified in the Communal Mercenary sub-quadrant within the Communal Culture.

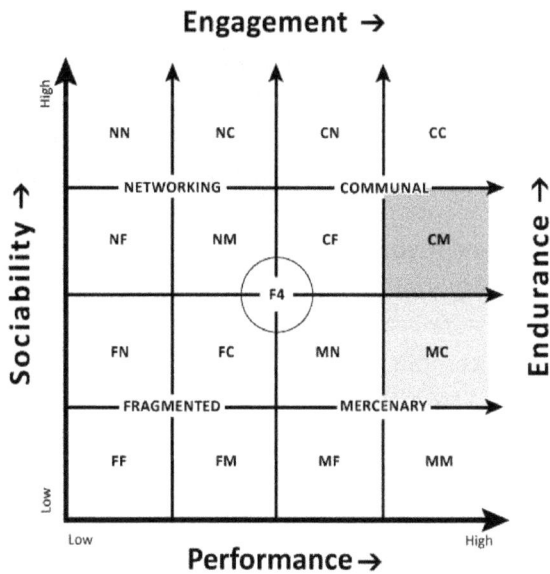

Mercenary Maverick – Dictator with Strength & Charisma

In Chapter 12, I shared the difference between the Maverick Mercenary Culture and the Miser Mercenary Culture. This becomes even more distinguishable when you look at the management styles of the Maverick Dictator compared to the Miser Dictator. Shultz is an example of a Mercenary Maverick.

Characteristics that distinguish the Mercenary Maverick include:

Practicing & Reinforcing Ethics: The Maverick Dictator continuously reinforces what is considered ethical and acceptable behavior and conduct within the organization, and is also willing to take a stance beyond the organization where deemed necessary. A high expectation of tangible results is carefully weighed against what is deemed ethical at all times, with no exceptions.

Being vocal and unbending in this regard is a hallmark of this management style. An example of this is demonstrated by Schultz's belief that the truly right conduct and policies would eliminate the necessity for union labor through fair and caring treatment of employees, farmers, and anyone associated with Starbucks. Named among the most ethical CEOs in Corporate America in 2012, Shultz also was recognized for his stance in 2011 urging Americans to withhold donations to politicians until they started running the government like successful businesses.

Innovation-Driven Confidence: Innovation for a competitive edge or for bringing to market the unexpected and then creating demand for it is a key characteristic of successful Mercenary CEOs and executives. There is a level of relentless pursuit of being the first and best that makes innovation paramount to the company's success in the eyes of its executive leadership. In the case of the Mercenary founders who bring a level of genius to the effort, they have such a sense of knowing that no-one can stop them from thinking or doing what they set out to accomplish.

In a 2012 article in Forbes Magazine, it was stated, "In a sense, Howard Schultz did what Steve Jobs and other great innovators have done, creating something that we didn't really know we needed until we had it."

Leveraging Power & Authority: A Maverick Mercenary executive will not hesitate to leverage his or her power and authority to achieve desired end results, but this is done out of their sense of passion and purpose over their ego or position as the motivator. As the example shared at the beginning of the chapter of Schultz demonstrates, the Maverick Dictator imposes authority and control through a fine balance of passion, focus, and confidence that considers what is being offered and the customer's experience are mutually essential for achieving excellence and profits.

A Mercenary Maverick will not hesitate to take back the reigns of the organization without notice if they deem it is in the best interests of performing to their standards of excellence. The critical difference, as you will understand later in this chapter, is that the Mercenary Maverick uses the position of power for leverage and effecting necessary change, not for their might and ego's sake.

Coveted & Revered: A common factor of the successful Mercenary Culture is that the leader is coveted and revered to the point of being worshipped by employees and customers alike. This extreme level of admiration is derived from a combination of charisma and genius that places the leader on a pedestal in the eyes of his or her followers. I use the word follower instead of employees because in many cases, customers and employees are best characterized as followers, who are willing to do whatever is necessary to be associated with and/or serve this type of leader because of how much he or she is revered. Apple's Steve Jobs, more extensively examined in Chapter 28, was a perfect example of this type of Mercenary Maverick.

Another example of this type of leader is Hugh McColl, when he was the effective CEO of Bank of America. Still admired and revered long after retiring from Bank of America, his management approach, considered tough and demanding with high expectations, has been a basis of comparison for succeeding CEOs, as well as those in other banking institutions.

Profit-Motivated Customer Obsession: Customers are considered first and foremost in the successful Mercenary Culture by its leaders because they understand that through this obsession, profits can be made and competitors can be squelched. The motivation is to serve and wow the customer versus screw the customer to realize sales and profits. Where the fine line is drawn between the Mercenary Maverick and the Communal Leader is that customers are considered priority and employees are secondary in the Mercenary Culture.

Under Jim Skinner's leadership as CEO from 2004 to 2012, McDonald's realized its best financial performance in history and had its stock price triple due to reinvented menus, modernized restaurants, and product innovations including smoothies, wraps and coffee drinks to better serve and satisfy its diverse customer base. While the obsession on more effectively competing for a family's diverse palate continues to be evident under Skinner's successor, Don Thompson, only 51 percent of employees would recommend McDonald's as a place to work to a friend. The focus is on the customers, and employees are a means to that end – task masters following the clearly defined protocol and procedures of product preparation and delivery to serve the customer.

Mercenary Miser – Dictator With Misguided Authority

There are far more Misers than Mavericks in a Mercenary Culture dynamic, which is why it can so easily go awry. The key differentiator is in where the focus on performance lies. When performance is only tied to sales and profits, and doesn't consider service or quality excellence as important, then you are entering into the realm of Mercenary gone bad by its key motivators. It's all about the short-term monetary gain at the expense or sacrifice of customers, suppliers, employees, and even other managers or leaders within the company.

Characteristics that are typical of the Mercenary Miser include:

Preaching Ethics versus Practicing Ethics: The saying "Thou protests too much" in being defiant about being ethical is one of the chest-pounding flaws of the less effective Mercenary Dictator. There is a surface level pretense of ethics for the sake of building customer confidence or public image, but intentional actions and unethical practices are occurring behind closed doors or in front of employees, who are expected to keep quiet and do as they are told, not as they are shown. The way I see it, if someone has to make a big deal about being honest and ethical, they have something to hide. Ethics is practiced day in and day out, not professed.

The unraveling of Bernard Madoff's reputation is a prime example. Considered a "shocking revelation" when the Ponzi Scheme was uncovered in 2008, Madoff had been considered among the most prominent and respected investment managers on Wall Street in having a "magic touch." Madoff's sons alerted authorities after their father confessed to them in 2008, and were estranged from their father from that point forward. His web of deceit was shocking because of all that he had professed, even to his own sons, in how to act and be as an investment manager, while underhandedly doing the opposite privately with others in his firm, who were also indicted and found guilty.

Ego-Driven Confidence: Dictators who have a superiority complex in which they deem themselves supreme masters are another example of the personality characteristics that undermine a Mercenary Culture. Believing that they are always right, and everyone else is wrong, they are also more likely not to admit having faults or ever making mistakes.

These executives or managers are stingy with compliments or acknowledgement, if any are given at all. When mistakes happen, they are quick to "throw others under the bus" or point blame elsewhere, including expecting managers to take the fall to maintain their own appearance of competency and supremacy. Their egos are the source of their confidence more than having a passion or purpose in what they are doing within the company.

In contrast to Howard Schultz's example, when Eddie Lampert of Sears Holdings took over as CEO in 2013 because the company was floundering, no investment in the stores or marketing was initiated. Instead, he cut costs, sold off assets, and then bought back stocks. With no attention to merchandising or store management, sales continued to fall to the tune of $800 million over three quarters. The takeover as CEO was more about ego for being a majority shareholder than about manifesting corporate initiatives to facilitate a turnaround. Lampert had to sell off some of his shares to meet investors' redemptions, and now owns less than 50 percent of Sears' stock.

Imposing Power & Control: A tyrant or bully is the best way to describe this Mercenary Dictator, who uses their might to intimidate and modify behaviors to get what is expected. The "my way or the highway" attitude is prominent, with work always coming first no matter what the personal circumstances may be of an employee. Money is used as a means of control and manipulation in many cases where high pay is tied to expectations of long hours and performance without exception to managers or employees within the business. The hierarchical mindset dictates treatment, privileges and the amount of power wielded and allowed by others. The concept of earning your stripes or gaining the "golden key" to the executive suite is typical in this environment, where status and power are considered synonymous and anyone else, including "underling employees" and customers, are viewed as pawns and as a means to a financial end for the select few who will ultimately benefit.

As CEO of my mortgage company in 2004, I would be wined and dined in Wall Street because of our success in closing subprime loans. We were making them money and they liked us because of it. We were skyrocketing in sales, and everyone wanted to get into our customer base to sell their latest products. The first thing that would come out of their mouths would be "this product is going to make us all a lot of money." When I would ask them to explain how the products they were pushing were going to benefit the customers, they would then camouflage their intentions under the guise that the product was something new and different – a product never seen before and we would be the first to offer it to our customers. I said "no thanks" and am glad that I did. We were growing just fine by doing what was right for the customers' confidence in what we believed to be the right thing to do as a business.

Control and power is not just limited to the money-making aspect of how some companies are managed in this Mercenary-gone-bad scenario. Numerous accounts of the historical leadership within Lehman Brothers illustrate this point all too clearly. In a book by Vicky Ward, *The Devil's Casino*, the author described Lehman Brother's culture as "terrifying" where people got fired for wearing the wrong clothes to play golf and disagreeing with top management practices. Top executives were expected to get married and stay married, and their wives were directed in everything from the clothes they wore to the charities and activities in which they were allowed to be involved.

Revered and Feared: While looked-up to by employees and their industry, these types of Dictators instill an underlying fear that one wrong move could cost employees their jobs or even make markets crash. Mercenary Dictators who are both successful and unsuccessful continuously test their employees' allegiance and abilities in order to achieve their desired performance results. They also test the industry as a whole in a multitude of ways. The difference is in the consequences with relation to cause and impact. When there are no exceptions or mistakes are not tolerated, a fear and tendency to hide mistakes occurs versus an attempt to learn and innovate from the experience. A motivation to please or not upset this executive takes precedence over best judgment by employees.

Microsoft's co-founder, Bill Gates, is an example of someone who is both revered and feared. Respected for his business acumen and feared for his cut-throat competitiveness, Gates built what has been described as an "800-pound gorilla" with billions of dollars in financial reserves in place to battle with any perceived threat. While investors wondered why profits weren't being paid out in juicy dividends, it soon became apparent that protection of the company's dominance and position were at the helm of decision-making.

Self Money-Motivated Above All Else: Greed rules all decisions, even at the expense of people, customers or what is sometimes in the best interest of the company. While Miserly when it comes to taking care of employees, these Mercenary top executives are likely to have a fat paycheck unbalanced with reciprocating results. Money is status and influence and, therefore, is revered as the end all to how and why decisions are made. Employees are expected to produce without necessarily reaping the benefits. Stinginess is reaping high pay for oneself while poor working and pay conditions for employees are also typical.

CEOs named among the worst CEOs in 2013 for the above reasons, according to Glassdoor.com ratings, include Bill Dillard II of Dillard's Department Stores and Mike Jeffries of Abercrombie & Fitch. Typical of many patriarchal family-founded businesses with Mercenary tendencies, Dillard's top three positions of CEO, president and vice president are all family members who paid themselves $54 million dollars, over a three-year period between 2010 and 2012, while paying employees poorly and settling a class action disability lawsuit. Abercrombie's Jeffries earned more than $79 million between 2010 and 2012 while employees earned low salaries. An attempt by large shareholders to oust Jeffries failed; however, he was stripped of his chairman role with a one-year employment contract in 2013. Further declines in performance and the overall market stock and market cap predicted his time to be limited according to industry analysts.

As introduced in the beginning of the chapter, a Mercenary Culture can be high performance with engaged employees when elements of the Communal Culture creep into the mix. When performance focused on money alone becomes the definitive measure, that's when the culture takes a nose dive or endures a roller coaster ride over time. I say this from personal experience as a CEO continually battling against the Mercenary tendencies in my industry.

In Chapter 28, I go into more detail about Apple as a company residing in the Mercenary Communal sub-quadrant with Steve Jobs having possessed many of the ideal characteristics, while also a few of the not so ideal qualities.

❖

The bottom line for a Mercenary Culture as stated throughout this book IS the bottom line. Its leadership sets the tone in either empowering in larger-than-life ways, or through enforcing ways where lives are considered meaningless and expendable, and work is expected to be everything.

CHAPTER 25

Defying an Industry Culture

My leadership team and I were in Santa Monica, California, attending an HSBC stakeholders meeting, and then were getting the red carpet treatment to enjoy the Grammy Awards in 2007. We were there as a part of the Sellers Advisory Board. Our mortgage company was among their top performers across the country. The unrest in the industry had already begun showing signs of turmoil in late 2006, so my team and I questioned the lavish all-expenses-paid event, but were assured that there was nothing to be concerned about...and exciting growth plans were going to be revealed. As I sat in on the morning meetings, listening to the analysts report their "turnaround" recommendations, as well as the North American President, reinforcing our critical role as their "partners," I became more and more uneasy with the entire scenario. Something in my gut was not computing. This was especially concerning because I knew the president very well, and his demeanor and body language were sending me a different message than what his words were professing.

After the meetings had concluded, to help clear my head I decided to go for a run along the beach of Santa Monica Boulevard that afternoon. My internal stress was continuing to build and I couldn't understand why. I lost track of time, and when I got back, the limos were waiting and my team was ready to roll. I rushed up to my room and quickly changed. The run had helped clear my head, but the uneasiness remained. In the middle of the Grammy's I was rushed to the emergency room in what was later defined as an anxiety attack after two days of tests.

My uneasiness was gut instinct and well founded, based on seeing so many signs that everyone else seemed to want to ignore or were choosing to ignore. Within days of the North American President of HSBC claiming that everything was fine and under control, the European CEO had released a letter of dire concern about the industry and HSBC's position being in grave danger. Two weeks later I received the infamous email, yes...an email, not a call or a personal meeting, from Washington Mutual stating that they were shutting down.

Industry Culture Gone Bad

Over the course of the following years, the implosion of the mortgage industry, as we all know, was astronomical. From 2006 through 2013, over 350 mortgage companies met their demise in the United States according to the Mortgage Lender Implode-o-meter, which is still tracking the number of companies that have gone out of business. The country and world as a whole is still reeling from the greediness, unethical decisions made, and short-sightedness of the industry. It wasn't as much, in my opinion, about taking the focus away from compliance as it was taking their pulse off of integrity. Greed was a stronger force than ethical obligation to peers or customers.

Earlier in this book, I shared examples of how the industry had shaped companies into being. The majority of companies in the financial sector were and are Mercenary, with an obsession on making money at all costs in any way, shape or form. Making money was a right of passage and worn as a badge of honor with pride.

Reporter and author of *Young Money*, Kevin Roose, was sharing his discoveries on an NPR interview of what it was like for new recruits of Wall Street immediately after the bailouts. In his book, Roose shares his account of shadowing eight young people during their first two years, shortly after the bailouts and when Occupy Wall Street was in the headlines in 2012. A particular example was chilling and all-telling about how the industry still had not learned from its greed-driven culture. One of the recruits, working at the commodities desk, was asked by his boss why he came to Goldman Sachs. The recruit passionately shared his view on "helping companies to hedge their fuel costs" and "eventually those savings would get passed onto customers." This was an unsatisfactory answer to the boss, who summed it up more succinctly to the recruit that if he wasn't there to make money for himself and the firm, it wasn't the place for him. Out of the eight recruits that Roose followed, only three are still in finance. This is not surprising, and it says a lot about the character of our younger generation. They are more purpose driven, and this is a very good thing.

I can relate entirely to the scenario that young recruits experienced on Wall Street as I was a young recruit myself in the late 80s. But it was even more corrupt with greed when visiting as a CEO of my mortgage company. It was all about the product, not the people, and how it was going to make them money. In 2005 and 2006, at the height of Ameritrust's growth, Wall Street was giddy with the money it was making. It was an addiction like an intravenous drug that was leaving tracks that no one was noticing. I would visit Goldman, and many of the others like them that had been bailed out or are no longer in business, where a room of traders would share their algorithmic formulas demonstrating how this product or that product was going to make both them and us loads of money. When we would pose the question of how this is in the best interest of customers, we were met with blank stares and further number crunching about the money. We were expected to market the whole kit and caboodle, regardless. We chose not to, and since we were making them tons of money on what we chose to market, we got away with picking and choosing.

We were literally doing business with the devil, and yet, our corporate culture dictated being able to sleep at night. We would choose the products to take to the market based on our own criteria, not theirs. We identified our own level of risk tolerance, always with our pulse on the value of our reputation, our customers, and our market share. We're still standing, and well, we all know who isn't. It became a war in our industry, and we had our share of battles.

Being in an industry driven by greed is also being in an industry with no accountability for its actions. We have endured and won countless disputes, including a law suit and appeal by none other than HSBC attempting to pass the buckshot onto us. A half a million dollars later, we won against their legion of attorneys that most likely cost them into the million mark or more. But they couldn't combat the one thing we had going for us — our integrity and decision from the inception of our company to make proud choices so that we could sleep at night. It's a story of David versus Goliath worth sharing. But not in this book, so stay tuned. Just suffice it to say for now, Right can win over Might. And that, my friend, is priceless.

Defiantly Grounded

I would have been remiss if I didn't have a chapter dedicated to the challenge of building a company that is going against the corporate culture norm in an industry. Is this you? Are you in an industry that seems to have gone wacko in the way it operates as a whole? Well, at least wacko from your perspective. I know how you feel, because I have been living with that challenge since starting Ameritrust in 1995.

Yes, industries have a dominating culture. Chances are that as you read the descriptions of the Networking, Mercenary, Communal and even Fragmented cultures, certain industries came to mind as well as specific companies. The financial industry is Mercenary in every facet of its being. The biggest problem with this is that it has been Mercenary in every way that discredits its value as a potential successful culture, by losing its heart in exchange for the almighty dollar.

The reality is that since entire industries can dictate a corporate culture, the finance and banking industry is certainly one of the most prominent in being Mercenary. The key for you as a CEO or leader of your organization is whether you are willingly accepting and going along for the ride, or willing to take a stand and defy what an industry is doing as a whole because your values, vision, mission, and purpose are guiding you in a different direction.

If you are questioning the practices and standards of your industry, go back and read Chapters Four through Eight. Consider the values, strategy, leadership, and communication practices of your industry as a whole compared to how you prefer and desire to operate. Determine what you believe is the best practice for you, regardless of what is being dictated as a best practice. Determine what choice is proud for you and your company, then embrace it.

❖

While many mortgage companies were being gobbled up and bailed out within banking restructuring to survive or be absorbed, my mortgage company got sold for all the ideal reasons. The sale was for it to continue to grow and build off of what it was already doing right. The CEO has changed, but the corporate culture was part of its appeal to the buyer. And that makes me feel like a proud papa watching his baby all grown up and leaving the nest.

SECTION V

Four Companies
Four Cultures

INTRODUCTION
Case Studies in Culture

While conducting hundreds of hours of secondary research to identify companies that best characterized each of the cultures, our team became fascinated by four companies in particular: Facebook, Google, Apple and Microsoft. With reams of articles, media coverage, case studies and books to reference, in addition to feature box office films recently bringing even more interesting facts (and assumptions) to bear, my research and assessment development colleagues and I were inspired to write a white paper entitled, "A Tale of Four Cultures: The Link Between Corporate Culture and Enduring Value" as it relates to these four iconic companies and the evolution of the Goffee Jones Two-Dimensional Culture Model to our Three-Dimensional CURx^2 Culture Model.

This section of the book delves deeper into each of these companies from the perspective of the CURx^2 Corporate Culture Model. Using the extensive secondary research, each company was analyzed based on its employee relations, teambuilding and professional development practices, management approach, hiring practices, industry and community engagement,, vision, mission, values, and track record in operating over the course of its existence from inception to today. As you will see by the diagram to follow, our research indicates that each of the companies currently fall into different Culture Quadrants. Movement within a quadrant or out of a quadrant was dictated by company practices or recent developments indicating the likelihood the company has shifted, where applicable.

Based on our analysis of the characteristics and operating practices of the four companies, we have identified them to currently be in the following Quadrants and Sub-quadrants:

Company	Quadrant	Sub-quadrant
Facebook	Networking	Networking Mercenary moving toward Networking Communal
Google	Communal	Communal Communal
Apple	Mercenary	Mercenary Communal on the border Of Communal Mercenary
Microsoft	Fragmented	Fragmented Mercenary

Engagement →

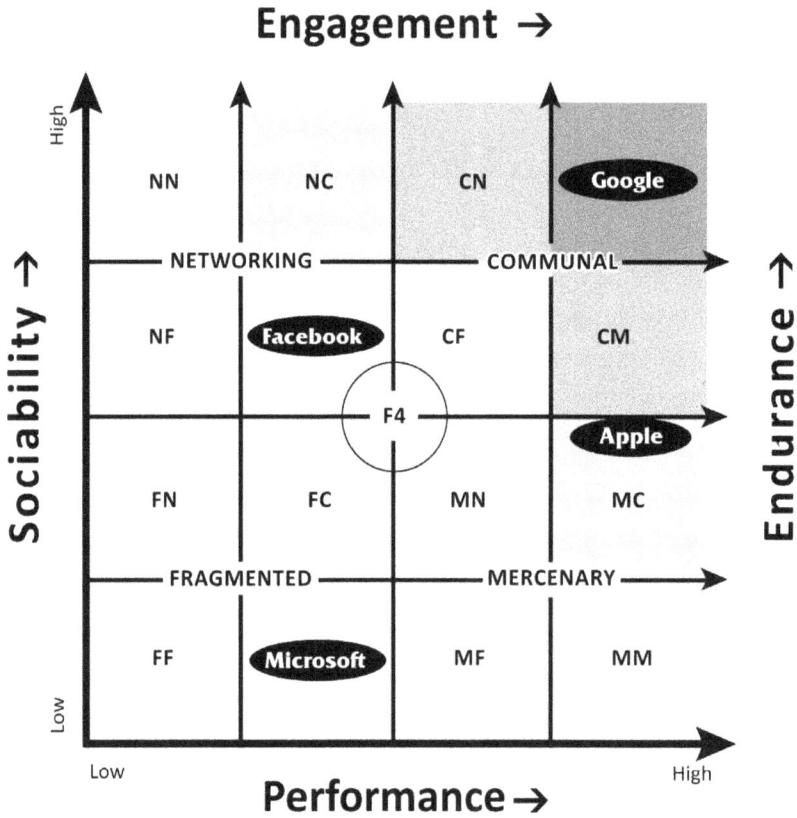

The above assigned quadrants and sub-quadrants were based on sound deductive reasoning using our assessment qualifiers as a guide in combination with the compiled secondary research findings for each company. We are continuing to study these companies, and others, from the standpoint of the correlation between enduring value and corporate culture. You should find the comparisons in this section of the book enlightening as it relates to decisions you make for your company in how it operates and strives to build the ideal corporate culture in order to be a company of endurance.

NOTE: This section of the book would not have been possible without the team effort in compiling, analyzing, and confirming the mounds of information gathered by my research and assessment development team of J. Kevin Toomb PhD, Sherré DeMao, and numerous college interns.

CHAPTER 26
Facebook
Networking in Conflict

Kegs of beer, Red Bull, and an array of snacks with a DJ blasting music in a corner at ramped up volume is the setting. Instead of feet dancing on the floor, you witness fingers dancing on keyboards at a rampant pace. This is not a nerd sleepover or a college frat party, but a three-day, two-night work fest. By 2 p.m. on Friday, the teams gather together to present prototypes to demo from the 43-hour marathon of programming innovation. Out of countless demos to be shared, a handful will make their way in front of CEO Mark Zuckerberg. Called Camp Hackathon, this particular hacker's dream was the first multi-day hackathon since Facebook's IPO. Innovation is the lifeblood of a technology company and shareholder returns are the lifeblood of Wall Street traders, so the pressure was growing to step it up in a significant way after the IPO had been considered a failure on many counts.

You could say that it was a hackathon, with Zuckerberg and geek friends, that sprouted the initial idea behind Facebook, which was based on a college prank, highlighted in the movie The Social Network. At Facebook hackathons, no one is allowed to work on what they normally work on in the company. And if you had never hacked before, you were expected to hack, period. Almost every major feature on Facebook was a hackathon project. The first official hackathon took place at Facebook in 2007, with them being all-nighters that occurred every six to eight weeks as a regular business practice. That is why the multi-day Camp Hackathon was raising the bar even further. It possessed a Mercenary Culture undertone of pressure and expectation to perform with Networking Culture perks like entertainment, food, and alcohol to emphasize it was something to be enjoyed among friends and colleagues, in spite of its pressure. The fact that the hackathon concluded on Friday, so that it doesn't interfere with the weekend, is another Networking Culture influence.

The Hacker's Way

The corporate culture at Facebook has been described by insiders as the Hacker's Way since its inception, even though hackathons didn't become an official initiative until later. To some in Silicon Valley, Facebook has been one long hackathon since its inception. Prior to this post-IPO hackathon, the hackathons averaged 20 hours. Facebook's approach to innovation is a marriage of the best practices of Microsoft and Apple in how these companies innovate. Microsoft's innovation process includes brainstorming, idea collection and team evaluation. Apple has made it a protocol to keep teams small and agile when working on specific development projects.

Hackathons at Facebook are a chance to try out crazy ideas. Everyone is to question the purpose of every feature and expect a logical answer from others. While it is one big room, small teams work together, with team members given the freedom to walk up to anyone else and engage or give them feedback. Facebook's hackathons are a company-wide endeavor, not just a coder's fest. Interns work alongside executives, and every function of the company is involved. For instance, the Finance department could manifest a multi-year budget. The whole idea for everyone is to think at a higher level than had been thought before.

Being a social network services business, on the surface it would only make sense that Facebook landed in the Networking quadrant of our corporate culture analysis. Some might even say that is where they belong. In the dot com era, all technology firms would have been stereotyped in the Networking quadrant because of their fun and fanatical camaraderie approach. Part of the reason we focused on technology companies in this section was to dispel the idea that certain industries dictate specific culture quadrants. Regardless of any industry, it is my belief and my assessment team's belief that the Communal quadrant is where every company should strive to be.

When Facebook was established in 2004, it quickly defined itself as a Networking Culture due to friends and family being the first hires and partners in the business when it launched. Early recruitment efforts focused on employee referrals with candidates being vetted by team members. In most cases, initial employees knew or had a personal connection with Zuckerberg in one way or another, with perhaps three degrees of separation at the most. As the company grew, engineers in the company wore recruiting hats, finding future peers through targeted efforts including making campus visits and attending meet-ups. They even put their technological adeptness to use in recruiting by creating an internal wiki that enabled everyone to share their feedback, recommendations, and ideas related to working efficiently together as new recruits joined the ranks. Zuckerberg's all-hands involvement, accessibility, and visibility was integral to the Facebook culture in everything from recruiting to programming and to business development, though his preference was being at the keyboard pounding out code.

Facebook's mission was and still is "to give people the power to share and make the world more open and connected." Just as Facebook wants its users to share more and more about themselves, the company aspires to have full transparency and communication across all boundaries. Communication and interaction is encouraged to be free-flowing within the company.

The Boy CEO

In 2006, Zuckerberg, coined the Boy CEO, courted with the idea of selling Facebook for $1 billion to Viacom and Yahoo. His absence wreaked havoc on the culture with communication no longer free-flowing and him not being visibly involved. The highly communicative and open environment had changed and the techno-natives were getting restless. The deal fell through, and Zuckerberg quickly recognized what the distraction had cost him. While the company was growing fast, at 19 million users in 2007, MySpace was the dominant social network. Zuckerberg's competencies were needed if Facebook was going to be the number one social network. Selling then was viewed as a very confusing, selfish and a Mercenary move by his loyal legion of hackers.

At age 22, Zuckerberg realized he needed help. Like any other project, he immersed himself in being a better CEO. He hired an executive coach in order to learn more about how to lead, build and let go in order to better run such a fast-growing company. Part of the outcome of that process was realizing where his strengths needed to focus and where his shortcomings needed to be replaced by complementary strengths. In 2008, Sheryl Sandburg joined the company as its new COO. Her immense success as VP of Global Online Sales and Operations at Google made her addition to Facebook's executive team to be seen around the globe as a smart, much needed move, and that the company was finally growing up.

Shortly after Sandberg arrived, Facebook implemented "hands on" meetings where people could hear directly from Zuckerberg. The previously coveted open communication began flowing again, as everyone had been accustomed, but with a bit more structure through Sandberg's guidance.

Due to Zuckerberg possessing Mercenary characteristics in the Networking Culture he created, when he was running both operations and product development, Facebook experienced high turnover of leadership including one president, two CFOs and one COO, as well as three of the company's co-founders. In contrast, Google lost virtually none of its senior staff until months after its IPO. Sandberg knew what needed to be done and began to bring stability and discipline to the business that was essential for global expansion.

A Diligent Duo

From the very beginning of this union, Zuckerberg and Sandberg were the perfect complement to one another. Sandberg focused on and was exceptional at all the things Zuckerberg didn't want to do. She integrated the two halves of Facebook, while also valuing the entrepreneurial problem-solving prowess that kept the company agile. They shared the same philosophy of hiring smart people regardless of whether there was a job opening, and then helped them identify top talent through strengths-based optimization within the company.

She knew how to leverage the agility of the firm by working in tandem with Zuckerberg's Hackers Way. When Sony Corp's CEO met with Sandberg, sharing his skepticism of promoting his studio's movies due to a lack of effective tools to measure effectiveness, Sandberg immediately formed a joint venture with Neilson to devise a way to measure how effective advertising was on Facebook.

As Sandberg grew the operational infrastructure, Zuckerberg grew as a leader. To carry out the "hacker ethos" to be a corporate-wide credo, he initiated training of a legion of leaders to rise to the challenge of middle management in an organization that aspired to be flat. The critical success of these middle managers was in how they interacted with their teams. They were coaches, not bosses. They were facilitators, not gatekeepers. Their main role was to spot and encourage ideas worthy of sharing with Zuckerberg for consideration. Grooming management was deemed important by both Zuckerberg and Sandberg, because like Zuckerberg, a majority of the Facebookers had never worked anyplace else. They were in their 20s with most joining the team directly out of college. They had no point of reference regarding what it took to build a sustainable enterprise. In some ways this was good, because they weren't tainted by traditional management practices. However, it still posed a challenge due to

Zuckerberg's desire that Facebook would not become too hierarchical, and his belief that the more "unmanaged" product development was within the company, the more innovative it would continue to be.

Tying One On

In 2009, the usually hoodie cladding Zuckerberg wore a tie every day that year as a symbol that it was going to be a serious year for the company. Facebook had grown to 1,200 employees and 400 millions users. They moved to their first grown-up campus in Palo Alto. While Facebook was growing up, Zuckerberg affirmed that the company was still an organization that questions assumptions, moves fast, takes risks, shares information, and learns from smart people. However, bureaucracy was creeping into the existence within the company. Code was developed and disappeared for days, weeks, and months. Communication was lagging and confusion around the company's priorities was beginning to surface.

There was an instance where one of the company's executives was standing in a café lunch line and met an engineer he did not know. More concerning, he was not familiar with the project the engineer was working on. The connectedness that the company preached in a total sharing philosophy was not being practiced.

Recognizing this among many other issues of concern, Facebook management took action. It was determined that to continue to honor its mission, they needed to respect efficiency above all else as it relates to everything from how their professionals interacted to how users interacted. They put systems into place to enhance everyone's ability to do their job faster, keep in touch on projects in an easier way, and communicate more fluidly within the company.

Six-week long Bootcamps for engineer recruits began to occur. The minute the new recruits opened their laptops, they were greeted with six emails, one welcome email and five task emails focused on fixing bugs on Facebook. Each recruit was paired-up with a mentor for the first few weeks of their employment. It was a win-win, enabling mentors to gain leadership experience while being an on-call resource for the new employee.

Amidst all the procedures, processes and efficiencies to eliminate bureaucracy, Facebook was still determined to remain as flat as possible and not become a hierarchical business model.

Serotonin Moments

By 2012, Facebook had grown to 843 million users and the design team alone had grown from 20 to 90 focused and determined people. For everyone working there, every day was focused on preparing for tomorrow's Facebook. Their goal was to continually find ways to make the Facebook experience easy and seamless to people. Most important, they wanted the sharing to continually bring "moments of delight," which was referred to as Serotonin, after the mood impacting neurotransmitter in our bodies.

The Hackers Way was about continuous improvement and iteration to achieve that "delight." It evolved employees to get comfortable with the power to push changes directly onto Facebook and embracing that there is never one way to solve a problem, but multiple ways. To keep fresh thinking, engineers were required to leave teams for a month to work on something different. Zuckerberg stayed hands-on, working directly with teams on products and helping them drill down to the details.

To keep everyone in the loop, Zuckerberg stayed on course with his every Friday Q&A hands-on meetings that included beer and reiteration of priorities, encouraged everyone to stay on course, and reminded them that the company's purpose of making the world a more open, connected place was not only transforming lives, but also industries, including entertainment, media and retail.

As the company's IPO became a major focus in the media, "Zuckerberg's meritocratic, coder-led organization" was focused on developing the Facebook site that its founder most wanted, and those charged with making money were still viewed as subordinate. The intense tension between the coding realm and the money makers within the company began resonating up to Wall Street, making Facebook questionable as an investment darling. Many people within the company viewed the IPO to be a threat to their culture of reinvention.

Wall Street Weary

The scuttlebutt on Wall Street questioned whether Facebook was ready for the big time months before its IPO. Financials released in February 2012, before the May IPO, caused further concern in being viewed as far below expectations in spite of making a $1 billion profit. This was further exacerbated by Zuckerberg writing "We don't build services to make money; we make money to build services." This line of thinking does not fare well with the minds of Wall Street. It is all about the money, period.

Furthermore, Zuckerberg's Mercenary insistence on retaining control was not what the Mercenary financial trading industry appreciated, as they expected to be the ones in control. This included Zuckerberg having 25 percent voting power based on stocks he would own, in addition to another 35 percent for a total of 60 percent voting power due to agreements made with other investors. The CEO and Wall Street people literally butted heads every step of the way up to the IPO. Zuckerberg was attempting to change the game by retaining his private interest leverage while attempting to gain public trading value enhancement. In the world of finance today, it just doesn't work that way.

IPOppressed

As one of the most widely anticipated IPOs in history, you would think that NASDAQ would have had its act together. A botched-up start causing a 30-minute delay due to "frenzied demand tripped a glitch in Nasdaq's software" causing the stock to pop nominally and then continuing to recede weeks after the IPO. While the Nasdaq's snafus and hindsight speculation about the style of the IPO potentially being to blame, the real bottom line is that with so much uncertainty about Facebook's potential growth and performance, it is unlikely that the stock would have performed much better with a pristine start at the bell.

As mentioned previously, the months leading up to the IPO brought Facebook into question on many fronts. Less than two weeks before the IPO, Facebook cut projections for revenue as a last-minute correction, which was unprecedented and raised skepticism in the investment community. As days drew nearer to the opening bell ringing, Wall Street research analysts were having to explain the revenue adjustments to investors waiting in the wings. Many large investors sensed an opportunity to bet against Facebook stock with a massive short, with the consensus among hedge funds on the West Coast to take this action on the first day of trading. Actions such as these along with countless trades that were ordered canceled, but then weren't due to Nasdaq's glitch, made big investors rich and individual or retail investors the big losers.

One year after its IPO, Facebook's stock still hadn't rebounded at $15 below its initial offering price. Two months later, it finally topped its IPO price.

Leaning Into Communal

With Sandberg as COO, Wall Street was looking to her to bring the company in alignment with what the financial district expected. Her success with Google proved in their eyes that she was the right person for the job. However, I believe the offering was played out too soon, and needed more time for Sandberg to continue to move it in the direction of Google on many fronts. First, she was operating under a founder with a strikingly different approach to leadership given his greater need for control than at Google. Second, the profits and revenue turnaround she helped manifest still needed more time to build a track record of stabilized growth. Author of the book, *The Facebook Effect*, David Kirkpatrick, said it best in an L.A. Times article just prior to the IPO: "It's a tall order to become a blue chip company in a business that changes as fast as Facebook's does. I am not saying Facebook won't achieve it, but if it's going to achieve it, Sheryl has to stay for a long time."

Kirkpatrick was astute in what needed to happen in Facebook. It needed to become more Communal and Sheryl Sandberg was the right person for the job to help make that happen. Google is the epitome of Communal and she was a core contributor to its growth while respecting and nurturing the culture that was inspired and coveted by founders Larry Page and Sergey Brin. You'll read all about it in the next chapter.

While disappointed in the lackluster IPO, Sandberg was more focused on staying on course in building the company, just as a COO should be. Facebook had rolled out several promising features and had grown to 1 billion users.

Interestingly, a team of mission-driven Facebookers is one of the key reasons Sandberg claimed that the IPO, while disappointing, did not ruffle employees' loyalty or their focus on innovating and reinventing. Her work to make the organization more Communal appeared to have passed a critical test in enabling it to continue to move forward in spite of what has been touted as the most failed IPO in history. But then, as Zuckerberg stated in the opening bell of the IPO, the company has always been more focused on making the world more connected, not making money and going public.

Mobile apps and premium services, among other new products and services, especially the mobile apps, seemed to be the key to turning Facebook back into an upward stock value mode. Another key factor is that while Sandberg took the hot-seat interviews, Zuckerberg was able to do what he preferred to be doing anyway, product development.

An indicator that the company was reinventing internally to realize the power of engaging its people to foster performance, Facebook was named the #1 Best Place to Work in 2013, beating out Google and Apple in the Glassdoor's annual compilation of employee feedback and ratings. In 2014, it remained in the top five in Glassdoor's rating, still edging out Google, which moved to the #8 spot on the list.

❖

More all-telling than being named Best Place to Work is what is occurring within Facebook with regard to making financial and product innovation also reach greater heights. While Facebook is only dipping its toe into the Networking side of Communal, coming together as an organization in more alignment with its purpose is a strong step in the right direction.

CHAPTER 27

Google
Banking on Communal

In 2007, Google's HR department noticed a problem. A lot of women were leaving the company in spite of their priority being to increase the number of female employees in a male-dominated tech industry. The departures weren't just a gender equity issue, they were having a significant bottom-line impact because of the costly, time-consuming recruiting process. Google was competing for top talent against Apple, Facebook, Microsoft, Amazon, and countless other tech start-ups. Competing to replace talent was costly and time consuming, whereas keeping employees happy is where Google always wanted to be focusing when investing its dollars in talent. Monitoring employees identified a happiness problem related to the female departures. Women giving birth were leaving at twice the average departure rate. Even though Google's average attrition was far below the industry standards to begin with, this particular data trend indicated a growing problem that needed to be addressed.

The first issue discovered by Google's HR department was an inconsistency in maternity plans. In California, new mothers received 12 weeks paid leave, while everywhere else in the country new mothers were given seven weeks paid leave. This was changed company-wide to 18 weeks paid leave for new mothers and seven weeks paid leave for new fathers. The second issue was related to when new mothers returned to work, they had separation anxiety. Google's revised maternity leave policy allowed the flexibility to use the time in increments versus all at one. New mothers could even use some of the time before giving birth for preparation. The solution resulted in reducing female Googler attrition back down to Google's low industry average. Another people problem was solved.

The monitoring that Google does to better understand what motivates and keeps its employees satisfied includes a Happiness Survey that is a standard part of its HR outreach. Google continuously monitors a slew of data related to employees' response to benefits, working conditions, and more. Their generosity to employees is actually documented on an ongoing basis in order to confirm that their ever-growing list of benefits is savvy investing in talent and the future of the company, not just whimsical or extravagant perks.

What can be learned from Google's obsession with its people and keeping them happy and engaged is that they truly have made the connection between people, engagement and performance, which is key to building an enduring, growing enterprise. They put as much emphasis on their people decisions as their tech decisions by living their mission in having "all people decisions be informed by data." They don't operate on assumptions, but get to answers quickly in order to make informed decisions swiftly.

You could almost equate Google as being human in how it operates as an enterprise. It is quick to admit to making mistakes and then just as quick to resolve or correct a situation with an even better solution or end result. How does it do it? By doing what it knows it does best ... analytics with a human touch.

In my opinion, as mentioned when referenced in Chapter 26, Google is the epitome of the Communal Culture.

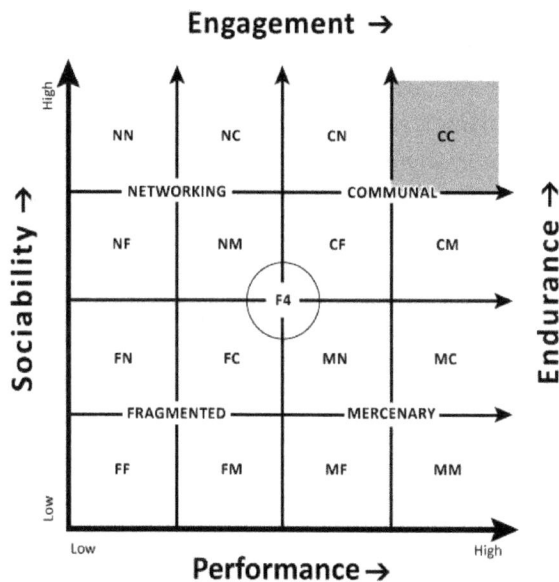

Data Equals Divine Intervention

Google's HR department functions more like a rigorous science laboratory than a compliance and policing department. The details of employee satisfaction have expanded as far as analyzing the length of lunch lines and the optimal size and shape of cafeteria tables. Every creature comfort, as it relates to optimizing the work environment, is considered for assessment and continuous improvement. Once the company grew to thousands of employees, Google hired social scientists to be on staff to study in the PiLab (People & Innovation Lab) and conduct dozens of experiments with employees to determine the best way to manage a large firm.

A couple of examples of this can be illustrated in how Google streamlined its hiring practices, as well as how it shifted its philosophy on middle management.

In its early years, the initial thinking of Google's co-founders, Larry Page and Sergey Brin, was that hiring the right people meant everyone in the company should interview the candidates. Prospective candidates endured what seemed like an unending gluttony of interviews, which was sending a negative message in recruiting. Then data mining came to the rescue. The firm conducted a study to find the optimal times a candidate should be interviewed. The end result was four interviews, and this is still their protocol to this day.

Another data mining gem, known as Project Oxygen (10,000 observations across more than 100 variables), identified the optimal behavior related to middle managers, overturning the presumption of the company's co-founders that a company could run without anyone being the boss of anyone else. Two-sided feedback revealed otherwise. The highest performing team managers had more productive teams because they were not only managing the team's performance, but also were coaching for productivity and results, communicating consistently, not micromanaging, providing a clear vision and strategy, supporting employees' career development, conducting problem-solving with employees, connecting with and being accessible to their entire team.

Analytics also played a role in understanding how to get employees to contribute more to their 401(k). What was discovered is that nudging employees wasn't enough. Guiding and directing employees was better with numerous reminders, including aggressive savings goals accompanied by a multitude of reinforcing reasons why saving for their future was taking better care of themselves.

I could cite countless more examples, but you are getting the idea. People and how to keep them engaged and performing at their highest levels, to Google, means taking care of them in every way, shaping and forming through leveraging information that provides valuable insight. Where you may not be making the connection with your team is in how your own data could be telling you so much more than you are allowing it to tell you. Don't overlook this important piece, simply because your company is not a technology analytics company. Every company has information readily at its disposal or could be tracking data to help management and employees make better decisions.

Communal is as Communal Does

In my opinion, Google is among a handful of companies that have consistently operated in the highest possible sub-quadrant, within Communal Communal. My research team intentionally went to the employer rating sites to garner what employees were saying about all four of the companies in this section of the book. Not surprising, Facebook and Google were scoring in the 90th percentiles by being recommended as great places to work. These companies are at the High Sociability and Mid to High Engagement related to their people, so this makes sense from a corporate culture standpoint.

When skimming through the reviews, we gained some additional insight regarding what were viewed as the pros and cons of working at Google. One of the cons mentioned several times was the fact that "you are working amidst the country's best and brightest." Of course, this was also cited as a pro about working there. What was stated as the negative side of working amidst the best and brightest is that an MBA from Harvard might be doing what could be viewed as a mundane, low-level job, such as providing tech support or applying basic code. Another negative is that it is hard to stand out when everyone is at the top of their game. This is why the company's culture plays such a pivotal role. Being a Googler, as team members are affectionately called, is about being a high performance team on a specific mission. If an MBA from Harvard is more concerned about standing out than about being part of an impassioned culture dedicated to changing the way the world receives and accesses information, then that particular Ivy Leaguer is not a good fit for Google. There are plenty of other MBAs from Harvard and elsewhere who will embrace and excel because they understand Google's entrepreneurial team workgroup dynamics. More on this is later in the chapter.

No longer being a start-up, Google is a big, big company with tens of thousands of Googlers worldwide. When a company gets big even into hundreds of employees, let alone thousands around the globe, there comes a certain level of bureaucracy that inevitably attempts to infiltrate the seams of the company. Often, this comes more from the mentality people bring in when coming from other big organizations, but the reality is as a company grows, it can get caught-up in its size more than in its mission. The critical difference in Google is what its co-founders started doing from its inception and then more formally in 2007 by continually looking at their "people operations" as much as their tech operations. It is because of this "communal" obsession that when a choice needs to be made, it will always lean toward what is in the best interest of engaging and inspiring people for optimal performance.

A Living, Breathing "Realosophy"

Too often, a philosophy is great in thought and in the written form, but is never really entirely embraced to be brought fully into reality. It remains a philosophy or theoretical goal, rather than an actualization through practice and ongoing initiatives. What Google's co-founders and the Googlers have accomplished is transforming the company's founding philosophy about what could make their company great into a "realosophy" that has truly made the company great. The company professes 10 Truths as keys to its philosophy.

Translating Google's 10 Truths as it relates to their Communal Culture underscores the importance of corporate values, vision, mission, strategy, communication, leadership and ethics discussed earlier in this book. To follow now is what our research team believes each of their truths mean from a corporate culture perspective.

Truth #1: Exceptional User Experience: The first truth states "Focus on the user and all else follows." While their website talks primarily about the end user, as in the person "googling" for this piece of information or a specific answer to a question or problem, Google's reference to "user" is just as much about its employees and anyone connected to the company as it is about its advertisers or the searching population. From a corporate culture standpoint, its presentation of unprecedented benefits to employees is a glowing example of the experience it strives to provide to its Googlers.

> **Take Care of Your People:** CEO and co-founder, Larry Page, has been quoted as saying, "It is important that the company be like a family, that people feel that they're part of the company and that the company is like a family to them – when you treat people that way you get better productivity." But, at Google, it is so much more than treating them like family. They actually treat them better than family on so many levels – more like royalty or, as some would aptly say, rock stars, with the unending perks, benefits and privileges with which most other companies can't compete.

Give People Opportunities: In the same interview, Page also stated, "My job as a leader is to make sure everybody in the company has great opportunities and that they feel they're having a meaningful impact and are contributing to the good of society." Since Google wants to be a leader, not a follower, Googlers are rewarded for their ideas and contributions that keep them leading and innovating.

Nurture Personal Passions: Google allows employees to spend 20% of their time working on their own project, independent from a work group. Google believes that no one should want to leave so they can pursue their personal interests. While paying them for time that is not directly related to assigned project work, this personal time allowance has resulted in over 20% of product launches stemming from personal projects. Respecting personal passions also relates to an employee's time with their family and having a life outside of work. That's why, even though you may witness Googlers on campus late at night, it is by their choice, not demanded. There are no late-night or early morning meetings imposed by management. Chances are the reason that many Googlers are working at night is because of the flexibility in their work schedules, since they can set their own schedules.

Truth #2: Excel at What You Do Well: The second truth cites, "It's best to do one thing really, really well." While Google started out focused entirely on search problems, it has realized that what it does really, really well is access, accumulate and provide information efficiently and effectively. Therefore, it has been a stellar example of being a company that uses it own core competency to make it an even better company.

Data Rules Supreme: Engineering talent is what has kept Google on top, and only the best employees are hired. From marketing, sales and business development to production development and management, the individuals most likely have an engineering background or education. This is why there is such a demanding thought process that questions assumptions, requires accurate data, and then uses data findings in their critical decision-making process. Decisions are based on information backed by data, not intuition or opinion.

Intense, Competitive Hiring: While you would think this means that hiring is left to headhunters, competitor poaching and the Ivy

Leagues in order to get the best of the best, this is where Google gets the power of a Communal Culture. Every employee at Google has recruiting and hiring great people as a part of their job, not just the HR department. The idea of excelling at what everyone does best unified by a "greater than one" purpose and mission helps Google continue to excel with each hire made.

Food for Thought: A company rule exists that that no employee should be more than 100 feet from food. A farmer's market, a cafeteria, snacking stations, gourmet meals -- whatever one fancies is literally steps or a bike ride away and at no charge. Several theories have been bantered about regarding why the free food is so important at Google. One school of thought is that many of the best and brightest people who are being recruited are coming right out of college. A free meal is considered gold to a college mindset, so it is viewed as a real perk by someone coming out of college. Another theory is that employees are more motivated if their basic needs are met. According to Maslow's hierarchy of needs, food and shelter are among the basic physiological needs that must be met before moving up the hierarchy to realizing self actualization and transcendence. But in my opinion, it is less psychological and physiological as it is practical from a bottom line standpoint. The employee that doesn't have to think about bringing a meal to work or knowing where to go out for a meal is using his or her brainpower on problem-solving and moving initiatives forward. Additionally, an employee who is putting in a long day is less likely to miss a meal when it is readily accessible, so they are more likely to take that much needed break because it is reinforced as acceptable because it is being provided by the employer. The bottom line for providing food is that it enables the employee to stay focused on and excel at what they were hired to do.

Truth #3: At the Speed of Right: The third truth cites, "Fast is better than slow." Time is precious and people are impatient. We all know this. Google seems to really understand this. They want to give people answers within seconds, and not just any answers, but the right answers in what they were seeking to learn, understand or know. This is also key to the company's internal approach to the problems they are trying to solve.

Quick to Shift: The agility in which Google still operates is why many in the world of big business will claim that it still feels like a start-up. But then, perhaps Google is proving that best practices are more about what you do in the beginning, and are able to continue to replicate because it worked in the beginning. Google is organized and prepared at any given moment to quickly adapt and redeploy people and resources to solve big problems or embrace emerging opportunities. Project cycles are short, yet continuous. What this basically means is that everyone is always in a mode of continuous improvement in everything they do, which is not to the detriment of innovation, but for the elevation of innovation.

Need for Speed: With technology advancing at a record pace, Google's deployment flexibility along with their information competency enables their team of super stars to respond or proactively move initiatives forward effectively and efficiently. The lack of hierarchy can be essential for always being able to leverage the best talent on any given project.

Truth #4: Democracy at Its Finest: The fourth truth cites, "Democracy on the web works." For Google, it also works by how it is operationally organized and functions.

Collaborate & Cooperate: Google is successful because of its purpose driven small work groups or "entrepreneurial teams" approach. If a Googler wants to work with another team, he or she can make the switch without asking permission or having to go through human resource channels. The company's Intranet, which is like an internal "Facebook," keeps everyone easily accessible to one another.

Collaborate to Innovate: At Google, innovation is not just about the service or products, but also about how to innovate in nurturing the relationship with employees. This means giving employees every opportunity to be the solution, regardless of the current role they are in at the time. Meetings for employees to present new ideas in a forum were established as a way of avoiding the conservatism that can set into more mature companies.

Good Ole' American Work Ethic: The work ethic at Google is driven by people loving what they do and where they are doing it, versus an expectation of long hours. And its leaders are truly leading by example, often seen eating at the cafeteria late at night for dinner, like everyone else. Everyone puts everything they've got into each working day by knowing they are doing it with team members that are considered the best in the world. Working at Google is viewed as a privilege that no one takes for granted. It is a cooperative spirit with competitive undertones that are healthy, effective and impressive.

Truth #5: Information is Where You Are: The fifth truth cites, "You don't need to be at your desk to need an answer." Recognizing that the world is increasingly mobile, Google also respects this about its employees. The environment at Google encourages employees to connect away from their desks and cubicles to further encourage free thinking. Googlers can escape to a thinking pod for private reflection or meditation, or teams can meet at any number of venues throughout the campus to stimulate ideas or discussion.

Truth #6: Greed is Not Necessary: The sixth truth states, "You can make money without doing evil." This particular truth is near and dear to Google's co-founders' hearts. Page and Brin did not want the traditional culture of "Greed is good," which was prominent in the 1980s, to exist within their company. The Google culture does not tolerate backstabbing, drama, neediness or general discord. Their belief was and still is that you can create a high-performance, profitable company without doing evil. They wanted an environment where people would want to come to work, have fun, dream big, and get rewarded for bringing big things to life.

Truth #7: Improving Access is Essential: The seventh truth cites, "There's always more information out there." Google realizes that cyberspace is an infinity and beyond reality.

Abstract Thinking: In the Google-based movie, The Internship, released in 2013, a Skype interview happened with the characters, Billy and Nick, played by Vince Vaughn and Owen Wilson, and the interviewers asked the question, "You are shrunken down to the size of nickels and dropped to the bottom of a blender. What do you do?." While theater goers may have thought this was scripted just for laughs, it is far from it. It is off-the-wall questions just like the one posed in the movie that helps Google understand how a potential employee thinks and would be able to contribute within one of its entrepreneurial work groups. Answers given and the demeanor of candidates when these questions are posed also shed light on attitude and aptitude.

Learn & Adopt: In the first year of its existence, the Google founders knew that they had a lot to learn about running and managing a company, especially one growing by leaps and bounds like theirs. Venture capital investor, John Doerr, introduced the Objectives and Key Results (OKR) system used at Intel to the founders and it was immediately adopted by Google and is still used today. The reason this made so much sense for the company was because of the definition of the objective in OKR, which was that it is ambitious and makes you feel a tad uncomfortable. For a company focused on achieving the impossible, this system was exactly the protocol required and that would be embraced. Google has added its Communal spin to make it powerful company wide. Every co-worker's OKR is viewable by anyone in the company with scores and outcomes. This keeps everyone aware of what everyone else is working on, as well as helps others potentially know who to tap into in order to collaborate on a problem they are trying to solve. This is strikingly different from Apple, where secrecy is coveted and expected at the threat of one's job if unapproved disclosure occurs.

Google has taken the aspect of Learn and Adopt seriously at every level, as well as Learn and Adapt. This has been described as the Thomas Edison Approach to problem solving and innovation development. The focus on what is impossible is built in with the expectation that one will discover what didn't work in their 5, 10, 100, 1,000 attempts until success is realized. As stated earlier, failure is not a negative or an option. It is a learning curve towards gaining achievement, plain and simple.

This can apply to problem solving in innovation or internally in operations. For instance, Segways and electric scooters were the norm initially around the California Googleplex campus. By 2008, these modes of transportation were replaced by bicycles. The Segways kept breaking down and employees kept falling off the scooters. Instead of just eliminating things, they adapted new ones based on what was learned. Additionally, using the bicycles reinforced another aspect of their values in healthy fitness activities.

<u>Truth #8: Need Crosses All Borders:</u> The eighth truth states: "The need for information crossed all borders." Facilitating access to information for the entire world is a mission that Google takes seriously, including the access they desire to provide to a diverse workforce for helping them achieve this outcome. For Google, it is not just about eliminating borders geographically, but also in how people think and perceive one another's value and worth.

Respecting Diversity: The earlier example related to increasing the number of female team members only scratches the surface of Google's diversity initiatives. The company also offers Employee Clubs to help connect specific segments of workers to one another socially and professionally, including the Black Googler Network, Google Women Engineers, and the GLBT (Gay, Lesbian, Bisexual and Transgender Googlers).

Respecting Individuality: Part of the reason why the benefits are so extensive is out of respect for the individuality of every Googler. Sure, many of them are engineers and programmers, but this doesn't mean they all get excited or motivated by the same things. Google gets this.

<u>Truth #9: Serious Should Be Comfortable:</u> The ninth truth proclaims: "You can be serious without a suit." Co-founders Page and Brin built Google around the idea that work should be challenging, but the challenge should be fun. Their belief is that creativity is stimulated by a balance of work and play.

Playing IS Good!: Work without play is like night without day to Google. This means some play time while at work is not only encouraged, but expected. Meal breaks are true breaks and play breaks often lead to breakthroughs. Why? Because a mind that is nourished and challenged by a variety of stimulation is a mind ready to tackle the toughest problems. Flashes of brilliance often come when the mind is at rest or not focused on what has been consuming it for long stretches of time.

Sense of Fun Builds Commitment & Camaraderie: Having a little fun and keeping one's sense of humor and adventure while on the job is important at Google. Their April Fool's Day practice is a prime example. It is a company tradition to design elaborate pranks to fool users and potential employees every April 1st. Some examples include a job listing for engineering positions on the moon and a fictitious brain-boosting energy drink called Google Gulp. To truly test Googlers' vulnerability and to keep them wondering, it launched Gmail on April 1st in 2004. However, this one wasn't a hoax at all. You simply have to appreciate a company's ability not to take itself too seriously, and to creatively keep everyone on their toes.

Truth #10: Great Is a Starting Point: The tenth truth declares, "Great isn't good enough." For Google, dissatisfaction is a challenge they love to conquer, and far exceeds what it believes it has an obligation to fulfill.

Social Responsibility: Google's social and corporate commitment to making a difference in the world extends far beyond access to information, which reinforces its belief in great being a starting point. Google has taken environmental responsibility as a corporation into every nook and cranny of its operations with a focus on reducing its carbon footprint. This included hiring on-staff engineers who were dedicated to improving solar power technology in its ventures investment division and sponsoring research to develop the first geothermal map. For its co-founders, this means "making the company stand for something other than making money." Charitable giving at Google is as diverse as its workforce, including empowering girls and women, protecting threatened wildlife, improving computer science education, responding to crises, fighting trafficking and child abuse, and issuing impact challenges around the globe to nonprofits for foundation funding. Google also matches employee contributions up to $3,000.

Achieving the Impossible: Google believes that an environment that radiates success, confidence, optimism, dedication, and hard work results in accomplishing the impossible. Everyone works harder because they know they are achieving more than they would anywhere else they may be working. Superstars are happy to take less prominent roles for understanding what it means to overall team success. Google sets high standards and measures them quarterly as a part of its OKR approach and generously rewards achievement. Notice that I said rewards versus incentives. "Impossible" goals are the standard expectation to challenge everyone beyond what can be imagined right now. No one accepts failure at Google, they believe it is just learning from what doesn't work and then trying again and again, continually learning, until a solution is discovered, tried, tested and proven. As Don Dodge, a Developer Advocate at Google and serial entrepreneur put it, the way Google sees it, "Achieving 65% of the impossible is better than 100% of the ordinary."

Counter Intuitive Intelligence

In many ways, Google is redefining 'big business" best practices. For instance, their reliance on data-driven decision-making would seem counter intuitive to the ability to be so agile. Too often, the need for data paralyzes management within companies into taking forever to make decisions, ultimately making agility impossible. Is this an area you fall victim to…analysis paralysis?

Another counter intuitive aspect of Google's operations is their work environment laden with "goof off" temptations at every turn. At least, this is the way some more mercenary management styles would view it. The bottom line is, all work and no play makes workers dull, desensitized, and unmotivated. They become robots instead of thinking, innovating, and being resourceful and inspired contributors. Which do you really want working for you?

Google is literally redefining what works and doesn't work in business. They also clearly understand how important nurturing and protecting a corporate culture is to their bottom line. Since 2006, one of the executive level positions is Chief Culture Officer, or Culture Czar, as it was referred to from its inception. Co-founders Page and Brin determined the need for this position, because as the company was growing, it was demanding more and more of their attention in a variety of areas. They didn't want to lose what they knew was at the heart of the company's unprecedented success.

Once a company grows beyond you as a CEO, one of your most prized and valuable executive level management positions should be that of a Chief Culture Officer (CCO). If you are finding it more and more difficult to maintain the corporate culture that has gotten your company to its current level of success, it is time to hand over the reigns to someone that can help you assure that it remains protected.

If you are thinking "My company is not a tech company, or my company could never be Google, so this would never work for us," you should think again.

❖

This isn't about the type of industry or the type of company, but its corporate culture. You have total choice about the culture you want to foster within your company and how you empower it to thrive.

CHAPTER 28
Apple
Mercenary At Its Best

Anxious young recruits in awe and wonderment at landing a position with Apple and the chance to brush shoulders with its legendary visionary co-founder, Steve Jobs, hadn't a clue exactly what they were going to be doing for the company. They were hired into "dummy position" roles that were not explained in detail until after they were officially hired. This air of mystery was and is intentional and is protocol for the iconic multi-billion enterprise. While Apple recruits the brightest stars from college campuses and elsewhere, the collegiate impression of Apple's 32-acre campus is all-deceiving, cloaking an internal society of secrecy that is the company's non-negotiable imperative for success. Even before knowing which building they will be working in, recruits are taught the importance of keeping secrets. A roundtable of introductions reveals many who can state titles, but not what project they are working on. Orientation reveals that new employees have not just joined a company that is revered worldwide, they have joined a cult that is coveted internally.

When the security briefing occurs, no Apple employee is left unshaken and reality sets in. According to various sources, this briefing is the most remembered and with good reason. Whoever is the head of security at the time comes into the orientation and clearly explains the reasons behind the importance of Apple's security and secrecy measures. The talk is not a pep talk, but is a matter-of-fact explanation of the end result with an ultimatum. Being quiet is worth millions of dollars to the company in successful product launches, and any breach by any employee will result in swift termination, period.

There is only one free lunch at Apple, and it is on a new recruit's first day of work during the orientation. Yes ... There is Caffe Macs, a centralized cafeteria serving exceptional food on Apple's sprawling multi-building campus, but employees are charged for every sip or morsel, with exception of the water from water coolers, I guess. There also are plenty of other amenities to enjoy as an employee of Apple at reduced or subsidized rates, including a health and fitness gym. Some freebies include an outdoor courtyard and volleyball courts that are rarely used as employees scurry from meetings to meetings that start and end on time, no exceptions. Apple does allow employees to take naps in one of their "user definable areas," at no charge. I am not sharing this to discredit the company; it is just to reinforce how strikingly different it approaches engaging and managing employees as compared to Facebook and Google.

Need To Know Basis

The secrecy at Apple is at the core of its success on many fronts. Aversion to pre-release publicity is constant because it is viewed as harmful to a product launch. There is a build-up to the release in a matter of days, not weeks or months. Many have compared Apple's product releases to how Hollywood approaches a blockbuster movie opening weekend. Even the slightest detail released would dampen the anticipation and, most important of all, the buying frenzy. The stealth mode around future new products and versions of current products is also to not steal the thunder from existing products. While Apple relies on its early adapter buyers, it still wants the buyers who will buy since they are unsure if or when an updated version will be released and they don't want to appear too far behind the loop, that "infinite loop" of mystery that Apple has so adeptly mastered.

Jobs also continuously reinforced the company's stealth ways in meetings including stating that anything disclosed would not only result in termination, but also prosecution to the highest extent of the law. Special agreements are signed by employees and anyone contracted by Apple acknowledging that they are working on super secret projects. Talking about any aspects of a project is strictly prohibited to anyone, including family members and others inside the company. While not confirmed, rumors also have circulated that plain clothed Apple security agents would visit local hangouts of employees so they could listen to discussions on the street and while socializing. Employees being heard sharing anything outside of the company were swiftly fired, as warned.

Obsessive Protective Productivity

Minding your own business and staying focused on what you have been hired to do is expected at Apple because an employee who is not butting into another employee's business is more productive. The depth of Apple's elaborate measures to enforce security includes giving teams only pieces of the bigger puzzle – the end product.

The aspect of testing versus trusting, as described in Chapters 2 and 3, is clear here. In many cases, teams are working on the same project and actually competing with one another for the desired end result. Teams are purposely kept apart and are not allowed to intermingle as is encouraged at Google. Only those working in the highest reaches of the company know what the completed puzzle looks like. New additions on a team are kept out of the loop for a while until trust is earned.

A small executive team and counsel of advisors to the CEO assisted by fewer than 100 vice presidents (out of over 80,000 employees) run the company. Across the rest of the organization, status fluctuates according to the prominence of the products being worked on.

There are no open doors at Apple. With silos being the norm, security badges allow your access to certain areas of the company that could literally change overnight. An employee's boss may not have access to an area the employee can access. When carpenters are seen, as one source described, employees know something big is in the works. Walls are relocated, windows are frosted, or rooms are built with no windows at all, called lockdown rooms.

In spite of what appears to be cogs of workers unconnected and blinded to any resemblance of a bigger picture, there is immense cooperation due to the continuous magical stream of products that these employees know they had a hand in. Their small piece of that solved puzzle is a source of pride and privilege.

The Top 100

While everyone that works at Apple is described as the elite when hired, they still are not as elite as the Top 100 of Apple. This group is the epitome of another aspect of the Mercenary culture, its hierarchy. What makes Apple's hierarchy unique is that it is not based on the status within the company, but the preference according to Jobs and now its current CEO. Selected within the company as the coveted few who help develop the strategy, these selected few attend an intense three-day annual strategy session. Shrouded in secrecy, it cannot be discussed with anyone else in the company. Attendees are not allowed to drive themselves to the gathering, but are bused to the intended location. Per Jobs preference, it needed to be a resort, with good food and NO golf course. This was not a company retreat; it was a base camp like a military unit would have for strategizing its next attack. Meeting rooms are swept for electronic bugs.

The group in attendance is considered an "extremely influential group," the innovators, the idea makers, and Movers and Shakers, as described in Chapter 15. Not based on rank within the company, a vice president could be excluded and someone under his or her management could be invited, and not allowed to discuss it with their direct reports. Attendees can be bumped from year to year, and being kicked out is humiliating. Not being invited also sends a message of where the hierarchy begins and ends. The "elite" left behind have been known to placate themselves with a "tongue and cheek" Bottom 100 lunch.

Career stakes are high for anyone presenting at the strategy sessions. Pressure is nerve-racking. When the Apple iPod was introduced at one of the Top 100 meetings, only a handful of people who had been working on it knew about it. The majority of attendees were learning about it for the first time.

All Work, No Play

Apple people come to work to work. In contrast to Google, where workers take breaks for ping pong and actually do use the volleyball court and extracurricular activities promoting on fliers and engaging employees in everything from a lecture series to weekend trips, Apple workers are there to work. While people at Google are called Googlers and Facebook people are Facebookers, Apple doesn't consistently promote a special moniker for its employees. They are a workforce, a very specialized and elite workforce.

Go to Apple's recruiting page on their website, and it is abundantly clear. They don't sugar coat their expectations. A certain level of arrogance that most certainly emanated from its most admired and feared co-founder is inherent in the copy on the page including, "We're perfectionists. Idealists. Inventors. .... A job at Apple is one that requires a lot of you, but it's also one that rewards bright, original thinking and hard work ... We're like a jigsaw puzzle. We each have our own expertise, and we all fit together."

The first day on their job, employees get a company-issued computer with no instructions on how to connect to the network. They are expected to figure it out as yet another test to their tenacity and ability to find solutions efficiently and effectively. Then they get to work. The long hours and dedication to the company above all else is not what employees' families signed-up for, in spite of the prestige and decent pay at the corporate level. In 2004, during the holiday season, an Apple employee's husband held an impromptu weekend protest demonstrating his frustration about overtime hours he said his wife was required to work at Apple. With teenage sons and dog by his side, a sign with "KAPAO: Kids & Pets Against Overtime" apparently brought applause from workers looking out windows.

For Steve Jobs, loving work didn't necessarily mean it was a fun place to work. He described working at Apple as "the most fulfilling experience" in any employee's life. This open arrogance, combined with a clear disclosure that an employee will work and work a lot, is actually a best practice of the effective Mercenary Culture. As secretive as Apple is, it leaves nothing in question about the loyalty that is expected of anyone who works for them. It is the Mercenary Cultures that broadside new recruits with unexpected and unending work hours that cause dissension and ultimately the most fragile of Shaken employees described in Chapter 16.

Control & Accountability

There is never any confusion about who is responsible at Apple. As a part of its accountability structure, a DRI, or Directly Responsible Individual, is assigned so that there is no question regarding who is to handle a particular task or oversee an initiative. As a result, the company's ability to be nimble, despite size, can be directly linked to this best practice. If the executive team decides to change direction, it's instantaneous because there is never any question about who is doing what or why from the top down. This level of agility is what has kept Apple operating like it did as a start-up under Jobs' leadership, even amidst being a company with tens of thousands of employees.

Additionally, the company is organized into function areas, not divisions with clear and specialized directives of focus and concentration by its leadership. Specialization is another critical success factor for Apple all the way down to those hired with a very specific specialty in mind. Examples include that only Apple's CFO has the P&L responsibility for costs and expenses that lead to profits or losses. Jobs determined that P&L was the finance executive's job and did not hold other managers and team members accountable for P&L because it was considered a distraction to innovation. Only the Finance Chief needs to consider its implications and, if doing his or her job, profit is the only acceptable end result of that position. The executive who runs the Apple Store has no authority over photography on the Apple Store website because photography is handled company-wide by the graphics arts function. The retail executive doesn't control inventory because that is handled by the supply chain management function.

Jobs saw this as having 'best-in-class" employees in every role. However, as one employee described the structure, "it created fiefdoms" with each functional leader operating as a feudal lord wielding power over his or her territory. Rising stars are invited to be guests at meetings where they will be exposed to "how thing are done" and the decision-making process. Apple is not concerned with developing a well-rounded executive, due to its specialization focus.

The organization chart reflecting the hierarchy at Apple was shared in a Fortune Magazine article in 2011. The acting CEO, then Jobs, is central to everything. Instead of the traditional hierarchical tree chart with branches flowing down from the top gun of the company, Apple's organizational chart is more like a solar system with, at the time, Steve Jobs as the Sun, and everyone else circling him like planets and their teams the stars and moons. No-one in the company was far removed from Jobs' access or wrath, and the same is likely true for Apple's current CEO if he wants to keep Apple's divine universe in orbit.

Product is King

An executive who worked for both Microsoft and Apple was able to share a fundamental focal difference between what drives each company's bottom line. According to this individual, "Microsoft tries to find pockets of unrealized revenue and then figures out what to make. Apple is just the opposite. It thinks of great products, then sells them. Prototypes and demos always come before spreadsheets." In the more effective Mercenary Culture, the product and striving for excellence truncates the focus on making money. Making money is expected, just not the primary focus.

"Cash is King" is the mantra of the greed-ridden Mercenary Culture, as discussed earlier in Chapters 12 and 25, and is at the heart of every decision being made to the detriment of quality and excellence in the product or service or even serving the customer if it will make an extra buck. This is why Apple has such a loyal following inside and outside its ranks. For Apple, product innovation and living up to Jobs' insistence to pioneer what people didn't even know they needed is sexy, seductive and lucrative.

A Divine CULTure Intervention

There is no company more definitive of Corporate CULTure with the cult aspect being magnified than Apple. From employees to the media to its customers, the company has been described countless times as having a cult following. As shared in Chapter 2, the aspects of Communal Beliefs, Unquestioned Allegiance, Leadership Coveted and Revered and Teammates Tested are Apple in every essence of its being.

Apple has claimed having relatively low turnover considering its pressure-cooker environment because employees are believers in what they believe to be the company's mission, even if they are not personally happy at work. They believe that they are working on something bigger than them. They have guzzled Jobs' Kool-Aid, and cannot get enough of the intrigue. They believe they are privileged to work in the company. Attrition is due more to people not measuring up, as opposed to leaving, because people get fired more than people leave.

Many rank-and-file technical employees who work at Apple have been diehard Apple geeks since childhood. In an environment that shuns coddling, most geeks are not all that people –centric anyway, so that is fine with them. "Shut up and do your job and you might get to stay," is viewed as a challenge to perform, not an assault on someone's character. You can ask anyone in the company what Steve Jobs would want and even if 90 percent of them had never directly met him, they could answer the question confidently. Cult minions, blindly loyal worker bees, or impassioned wanna-bes with the arrogance to match, all are in awe of their fearless role model who is now viewed as a martyr and saint that anyone else could only dream to mimic.

The challenge now that Jobs is no longer alive, is can this CULTure survive and continue to thrive without its idolized deity? Leave it to Jobs to have considered this and anticipated what needed to be done. The Human Resources function was not an area that Jobs found interesting. During his second medical leave, he hired Joel Podolny, Dean of Yale University, to head Apple University. A widely renowned management guru, Podolny disappeared for two years, and then was resurfaced and was named VP of HR. He was joined by other crème de la crème from academia, hired to write internal case studies on all critical decisions made at Apple. These case studies would be for Apple employees' eyes only for the day when Jobs was no longer going to be around.

Dissension among its worker bees, however, was evident when, in 2011, amidst Jobs second leave of absence, in conjunction with the Apple Store's 10th Anniversary week, store employees were campaigning to unionize for better compensation and benefits, further reinforcing that Apples to Apples were not considered equal. While big bucks were being paid to corporate innovators and developers, barely minimum wage was being paid to its retail employees. Employees with years of service learned they were being paid less than those who were recently hired. During one-on-one meetings with management, longer tenured employees asked about pay disparities, only to receive a response of "money shouldn't be an issue when employed at Apple." The privilege of working at Apple was to be coveted with the threat that many others were waiting in line and, therefore, the job should be appreciated for the experience. Basically, they were expendable.

Apple defined retail employees working 40 hours a week as part-time, so benefits were limited. Most employees had to work other jobs to make ends meet, and even the part-time healthcare plans couldn't be afforded. Interestingly, after the national publicity of the union campaign, the effort appeared to be squelched. However, union rumblings in other function areas appeared to be occurring when, six months later, Apple required all managers in that function area to attend a mandatory "union awareness" training session. Time will tell as more and more retail workers as a whole are seeking union protection and advocacy for better working conditions as the primary complaint over better pay.

Where's the Mission?

In most Mercenary Culture companies, there is a cry from the top that is demanding, "Where's the Money?" Since Jobs is no longer at the helm, the cry is coming from the bottom up imploring "Where's the Mission?" The purpose that everyone believed they knew to be true was the internally stealth glue that kept Apple's employees driven against angst, hierarchy and threats of termination by its revered and coveted leader.

Jobs acknowledged his autocratic ways, but insisted he was not the only person who could wield the same power for the company. He described Apple as a complex, multi-cellular organism, not a single cell organism. As Doris Burke described in a May 2011, Fortune Magazine article, "Apple may be a multi-cellular organism, but its life source was Jobs."

With Apple University's primary charge to ensure that his management style of attention to detail, secrecy, process for innovation, and constant feedback would live on beyond him at Apple, the jury is still out as to how effective this has been captured. While Jobs focused his remaining days institutionalizing his way of doing business, it is unclear how far his appointees actually got in recording his practices and beliefs. After all, it is shrouded in secrecy. And secondly, Jobs was one of a kind. His eccentric genius was beyond what could be bottled, processed, systemized, or replicated.

Jobs was larger than life. He was idolized, and feared if he was disappointed. Considered a divine being on many levels, he has been metaphorically compared to Jesus Christ, Moses, Prometheus, and Zeus.

❖

For the culture to carry on Jobs legacy, it would require almost Bible-like teachings to have been collected, curated and preserved for future Apple generations. As Burke concluded in that same Fortune article, "… that is all a savior could possibly ask for." The question is, has it been done and, more importantly, is Apple's current CEO effectively shepherding the Jobs legacy into Apple's future?

CHAPTER 29

Microsoft
Force to Fragmented

A software engineer exits his annual review befuddled, feeling berated and undervalued. First, he learns that he has been ranked at the bottom of his team from a performance standpoint in comparison to peers within his department. He knew he had been a valuable contributor to projects and a dedicated worker, and could defend this, at least he thought he could. Then, he is informed that he is fired as a result of his unacceptable low score. He wasn't the only employee frustrated and shaken. There would always be a percentage of employees deemed sub-standard because of a stack ranking program dictated to management as a means of reviewing and rating their team members. Every department across the company would always have top performers, good performers, mediocre performers, and poor performers designated by its management, regardless of how the overall team performed as a whole within the company or the specific contributions that were made. The environment was a feeding frenzy of back stabbing and worker pitted against worker, focused on jockeying his or her position to ultimately be ranked higher when review-time grew near. Those who were ranked in the good to mediocre ratings would be kept on board. However, the discussions between managers and these employees would focus on a need to improve their visibility among other managers to gain a more favorable ranking. Providing insight on how to improve and perform better within their specific job function was not the focus.

The idea of stack ranking is nothing new in Corporate America. In my opinion, it is a performance rating system that has never served companies well. In the case of Microsoft, it resulted in a Mercenary competitiveness that Fragmented the organization as a whole instead of stimulating healthy competition among co-workers. When you reduce an employee to being a statistic of any kind, you are effectively kicking credibility and commitment to the curb. You are also kicking engagement and any morsel of teamwork in the gut.

Microsoft wasn't always so Fragmented. Mercenary, yes, but its fragmentation has been the result of dysfunction that began to show its weaknesses in the mid 1990s. When established by co-founders Bill Gates and Paul Allen in 1975, Micro-soft (yes, the hyphen was part of the name in its beginning) was a partnership between two impassioned and idealistic techno-geeks who saw something no one else could see – the revolution of personal computing.

The company grew from three employees and $16,000 in income to 40 employees and $7.5 million in sales in five years. By 1990, the company had grown to $1.1 billion and 5,635 employees. Its focus on products and bottom-line performance dictated an emphasis on profits and sales from the very beginning. As the company grew beyond its co-founders, the internal dynamic was more competitive than the external dynamic. Long hours and employees competing for attention and privilege helped the company realize year-over-year sales growth in the Mercenary Mercenary sub-quadrant. Continuing forward into the late 90's and 2000's, it was evident that products performing for the bottom line superseded products being designed to perform as intended for users. After all, updates can fix any problem. As a consumer, you know this all too well. At times what seemed like a daily deluge of updates and patches would take over your computer to fix, protect, and sometimes enhance. Our dependency upon Microsoft, due to its brilliance in its earlier years, became a love-hate relationship among customers, was disenchanted by features that were valued going missing with newer versions, and the necessity to sometimes learn the program all over again, or at least it felt that way.

The morale among employees took its toll, according to several sources studied, beginning in the 1990s. First in 1988, long-time customer, Apple, filed a copyright infringement claim against the resulting applications from a Microsoft and Hewlett Packard joint collaboration. It wasn't until 1993 that the case was dismissed, but the 63–month battle impacted the company as one of a series of distractions that would play out more extensively as time wore on. Named the Fortune's Most Innovative Company Operating in the U.S. in 1993, Microsoft's successful win over

Apple appeared to be a minor distraction in their dominance as a technology innovator.

However, employees were being sent mixed messages during the Apple litigation. When Michael Hallman stepped down as President and COO in 1992, a replacement was not named. Previous Presidents had not fared well in the role previously. Instead, the Office of President was filled jointly by three Executive Vice Presidents: Steve Ballmer, Frances Gaudette, and Mike Maples. With all three reporting to Gates as Chairman of the Board, in my opinion, it was telling the then 11,000 plus workers that there was a lack of confidence in leadership by its visionary founder. This organization of leadership continued through the end of 1996.

In 1994, Microsoft's attempt to merge with Intuit fell through. Then in 1995, the U.S. Court of Appeals reinstated the anti-trust settlement between Microsoft and the U.S. Justice Department. Microsoft had been under investigation by the Federal Trade Commission beginning in 1991, but the commissioners deadlocked and closed the investigation. Then the Department of Justice opened its own investigation, ultimately reaching a settlement with Microsoft that dragged on until a final judgment in 2002. Impassioned workaholics who had signed-up for and openly embraced the Mercenary culture of dog-eat-dog to realize achievement and financial gain had lost its allure. Their pride of being a part of a company that seemed to be the almighty ruler in the technology arena was being challenged and was losing its king-of-the-hill status. The settlement brought to bear the reality that competition from the outside needed to be more of a focus than competing on the inside.

However, the real issue from a corporate culture perspective was a lack of clear leadership, and the appearance of a lack of confidence by Gates himself in naming a president. In 1996, instead of a president being named, the Office of President was reorganized into an Executive Committee that had grown to eight executives reporting to Gates. Yes, the company was continuing to grow and increase sales year-over-year, but the passion that had prevailed in the early years continued to diminish at the employee level.

In 1998, Ballmer was appointed President, with Gates remaining as Chairman of the Board and CEO, working more closely with development teams. While this would appear to have offered the company's morale an overall confidence boost, Ballmer's finance focus was at the forefront of every decision being made, including protecting the "cash cows" of Windows and Office at the detriment of innovation in other areas. Additionally, there continued to be unrest at the top, with Ballmer being shifted to CEO in 2000. A president was named, but resigned in less then two years, while Gates added to his role, Chief Software Architect, again showing signs of disheveled and dysfunctional leadership.

The Bill and Melinda Gates Foundation, established in 1997, reinforces a Communal aspect of Microsoft beginning to surface more prominently. Coincidently, this also was the year that Microsoft was named the Most Admired Company by a consumer voluntary voting poll conducted by Pollsters Hart and Teeter. While Microsoft had a giving program in place beginning in 1983 that was encouraging employee-giving, it was not emphasized as much until its more recent years and after the Foundation was established. However, concerns were raised that the Foundation was becoming more of Gates' passion than Microsoft. Under Ballmer's leadership as CEO, while the company continued to impressively grow in sales, profits and employee girth, the company's market value plummeted from an all-time high of $520 billion in 2000 to a market cap value of $249 billion in 2012. In comparison to the same 10-year period, Apple's market value had grown to $541 billion, when it wasn't even recognized on the list in 2000.

While Windows and Office advancements continued to build impressive cash flow, other innovations were hit or miss, or squelched in favor of a continuing focus on its core applications. A New York Times article published in 2009 provided insight as to "Why Microsoft no longer brings us the future." According to the article, "greed and its monopolistic ways had caught up with the giant." The continual advancement of the Internet, smart devices and digital technology, was being embraced by other companies more effectively than Microsoft. The company was making money, while losing market share in areas such as web browsers, high end laptops, and smart phones.

Stack ranking was becoming more of a demoralizing issue and, in spite of continued sales growth and profit, salaries to employees were stagnant or only slightly nudged upward. Talented engineers were being courted away by Google and Yahoo. Microsoft was no longer the cool, cutting-edge place to work given many of its best talent exiting the company. According to the New York Times article by Dick Brass, who had been a former vice president at Microsoft from 1997 to 2004, "Microsoft has created a dysfunctional corporate culture in which the big established groups are allowed to prey upon emerging teams, belittle their efforts, compete unfairly against them for resources, and over time hector them out of existence." It is no surprise then that over a decade, executives overseeing eBooks, phone, music, online search, and tablet efforts left the company.

By 2010, from the outside looking in and the inside looking out, Microsoft appeared to have lost its way and was no longer the admired, revered company. Media coverage was more focused on what appeared to be going wrong under Ballmer's leadership, and employees openly sharing their discontent, with an approval rating of the CEO at that time of 51 percent. There was no correlation, in the minds of employees, between hard work, compensation and rewards. There were no longer dedicated legions of workers staying late into the night with sleeping bags on floors, but a mass exodus at 5 p.m. Access to the executive suite was viewed as being surrounded by a moat with management tucked away in a castle and inaccessible, as employees continued to battle among themselves due to the review process that was in place.

When Microsoft announced that it would not be an exhibitor in the 2013 International Electronics Show to showcase any innovation, despite claims of the timing being wrong for the company, the underlying consensus was that Microsoft was being led further astray. While Ballmer was continually being blamed for Microsoft's fall from grace as a technology leader, the real culprit was a total lack of understanding and regard by its founder and its overall leadership about how a corporate culture impacts a company. The only time there was any emphasis in the area on human resources and employee relations was in relation to the stack ranking review process unfairness. In spite of this being an area of contention for employees, it took decades for the company to finally eliminate the practice.

However, there is a silver lining to this study of Microsoft's corporate culture that is encouraging and proving that paying attention to employee Sociability and Engagement along with Performance really does matter. There are many positive signs that Microsoft is evolving out of its dysfunctional funk into a more communally-driven organization. This was first reflected in numerous awards the firm has gained in everything from being a best place to work and ethical company to sustainability, green initiatives, diversity, and corporate responsibility since 2012. In 2013, its #4 ranking as among the World's Best Multinational Companies (Top 100) to work for by Great Place to Work® Institute, taking the #1 Great Place to Work position in Europe, and CareerBliss.com's #9 ranking of Microsoft as among the Top 10 Companies Doing the Most to Make Their Employees Happy, further supports that there is a valiant effort being made to change the dynamics of the company's culture for the better.

Another sign of a more Communal Culture being emphasized is the fact that Microsoft eliminated its ranking system of individual performance measurement in late 2013. According to a reported memo from Microsoft's HR chief, the reason for the elimination of the program was to bring greater emphasis on teamwork, collaboration, employee growth, and development. Additionally, Microsoft released its findings of Best Practices for Innovation in June of 2013. What became glaringly clear in this report was the importance of engagement as a critical success factor in the innovation process. This included creating an environment where people are encouraged to participate with incentives and rewards for participation. Transparency was also identified as a recommendation for making ideas visible and accessible so that other thought leaders can contribute, as well as allowing people to link or combine ideas. Even though Google and Facebook were not a part of the best practices consortium, this has been par for their course when it comes to innovation.

In early 2014, Microsoft and Facebook conducted a joint hackathon event at Facebook's Menlo Park location focused on its phone applications. This wasn't the first time the two had hacked together. In late 2012, they conducted a joint hack fest concentrating on Window 8. Who knows? Perhaps the blossoming strategic partnership is just what both companies need to push them into the Communal realm with Google. Facebook already has their toe in the Communal water. It's Microsoft that has some work to do to make up for numerous lost opportunities, but the fact that they recognize they can still learn a thing or two from others gives me hope that its Fragmented days are soon going to be behind them.

Probably the greatest indicator that the company can enter the realm of Mercenary Communal and perhaps even Communal Mercenary is the result of the selection of Sataya Nadella as its new CEO. Described as a more inclusive and collaborative leader, Nadella is viewed as a sincere, honest human being who is calm under pressure. With the technological and business genius that matches Microsoft's founder, he is re-energizing the company's brain trust of talent. His management style inspires people while pushing team members out of their comfort zones. Nadella was also described as being thoughtful and considerate, while also being calculating, with an ability "to connect with people and understand the impact something might have," not just from a product perspective, but from a people perspective, including developers and users.

When 30-year Microsoft veteran Steve Ballmer announced his retirement, stock shares soared 7 percent. Within 30 days of Nadella being in office, the stock price rose another 11 percent. Even more all telling is the confidence factor of Microsoft employees. At the end of his reign, Ballmer's approval rating among employees on Glassdoor was a dismal 47 percent. In just two months, the CEO approval rating jumped to 82 percent for Nadella. According to Glassdoor, if this is maintained, it would launch Microsoft into the top 50 best rated CEOs. While there is a bit of catching-up to do to reach the 90th percentile that Apple's Tim Cook, Facebook's Mark Zuckerberg, and Google's Larry Page enjoy, there is reason to have hope once again in Microsoft.

❖

Perhaps these efforts indicate that the days of "stack ranking" the deck of success against its own employees has been conscientiously replaced by stacking the opportunities for growth, innovation, and overall employee and customer satisfaction in the company's favor. I am most interested in watching Microsoft's cap market value increase as it gets its corporate culture in order. I have no doubts that it will, if it continues on its corporate culture correction course.

Conclusion
A Case for Enduring Value

Of particular interest when preparing the comparisons of the four companies for the white paper is the comparison of the companies from a price-per-share stock value. When we began to write the white paper and present some of our preliminary conclusions in presentations during beta testing, we were focusing on endurance from the standpoint of longevity of the company as a whole, which is still our primary assertion related to the positive effect of high sociability and high performance combined with high engagement.

However, when reviewing the historical record of the stock performance of each company, it compelled us to form another hypothesis related to the enduring value of a company in association with its ability to endure over time. Our white paper, "A Tale of Four Cultures: The Link Between Corporate Culture and Enduring Value" concluded with the proposal that there could be a direct correlation between building a company of endurance, specifically in the Communal Corporate Culture quadrant, and the company's return on investment and market value.

For basis of reference, consider the following statistics of the four companies from their Initial Public Offering (IPO) to year-end 2013. The year in parenthesis is the year of the Initial Public Offering for each company, not the year in which the company was founded.

COMPANY	IPO Share Price	Per Share +Five Years	Per Share 12/31/13	All Time Low	All Time High
Microsoft (1986)	$28	$100	$37	$19 (1998, 2008)	$116 ($58 split adj. -1999)
Facebook (2012)	$38	n/a	$54	$18 (2012)	58 (2013)
Apple (1984)	$26	$44	$561	$13 (1997)	$648 (2012)
Google (2004)	$86	$443	$1,120	$100 (2004)	$1,120 (2013)

With Google being identified to operate with characteristics of a Communal Culture in the Communal Communal sub-quadrant and Apple being identified to operate with the characteristics of a Mercenary Culture in the Mercenary Communal sub-quadrant, the impact of the Communal

Culture influences are a common factor in both companies. Most interesting, however, is that Google's stock price per share has never dipped below its initial offering closing price, which cannot be claimed by the other three companies. Could corporate culture be an indicator for stock performance?

❖

The idea that corporate culture could be an indicator of stock performance is fascinating. Our research team is now studying other publicly traded companies that can be classified with a corporate culture dominant in the Communal quadrant. The bottom line for now is irrefutable, in our opinion. The more Communal your culture, the more enduring the company and the more endearing it is.

As for enduring value, stay tuned. The premise that a company's corporate culture could predict its marketplace value is an exciting prospect. My research team and I look forward to seeing just how plausible this theory might be.

The CURx^2 Assessment

When I began writing this book in 2012, my corporate culture research team came to me with an exciting idea. The impetus for developing the assessment was inspired by the S&P 500 statistic we uncovered, which is shared in Chapter 21 on Building Endurance. We thought to ourselves, "What if we took all this research and developed an assessment tool to gauge corporate culture disparity and perceptions and then help an organization define and align its culture?" That "what if" turned into a "Heck yes!" and we embarked on a higher level of intense R&D to develop the assessment tool.

Head researchers, Sherre' DeMao and J. Kevin Toomb Ph.D. co-designed the assessment with the following objectives in mind: 1) gauge perception versus reality of a company's corporate culture; 2) gauge alignment among management and team members, 3) define the actual state of the existing culture in the company, 4) confirm the desired culture and ability to achieve; and 5) provide success factors for shifting and/or embracing the desired culture for effective leadership development and strategic focus. The assessment was branded as CURx^2 in Spring of 2013, and actually resulted in me changing the working title of this book to its current title of Corporate Cure.

Ready for its first beta test in July 2013, I used one of my Owens Management clients to kick off the beta testing. CURx^2 was then successfully beta tested on other companies from summer 2012 through fall of 2013. The countless "Aha's" realized throughout the beta testing was invigorating. Our assessment focused on small to mid-market sized companies in order to be manageable, and we tested it in a multitude of ways to define the scope and variable ways the assessment could be used as a business-building management tool. CURx^2 has been as exciting of a journey as defining the best practices of corporate cultures that work has been. With each beta testing, we found numerous applications for how the assessment could be used on both a micro and macro level.

CURx^2 PULSE: We branded this "Pulse" because it is literally taking a pulse on CEOs of companies to gauge how they perceive and have actualized their company's corporate culture from their perspective. This assessment is an individual assessment which then provides the Top 5 Positive Indicators for Success and the Top 5 Negative Indicators that could be derailing or are counter to the CEO's desired corporate culture. It allows the CEO to understand any gaps from what they think is the culture versus what is actually the culture, based on how they completed the assessment. A Pulse can also be taken with each of the executive-level team members to show variables of the indicators from one executive to another.

CURx^2 CONNECT: This assessment process is conducted with all leadership team members at the executive level and middle management level to gauge alignment and potential challenges to leading and managing within the desired culture.   We even included in some of our beta testing of larger organizations team leaders and project managers as a third tier of managers to confirm alignment with upper and mid-level management. You can see some of the results shared from this process in Chapter 18.

CURx^2 COMPLETE: This assessment process involves every team member within the company from top-level executives to entry-level employees. The assessment analysis compares management alignment to employee alignment from a perceived, actual and desired corporate culture standpoint. The comprehensive analysis and recommendations report that accompanies this assessment is why this phase is called "Complete."

- Confirm perception versus reality of a company's corporate culture.

- Confirm gap between desired corporate culture and current corporate culture.

- Confirms if leadership is aligned in practicing desired corporate culture.

- Confirms departmental alignment with desired corporate culture.

- Confirms critical issues affecting performance and teamwork.

- Confirms discrepancies in what is practiced versus what is preached.

- Confirms employees' perception of management.

- Confirms management's perception of employees.

- Provides answers and action steps to effectively align to desired corporate culture.

CURx^2 PLAYBOOK: This workbook is used in the facilitation process throughout the assessment phase and then, based on results, helps management transition into the implementation and alignment action phases towards achieving the desired culture.

As this book goes into pre-publication, our beta testing confirmed other complementary assessments and products to enhance the CURx^2 culture-building program. These were determined based on what companies requested as a next phase of awareness of corporate culture enhancement and sustainability.

CURx^2 360: This assessment involves both internal and external stakeholders taking the assessment including vendors/suppliers, board of director members, a select group of customers, and potential community or industry contacts. Each assessment is designed according to the specific segment audience.

CURx^2 HIRE: This assessment helps gauge a prospective employee's likelihood in fitting within the company's corporate culture. It's primary focus will be to confirm what is the individual's preference from a values and working environment standpoint.

The possibilities are truly endless to what will be added beyond the above cited assessments, programs and products.

For more information, go to www.owensmanagement.com.

About the Author

John Owens is a serial entrepreneur as CEO of Ameritrust Wealth Management, Showcase Baseball Academy, and Owens Management Group. His passion for the critical success factor that corporate culture plays in a company's survival has become his mission to share with and educate other CEOs. His belief that corporate culture is at the core of a company's potential to thrive was born out of his own experience in building his Ameritrust Mortgage, Insurance and Wealth Management companies amidst turmoil, market unrest and unethical industry practices.

Established in 1995, Ameritrust began as a mortgage lender. Ameritrust Insurance was incorporated in 2004, and then Ameritrust Wealth Management was incorporated in 2010. Through Owens' leadership, his companies received numerous awards including INC 500 Fastest Growing Companies (two consecutive years – 2005, 2006), Ernst & Young finalist for Entrepreneur of the Year, Parent Magazine's Top 40 companies for three consecutive years , and Charlotte Business Journal's Best Places to Work.

Experiencing first-hand the roller-coaster ride of his Ameritrust companies growing, failing, and then growing again, Owens embarked on a passionate pursuit to document the secrets to enduring success regardless of what a marketplace or the economy brings. Believing in his gut and heart that corporate culture was at the core of building a company of endurance, he began his own journey of discovery in 2000, with corporate culture being his unwavering focus. His insistence on honoring corporate culture above all else is why he believes he was able to protect and nurture the Ameritrust brand, while companies all around him either imploded or lost consumer and marketplace confidence amidst the Great Recession the country experienced beginning in 2007. In 2013, he successfully sold

Ameritrust Mortgage and Ameritrust Insurance, retaining the Ameritrust brand for his wealth management company.

Owens' vision and integrity tied to corporate culture have been pivotal to achieving success in multiple enterprises. His successes resulted in demand as a management consultant to other CEOs, resulting in Owens Management being established in 2009. He brought on a research team to validate the best practices around corporate culture in 2012. The end result was the development of a corporate culture assessment tool and teambuilding program, CURx^2, which was successfully beta tested and officially introduced in 2013.

If you ask Owens what attributes to the phenomenal growth of Showcase Baseball Academy, he will proudly proclaim that it was its corporate culture being its foundation from its inception. His love of baseball began as a child, but parlayed into a baseball career as a college team pitcher for Palm Beach before he transferred to take the mound for University of North Carolina at Charlotte. In 2002, Owens started the Charlotte Hurricanes Baseball Organization (now SBA CANES) with the dream of exposing a select group of players to the best competition in the nation, while teaching an advanced level of play. The organization grew to 30 teams competing nationally in every age group. In 2010, Owens decided to take his vision to another level by opening Showcase Baseball Academy, where athletes can develop their leadership, life and athletic skills in order to "showcase" their talents to best serve their TEAM on the field and later, in the workforce.

Owens attended UNC Charlotte and graduated with a BS in Economics. In spite of juggling the responsibilities of being CEO of multiple thriving companies, he makes his family a priority – enjoying quality time with his wife, Stacey, and their three children, Alexa, Nicklaus and Jack.

Acknowledgements

As any CEO knows, or any person for that matter, we are not in this life alone. Our triumphs, our ability to overcome challenges, or reasons to celebrate and give thanks are always because of the people we surround ourselves with or who bless us with their unwavering support, belief, abilities or friendship. This book and the successes I have had the privilege and pleasure to enjoy would not have been possible without these people.

Stacy Owens, my wife and lifelong partner: For giving me the support and confidence to "go for it."

Mike Whitehead (Center for Intentional Leadership): For bringing out my "intentional" and authentic leadership style.

Carol Gray and Bob Morgan (Charlotte Chamber of Commerce): For helping me connect with the Charlotte Chamber and community

Judy Rose (Athletic Director for UNCC): For demonstrating to me how "family" was important to her culture, and should be in everyone's culture.

Mac Everette (Community Leader / Wells Fargo Championship): For helping inspire "class" into my leadership style.

Frank Kowar (Bank of America Exec and teammate): For helping keep me "grounded" as a leader. He was always there to listen when I needed to talk.

Jim Mitchell and Chris Coram (Former HSBC executives): For being true partners with Ameritrust, believing in and supporting our culture and integrity-based decisions.

Gloria Richardson, Jim Acuff, Kathy Taylor, Tim Hilton, Glen Holden, and April Williams (Executive Leadership Team, Former Ameritrust Mortgage): For embracing and supporting the Greatest Culture evolution and then living it, working it and being it.

Joe Badgett, Eric Tillman, Ted Wilson, Jessica Cook , Courtney Martin, Erin Zelch (Former Ameritrust Employees): For having my back and refusing to throw in the towel.

Sherre' DeMao (GreenCastle Publishing/SLD Unlimited Biz Growth Inc.): For giving me the courage and confidence to tell my story. For guiding me through this process and making it happen. For partnering with our CURx[2] assessment and helping me build companies with endurance.

J. Kevin Toomb Ph.D. (Former Director of Entrepreneurship Certificate Program at UNC Charlotte): For being such a pivotal part of my research and assessment development team, and connecting me to resources instrumental in the publication of this book.

Rob Goffee and Garrett Jones (Authors of *The Character of a Corporation*): For introducing the Communal Culture through your brilliant two-dimensional model, which inspired me to evolve it into a three-dimensional corporate culture model that is changing the way companies are approaching building businesses of endurance.

Joshua Bredeman, Alexis Brethauer, Tyler Broadnax, Jasmine Davis, Rebecca Knapp, Brittany Moffitt, Katherine Newman, Laura Schaffer, and Zachary Shrader (Interns from UNC Charlotte), Robin Salmi (Intern from Belmont Abbey), and Alison Thomas (Intern from Eastern Carolina University): For being instrumental in our primary and secondary research and assessment beta testing efforts.

Bibliography

General References

10 most ethical COEs in corporate America. (2012, March 28). www.onlinemba.com.

Berfield, S. (2006, December 17). The best and worst leaders of 2006. www.Businessweek.com.

Bradford, H. (2011, May 25). Ten companies with the best reputation in America: Harris interactive. www.Huffingtonpost.com.

Bragg, S. (2013, April 04). HF survey suggest insider trading here to stay. www.integrity-research.com.

Bresslour, M. (2013, July 29). Appreciation in the workplace, wins. www.Switchandshift.com.

Campbell, A., Whitehead, J., & Finkelstein, S. (2009, February). Why good leaders make bad decisions. www.Harvardbusinessreview.org.

Coddington, R. (2007, July 30). 25 most influential business leaders. www.UsaToday.com.

Deragon, J. (2012, September 10). Suddenly corporate culture matters. www.Relationship-economy.com.

Farfan, B. (2013, October 22). 2013 retail brands with best reputation-customer survey, ratings and rankings. www.About.com.

Feeley, J. (2012, October 09). Revlon to pay 9.2 million to settle share-exchange suits. www.Bloomberg.com.

George, B. (2011, June 10). Why talented leaders are driven by bad behavior. www.BusinessInsider.com

Goffee, R. & Jones, G. (1998). The character of a corporation: How your company's culture can make or break your business. New York, NY: Harper-Collins Publisher.

Head, S. (2014, April 06). Goldman Sachs' sick con: How they made money off your misery. www.salon.com.

Highest rated CEO's 2014. (2014, January 31). www.glassdoor.com.

Kotter, J.P., & Heskett, J.L. (1992). Corporate culture and performance. New York, NY: The Fresh Press.

Lenzner, R. (2008, December 12). Bernie Madoff's $50 billion ponzi scam. www.Forbes.com.

Lipman, V. (2012, December 14). Study explores drivers of employee engagement. www.Forbes.com.

McIntyre, D. & Calio, V. (2014, April 04). Nine CEO's with the worst reputation. 247wallstreet.com.

Newport, F. (2012, August 16). Americans rate computer industry best, oil and gas worst. www.Gallop.com.

Ranker.com. Companies with the worst reputations. (n/a). www.ranker.com.

Rose, Kevin. Exclusive first read: Young money. (2014, February 11). www.NPR.org.

Sauter, M., Hess, A., & Weigley, S. (2013, March 05). Companies with the best and worst reputations. www.247wallst.com.

Smith, J. (2013, July 25). How to deal with cliques at work. www.Forbes.com.

Stemple, J. (2013, June 06). Perelman company reaches another settlement with company. www.4-traders.com.

Team Editorial, Top five worst business leaders of 2012. (2012, December 27). www.Leadership-idn.com.

The mortgage lender implode-o-meter. (2007, January 01). www.ml-implode.com.

Welch, Jack. Excerpt, The Welch Way. Twelve lessons from Jack Welch's leadership style. (n/a). www.vietnamworks.com.

WorldatWork. (2013, June). Trends in employee recognition. ITA Group. 1-29

Amazon References

Gerard, J. (2010, July 06). Best practice in corporate culture: Zappos. I-Sight.

Harris, D. (2013, November 18). The secret to Amazon's cloud success might be Jeff Bezo's corporate culture. www.Gigaom.com.

Huang, G. (2010, February 25). How Amazon innovates: Lessons in strategy for Microsoft and others. www.Xconomy.com.

Jackson, L. (2012, May 02). How to develop a successful corporate culture formula. www.Corporateculturepros.com.

Machado, S. (2013, March 23). Amazon's culture: How to shape an enduring organizational culture. Stephen Blandino.

Stone, B. (2013, October 15). Why is it so difficult to climb Amazon's corporate ladder. www.Bloomberg Businessweek.com. Bibliography Heading

American Express References

American Express CEO Kenneth Chenault: Valuing EQ over IQ. (2013, November 08). www.Wharton
University.com.

Bulygo , Z. (n/a). Business lessons from American Express CEO, Ken Chenault. Kissmetrics.com.

Kavoussi, B. (2012, December 18). Kenneth Chenault, AmEx CEO, approached by White House about treasury secretary job: Report. www.huffingtonpost.com.

Kenneth Chenault: Chairman and CEO of American Express. (2013, March 13). www.Observer25.com.

Mendonca, J. (2013, January 10). American Express cut 5,400 jobs, take charges in fourth quarter. www.CEO.com.

Tseng, N. (2011, December 06). American Express CEO: Pay attention to OWS. www.CNNMoney.com.

Apple References

A look back at the early days of Apple. (2013, August 29).
    www.Finansure.net.

Blodget, H. (2013, August 03). Apples "mission statement" is making
    people worry that the company has gone to hell.
    www.BusinessInsider.com.

Buckley, S. (2012, August 04). Apple execs talk about the iPhone early
    days, the secrecy of "product purple" www.Engadget.com.

Burrows, P. (2011, October 12). Working with Steve Jobs.
    www.BloombergBusinessWeek.com.

Confessions of an Apple employee. (2012, December 21).
    www.Popularmechanics.com.

Dennings, S. (2012, June 25). Apple employees have a hell of a ride. Forbes
    Magazine.

Devine, R. (2013, January 17). Google tops the Fortune 100 best companies
    to work for, Apple doesn't even place. Android central.

Eidleson, J. (2011, June 24). Apple store workers share why they want to
    'Work different.' Working in these times.

Faas, R. (2012, May 01). Are people who work at Apple actually happy?
    www.CultofMac.com.

Farfan, B. (2011, June 29). Union activity in the retail industry is a
    significant trend: Biggest issues motivating retail employees in
    unionization efforts are not pay or work conditions. www.About.com.

Fiegerman, S. (2012, June 14). The biggest complaint employees have
    about working at Apple. www.Business Insider.com.

Fiegerman, S. (2012, June 18). Here's what employees really think about
    working for Apple. www.Business Insider.com.

Finansure. Allsop, A. (2012, April 14). Steve Wozniak speaks of Apples
    early days. www.PCWorld.com .

Gibson, B. (2004, December 12). Apple employee spouses protest long
    work hours. www.Macobserver.com.

Hafner, K. (2005, April 30). Steve Jobs reviews his biography: Ban it.
    www.TheNewYorkTimes.com.

Jobs, S. (2011). Apple worldwide developers conference at the Moscone
    center. Online Video.

Lashinsky, A. (2012, February 06). From inside Apple. Fortune Magazine. P
    86-94.

Lashinsky, A. (2011, August 25). How Apple works: Inside the world's
    biggest startup. www.CNNMoney.com.

Lowensohn, J. (2011, November 07). Apple to train managers on "union
    awareness". www.CNet.com.

Macworld Staff. (2011, October 05). Remembering Steve Jobs, the man
    who saved Apple. MacWorld.

Markoff, J. (1993, April 25). Where the cubicle is dead.
    www.TheNewYorkTimes.com.

Moll, C. (2006, February 21). Why I passed up the chance to work at Apple. Authentic Boredom.

O'Grady, J. (2011, February 07). Working at Apple vs. Working at Google. The Apple Core.

Siegal, D. (2012, June 23). Apple stores army, long on loyalty but short on pay. The New York Times

Spiegeiman, P. (2012, December 13). Tim Cooks's attention to culture will grow Apple even more. www.INC. com.

Stern, J. (2012, February 15). Apple CEO promises monthly updates on working conditions. www.ABCNews. com.

Steve Jobs and the early years of Apple. (2013, June 16). I-Programmer.

TheOLigarch.com. A Short History of the GUI and the Microsoft vs Apple Debate. (2013,November). www.TheOligarch.com.

Bank of America References

Ackerman, D. (2001, January 24). Forbes face: Hugh McColl Jr.. www.Forbes.com.

Bank of America chairman and CEO, Hugh L. McColl to retire in April: Board names Lewis successor. (2001, January 24). www.Bankofamerica.com.

Bank of America CEO: Feds pressured bank to buy Merrill Lynch. (2009, June 11). www.FoxNews.com.

Henning, P. & Davidoff, S. (2012, September 28). For Bank of America, more trouble from Merrill Lynch merger. www.TheNewYorkTimes.com.

Malik, S. (2013, August 23). Bank of America reviews long-hours culture after intern's death. TheGuardian.com.

Chic-fil-A References

BAronoff, C. (2011, February 07). Chic-fil-A controversy gives insight to family owned business's powerful culture. Family business wisdom, thought and education.

Buchanan, P. (2012, August 03). On the Chic-fil-A front of the culture war. www.YahooNews.com. 2014

Cathy, Dan and Cathy, Truett. Are customers hungry for old fashioned values in today's quick-service restaurant era? (2002, November 20). Strategic Management.

Satler, C. (n/a). Chic-fil-A's recipe for customer service. www.FastCompany.com.

Waldmen, M. (2012, December 29). Dan Cathy's bag of leadership. www.TerrycollegeofBusiness.com.

Costco References

Byrnes, B. (2013, August 21). Costco Co-Founder: Culture is not the most important thing—it's the only thing. The Motley Fool.

Cardenal, A. (2013, November 30). Why Costco will manage to outgrow Wal-Mart and Target. www.Fool.com.

Gerard, J. (2010, March 25). Employee relations best practices: Costco's approach to HR. I-Sight.

Lewis, L. (2010, July). Talking Turnover. Nfrstores.com.

O'Toole, J. (2009, October). Connecting the dots between leadership, ethics and corporate culture. IveyBusinessJournal.com.

Stone, B. (2013, June 06). Costco CEO Craig Jelinek leads the cheapest, happiest company in the world. www.Businessweek.com.

Weinmann, K. (2011, December 27). What Costco CEO James Sinegal can teach you about management. www.AmericanExpress.com.
Bibliography Heading

Daimler References

Daimler- Chrysler merger: a cultural mismatch? (2001). Icmrindia.org.

Daimler, Chrysler and the failed merger. (2010, January 08). Casestudy.com.

How culture ended at Daimler-Benz Chrysler merger. (n/a). www.kwintessential.co.uk.

Facebook References

Array (2013, January 05). Confessions of a Facebook employee: What it's really like working for Zuckerberg.   www.BusinessInsider.com.

Boorstin, J. (2012, October 01). Where Facebook is looking to grow: COO Sheryl Sandberg. www.CNBC.com.

Burke, D. (2011, May 23). Apple doesn't often fail. Fortune magazine. P 126- 134.

Drell, L. (2011, October 17). The perks of working at Google, Facebook, Twitter and more. www.Mashable.com.

Gallagher, R. (2010, March 28). Want a free lunch? Work for Facebook. www.NPR.org.

Grandoni, D. (2012, December 12). Facebook rated best place to work in Glassdoor's 2012 survey. www.HuffingtonPost.com.

Guynn, J. (2012, April 11). Facebook's Sheryl Sandberg has a talent for making friends. Los Angeles Times.

Helft, M. (2013, October 10). Sheryl Sandberg, the real story. www.CNNMoney.com.

James, G. (2013, May 15). Sheryl Sandberg: is she the real brain of Facebook. www.INC.com.

Jana, R. (2013, March 07). Inside Facebook's internal innovation culture. Harvard business review blog network.

Keating, C. (2012, March 19). Inside Facebook. Fortune magazine. 114-122.

Kim, S., Stuart, E. & Vargas, E. (2013, March 12). The best advice Sheryl Sandberg received. www.ABCNews. com.

Leopold, T. (2013, March 11). Facebook's Sheryl Sandberg suddenly in crossfire. www.CNNTech.com.

Miller, A. & Carlson N. (2009, December 14). What is it like working at Facebook? www.BusinessInsider.com.

Roberts, Y. (2013, March 16). Is Facebook's Sherly Sandberg really the new face of feminism? The Observer. 14.

Smith, C. (2011, July 04). Facebook COO Sheryl Sandberg: "I feel guilty working because of my kids." www. HuffingtonPostcom.com.

Smith, K. (2013, April 18). This is what life is actually like working at Facebook. www.BusinessInsider.com.

Stillman, J. (2012, April 09). Sheryl Sandberg leaves work at 5:30. Why can't you? www.INC.com.

Su, P. (2012, August 15). Ten things I hate about working at Facebook. The world as best as I remember it.

Vance, A., Satariano, A., & Bass, D. (2012, May). Bloomberg Businessweek. 62-67.

Vickery, J. (2013, February 17). Facebook voted #1 place to work in America – Why millennial FB employees love their job. www.Policymic.com

Google References

Carlson, N. (2014, January 10). A Google programmer blew off a $500,000 salary at a startup. www.Chron.com.

Cook, J. (2013, May 27). How Google motivates their employees with rewards and perks. Thinking leader: Hub pages.

Creative Tension: The internet giant seeks new ways to foster innovation. (2009, September 17). www.the economist.com.

Dodge, D. (2010, January 28). How Google sets goals and measures success. The next big thing: Thoughts on Business and Technology.

Dodge, D. (2010, June 18). Working at Google- the first six months. www.VatorNews.com.

Edwards, J. (2013, November 03). Google employees confess the worst things about Google. www.BusinessInsider.com.

Grant, J. (2013, January 11). It's fun to work, and play, at Google. www.TeachingKidsNews.com.

Manjoo, F. (2013, January 22). Here's how Google became such a great place to work. www.HuffingtonPost.com.

Mills, E. (2007, April 27). Meet Google's culture czar. www.Cnet.com.

News.com.au. The worst thing about working for Google. (2013, November 05). www.News.com.au.

Peptone, J. (2014, January 14). Google house: Tech giant spends billions to get inside your home. www.NBCNew.com.

Strickland, J. (na). How Google works. www.HowStuffWorks.com.

Warren, T. (2008, October 17). What it's like working at Google. www.Neowin.net.

Yarow, J. (2014, January 06). This is the internal grading system Google uses for its employees – and you should use it too. www.BusinessInsider.com.

Yen W. & Lev-Ram, M. (2008, January 22). Nine things you didn't know about Google. www.CNNMoney.com.

IBM References

Burt, J. (2011, October 26). IBM, Aoole: Stark contrasts in CEO succession. www.Eweek.com.

IBM. (2011, September 20). A forum of the future of leadership. Think.

Johnson & Johnson References

Denzil, M. (2010, February). Team two: Ethical business practice of Johnson and Johnson. Slide boom.

Diamond, M. (2011, November 20). Woes for Johnsons & Johnson. www.USAToday.com.

Gerard, J. (2010, April 15). Crisis management and ethics best practices: Johnson & Johnson. I-Sight.

Gurowitz, M. (2013, December 18). The story behind Johnson & Johnson and its people. Kilmer house.

Josephson, M. (2012, February 11). Business ethics insight: Johnson & Johnson's value-based ethical culture: Credo Beyond compliance. Business, Ethics & Leadership.

McDonald's References

Dewan, S. (2012, March 21). McDonald's chief, Jim Skinner, to retire this summer. www.NYTimes.com.

Don Thompson, McDonalds CEO, feeds his kids burgers, fries and vegetables. (2013, July 25). www.huffingtonpost.com.

Ellwood, M. (2013, October 16). Dynamic duos: Don Thompson and Melody Roberts of McDonalds on serving billions. www.Fastcompany.com.

Fairchild, C. (2013, July 24). McDonald's CEO: We've always been an above minimum wage employer. www.huffingtonpost.com.

Jacobs, D. (2012, March 22). McDonald's recipe for success brought new CEO to the table. www.forbes.com.

Lewis, A. (2013, July 21). Put McDonald's CEO, Don Thompson, on a Mcbudget. www.wallstreetjournal.com.

Suhay, L. (2013, May 30). "We don't sell junk food" McDonalds CEO comment sparks backlash against 9-year-old. The Christian science monitor.

Microsoft References

100 Best companies to work for. (2010). www.CNNNews.com.

Amin, S. (2013, July 31). Microsoft Bans Steven Sinofsky From Working At Amazon, Apple, EMC, Google, Facebook, Oracle and VMware. www.Microsoft-new.com.

Bass, N. (2014, March 03). Microsoft CEO Satya Nadella shakes it up at the top: 'Scroogled' operative Mark Penn evaluated, sources say. www.vancouversun.com.

Beattie, A. (2009, October 29). The 5 most feared figures in finance. www.investopedia.com.

Bishop, T. (2003, July 07). Microsoft to end stock options for employees. www.seattlepi.com.

Brass, D. (2010, February 04). Microsoft's creative destruction. www.TheNewYorkTimes.com.

Chang, A. (2012, July 20). Deep inside a Facebook hackathon, where the future of social media begins. www. wired.com.

Circeo, K. (2004, March 31). Myths about working at Microsoft. www.PCMech.com.

Cohen, D. (2014, January 07). Microsoft, Facebook team up on hackathon. www.allfacebook.com.

Cook, J. (2002, April 03). Microsoft President and COO Belluzzo resigns. www.seattlepi.com.

Dennings, A. (2014, February 03). Microsoft, Facebook hackathon: Recap. Windows Phone Developer.

Dickey, M. (2013, January 09). Some of Facebook's best features were once hackathon projects. www.business insider.com.

Dvorak, J. (2008, July 17). Microsoft, the spandex granny: While the most popular kid in class in its heyday, Microsoft charm has started to wear thin. www.pcmag.com.

Eichenwald, K. (2012, August). Microsoft's lost decade. www.vanityfair.com. Fried, I. (2009, June 11). How Intuit managed to hold off Microsoft. www.CNet.com.

Facebook and Windows 8 hackathon. (2012, November 30). Channel 9.

Gallagher, D. (2014, March 30). New CEO opens window on Microsoft's future. www.wallstreetjournal.com.

Gates, B. (2013). The early days of Microsoft. It world news times. Online Video

Goldman, D. (2013, August 23). Microsoft CEO Steve Ballmer to retire. www.CNNMoney.com.

Great Place to Work. (2013). 2013's worlds best multinational work places. www.greatplacetowork.com.

Guggenheimer, S. (2014, January 06). Facebook and Microsoft hackathons. MSDN .

Heim, K. (2011, April 24). Book a look at Microsoft's early days. www.TheWichitaEagle.com.

History of Microsoft Corporation. (2004). International directory of company history.

Johnson, B. (2011, November 01). Microsoft named the best place to work in the world. www.Komonews.com.

Knies, R. (2006, September 26). Why I work for Microsoft. www.Microsoftresearch.com.

Lacombe, R. (2010, December 30). Microsoft history: what were the four or five key decisions Bill Gates made in the early days of Microsoft? www.Quora.com.

Machlis, S. (2011, April 19). Apple v Microsoft by the numbers: Wall Street thinks one company is more compelling that the other. www.computerworld.com.

Matyszczyk, C. (2014, January 12). Microsoft more trusted than Apple, studies say. www.CNet.com.

Metz, C. (2014, February 14). Why Microsoft got it right with the new CEO Satya Nadella. www.wired.com.

Microsoft Corporation. (2014 April 02), Yahoo Finance, www.yahoo.com.

Microsoft Corporate Citizenship. (2014). Citizenship awards. www.microsoft.com.

Microsoft's Downfall: Inside the executive e-mails and cannibalistic culture that felled a tech giant. (2012, July 03). VanityFair.com.

Microsoft Facebook hackathon recap. (2014, February 04). MSDN.

Microsoft timeline (2013, March 14). www.thocp.net.

Misfitchic. What is it like to work at Microsoft? (2013, September 26). Bubblews.com.

Nachtigal, J. (2006, March 09). Rising frustrations with Microsoft compensation and reviews system. www.WashTechnews.com.

Perlow, J. (2012, December 15). I use to be with IBM, now I work for Microsoft. www.ZDNet.com.

Phadnis, S. (2014, March 28). CEO Satya Nadella brings Microsoft closer to Apple. www.timesofindia.com.

Popa, B. (2013, November 04). Bill Gates to work closer with new Microsoft CEO, refuses full time job. www.Softpedia.com.

Riesinger, D. (2013, June 03). Ballmer at work on Microsoft reconstruction. www.CNet.com.

Rivlin, G. (2011, March 31) Microsoft's office: Why insiders think top management way. www.CNNMoney.com.

Rosoff, M. (2011, April 19). Bill Gates: 10 Crazy stories. www.BusinessInsider.com.

Shewchuk, J. (2014, January 30). Recapping the Microsoft Facebook hackathon. MSDN.

Shifrin, T. (2005, July 29). Microsoft prevents former employees from working at Google. www.ComputerWeekly.com.

The 10 companies doing the most to make their employees happy. (2014). www.Forbes.com.

Usher, W. (2014, March 20). EA and Microsoft both nominated for 2014's worst company in America. www.cinemablend.com.

Vijay. (2013, November). Microsoft axes stacking ranks for good. www.yosny.com.

Wallaert, M. (2013, October 09). What is the worst thing about working for Microsoft? Forbes Magazine. : PP

Wingfield N. & Guth, R. (2011, March 30). Microsoft Co-Founder hits out at Gates. Wall Street Journal. : PP

Nordstrom References

McGowan, P. (2009, August 28). The Nordstrom effect- What it does and why you are better start adapting it to your online business. www.PRlog.com.

Nordstrom: Focusing on a culture of service. (2013). Icmrindia.org.

Spector, R. (2000, October 01). Nordstrom is more than name, it's a culture. www.BusinessJournal.com.

SAS References

Cherian, A.R. (2009, October 08). CEO style at SAS institute. The business of life. 2014

DiRomualdo, T. (2004, April 07). Seven leadership lesson of next generation companies. www.WTNNews.com. 2014

Goodnight, J. (2006, June 01). The founder of SAS explains how to be progressive on a budget. www.INC.com. 2014

Harvard Business School leadership. (n/a). James Goodnight.

Lichtenwalner, B. (2010, June 07). Servant leadership lesson: Ed Bastian & Jim Goodnight at leadercast. Modern servant leaders. 2014

Maney, K. (2004, April 21). SAS workers won when greed lost. www.USAToday.com. 2014

Starbucks References

Anonymous. Leadership approach and style in Starbucks. (n/a). www.ukessays.com.

Colona, K. (2013, September 13). How culture can drive returns. Fool.com .

Ellwood, M. (2013, October 10). Dynamic duo's Howard Schults and Arthur Rubinfield on sharing a Starbucks order. www.Fastcompany.com.

Feitelberg, R. (2012, November 30). Starbuck's Howard Schultz of responsibility and leadership. www.wwd.com.

Gilbert, S. (2011, April 13). Starbucks CEO Howard Schultz: Reinvented and just the same. www.dailyfinance.com.

Rien, D. (2007, February 10). The Starbucks culture.Yahoo.com.

Stern, G. (2013, November 08). More than coffee is driving revenue at Starbucks. www.Investors.com.

Walton, A. (2012, May 29). Starbucks power over us is bigger than coffee: It's personal. www.Forbes.com.

Southwest Airlines References

Lapin, D. (2012, June 20). How intangible corporate culture creates tangible profits. www.fastcompany.com.

Larson, M. (1997, January 12). Corporate culture is Southwest's edge. www.bizjournals.com. 2014

Mac, R. (n/a). Information for the world's business leaders. www.forbes.com. 2014

Nisen, M. (2013, January 16). Southwest's founder explains why there's no secret behind its culture. www.BusinessInsiders.com. 2014

Smith, G. (2005). Culture is key to Southwest airlines. Emerald for manager. 1-3

Soloman, M. (2012, April 03). What you can learn from Southwest airlines culture. www.washingtonpost.com. 2014

Trading places: Orlando magic and Southwest airlines employees. (2013, November 19). www.swamedia.com. 2014

Wells Fargo References

Business person of the year: Readers choice. (2013, November 21). www.CNNMoney.com.

Desmond, P. (2011, December 06). GDC: Anatomy of Wells Fargo-Wachovia acquisition. www.nttcom.tv.

Dunn, J. (2001, December 01).Wells Fargo completes final transition of Wachovia banking locations. www. Wellsfargo.com.

Jo, H., Durairaj, V., Driscoll, T., Enomoto, A., & Ku, J. (n/a). A tale of two bank mergers: A case study in corporate governance issues during acquisition. Santa Clara University.

Murphy, C. (2012, June 01). Five critical tactics in the Wells Fargo-Wachovia integration. www.Information week.com.

Recognitions and awards. (n/a). WellsFargo.com.

Wells Fargo recognized for diversity, corporate citizenship. (2012, May 01). Oregon Opportunity Network.

Yahoo! References

Fernandez, L. & Schuppe, J. (2013, April 30). Yahoo expands maternity leave after banning telecommuting. www.CNBC.com. 2014

Krasny, J. (2013, May 08). Yahoo CEO: Why I was right about telecommuting. www.Inc.com. 2014

Morphy, E. (2013, February 26). Could Yahoo's telecommuting policy be another form of insourcing? www.Forbes.com. 2014

Tkaczyk, C. (2013, April 19). Marissa Mayer breaks her silence on Yahoo's telecommuting policy. www.CNNMoney.com. 2014

Zappos

Carney, M. (2012, September 13). For Tony Hsieh, Zappos success has been all about culture and control. Pando Daily.

Evans, T. (2013, May 19). The experimental nature of Zappos CEO Tony Hsieh. www.entrepeneur.com.

Fass, A. (2012, November 15). Tony Hsieh: I fire those who don't fit our company culture. www.inc.com.

Gerard, J. (2010, July 06). Best practices in corporate Zappos. I-sight.com.

Hsieh, T. (2010, May 24). How Zappos infuses culture using core values. Harvard Business review.

Hsieh, T. (2010, November 17). Your culture is your brand. www.huffingtonpost.com.

Luther, A. (2013, April 21). Firms need good company culture to succeed, Zappos CEO Tony Hsieh says. www.Milkwakee-WisconsinJournalSentential.com.

Index

Dillard, Bill, II, 183
Dillard's Department Stores, 183
Directives, inconsistent, 114–115
Disengaged employees, 121–122.
    See also Employee engagement
Diversity, respect for, 210
Documentation, 46
Dodge, Don, 213
Doerr, John, 209
Drop-ins, 48

E

Efficiency-based performance, 151–152
Effort, 73
Ego-driven confidence, 180–181
Employee engagement, 112–126
    Ameritrust Mortgage, 112–113
    cliques, 122–124
    Communal Culture employee, ideal,
        125–126
    Cynical level of, 115–119
    disengaged employees as fragmenting
        employees, 121–122
    Hopeful level of, 113–114
    Hopeless level of, 119, 120
    levels of, 113–119
    Mercenary Culture employee, ideal, 126
    Networking Culture employee, ideal,
        124–125
    re-engaging, 122
    Resigned level of, 119, 120–122
    SHAKEN employees, 119–122
    Skeptical level of, 114–115
    Employees. See also Employee
        engagement
    amenities for, 215
    attrition of, 130–131, 226
    best and brightest, 203
    disengaged, 121–122
    dissatisfied, 226, 227
    food for, 206
    401(k) contributions, 201
    as partners, 107–108
    perception versus reality, 94
    relations with, 130
    satisfied, 201–202, 204–205
    stack ranking, 223–224, 226, 227–228
    validating with, 132
Empowering others, 173–174
Endurance:
    about, 155–156
    business relationships, managing, 157–
        158
    in Communal Culture, 78
    corporate culture, managing, 156–157
    CURx² Corporate Culture Model, 65–66,
        68
    fiscal responsibility, managing, 160–161
    in Fragmented Culture, 89
    leadership success, managing, 158–159
    in Mercenary Culture, 83
    mergers and acquisitions and, 161

    in Networking Culture, 71
    social relationships, managing, 159–160
Enforcers, 110
Engagement.
    See also Employee engagement; Leader
        engagement
    in Communal Culture, 77
    Communal Leaders and, 173–174
    CURx² Corporate Culture Model, 63, 64–
        65, 66
    in Fragmented Culture, 89
    Networking Directors and, 165
Enterprise-wide performance, 148–152
Ethical leaders, 59
Ethical leadership, 57–59
Ethically passive leaders, 58
Ethics:
    Ameritrust Mortgage, 55, 56
    Communal Leaders, 172
    communication and, 60
    corporate values and, 54–56
    defined, 52
    degrees of, 53–54
    financial services industry, 52, 56
    Golden Rule, 165
    importance of, 52–53
    leadership and, 52–53
    legality and, 59–60
    Mercenary Culture and, 59–60, 177–
        178, 180
    Mercenary Mavericks, 177–178
    Mercenary Misers, 180
    morality and, 56–59
    transparency and, 53–54
    trust, building through vulnerability, 60
    values and, 54–56
Evolution of corporate culture, 62–68
Excellence:
    Communal Culture, 79
    at core competency, 205–206
    expectations around, 24, 102
    Google, 205–206
    Mercenary Culture, 85
    Networking Culture, 73
Exclusivity, 85
Execution, 79
Executive coaching, 39–40
Expectations around Excellence, 24, 102
External communication, 47–48

F

Facebook:
    Bootcamps for engineer recruits, 195
    communication, 193–194, 196
    corporate culture overview, 189, 190
    Google compared to, 194, 197–198
    hackathons, 191–192, 228
    IPO, 191, 194, 196–198
    Microsoft and, 228
    middle management, 194–195
    mission, 193
    recruiting, 192–193

www.ingramcontent.com/pod-product-compliance
Lightning Source LLC
Chambersburg PA
CBHW080525220326
41599CB00032B/6205